BE CAREFUL WHAT YOU WISH FOR

A true story of an American family's five
year adventure living on the high seas.

KAY MOON

authorHOUSE®

AuthorHouse™
1663 Liberty Drive
Bloomington, IN 47403
www.authorhouse.com
Phone: 1 (800) 839-8640

Published by AuthorHouse 09/04/2019

ISBN: 978-1-7283-2629-0 (sc)
ISBN: 978-1-7283-2628-3 (hc)
ISBN: 978-1-7283-2627-6 (e)

Library of Congress Control Number: 2019913340

Print information available on the last page.

In memory of my mom and dad who always supported me no mater how crazy they may have thought my ideas were.

This work is dedicated to those brave souls who have the faith and determination to make their dreams come true.

CONTENTS

Foreword

This book has been a long time in the making. When I first told my family and friends about this sailing idea they thought I was crazy. It was the mid 80's and no sane person would consider taking their children out of school to home school them, and on a sailboat no less. There were even some parents who had been jailed in those days for removing their children from the school system. And go sailing to foreign lands; I had never even been on a sailboat let along take off and live on one. I knew absolutely nothing about sailing. What was I thinking? This had to be all Daryl's idea and I was just going along with it. How very wrong they were.

I have always been impulsive, headstrong, and adventurous. That's just who I am. Every day to me is a new adventure. I love life and try to live it to the fullest, so to me this wasn't crazy, it was just another adventure. I was told that I was going to ruin any chance my sons would have at a social life. Their education would suffer, and on and on it went. Again, how very wrong they were.

I'll admit I may not always make the best choices in life but I won't go so far as to say that they were bad or wrong choices either as everything I have done in my life has led me to be the person I am today, and today I am quite comfortable with myself. I actually like myself and not everyone can say that. If I could go back and have a do-over here and there would I do it. Of course. I think everyone would. But we can't go back so we just go on.

The stories I tell in this book are all true. Some funny and some sad. Because my sons were young at that time they didn't question what we were doing. They were excited by the idea of living on a boat and especially liked the fact that they wouldn't have to attend school any longer. Today, however, with children of their own they say things like, "Mom, what in the heck were you thinking? We're lucky to all still be alive. Do you realize all of the terrible things that could have happened to us?" Well, yes. If you look at the things we did then and look at what the world has become today it does seem insane. But back then we didn't lock our house or car. I let the boys explore the high desert foothills for hours on end or sometimes even venture out on overnight campouts with their friends. We had never heard of a school shooting or a terrorist attack. Going through an airport was quick and easy. No removing shoes and jackets and being subject to searches and scans. In short, the world in the mid eighties was a kinder, safer place than it is today. My heart aches for my grandkids who have to be driven the few blocks to school rather than walk, who can't play in the front yard without the watchful eye of a parent always on them, and who are exposed to so many evils via TV and the internet.

I do have one huge regret though. That was to allow my oldest son, Michael, to choose not to go on this adventure with us. It broke my heart and I cried for days when he told me he had decided to stay with his dad in California rather than travel with us. But Michael was 17 by the time we left. He had a girlfriend, a truck his dad had bought him, and by then he wanted nothing to do with his step-father, Daryl. It was his choice to stay behind and I had to honor that choice.

My parents had always been extremely supportive of anything I did, and this time was no exception. If this was what I wanted to do then they would stand behind me. My mother made one request though. If I did take this trip she asked that I write a book afterwards telling of my experiences. I promised her I would. She made this job easier for me by saving every letter I wrote home which detailed a lot of our everyday lives during those years. Michael saved his letters, too, which I truly appreciate. In addition to the letters I kept a daily journal during that entire time. Some days it was only a couple of sentences but enough to remind me of what was going on.

I have also asked my sons Dustin and Jerad to write their version of a couple of periods of travel when they were left "in charge". Over the years their telling of these times have become more and more sensationalized. Or maybe it was just that over time they revealed more of the things they really did in my absence knowing that they were far beyond getting in trouble for the things they did. They delight in making me sound like a derelict parent which makes for a good story but I know that that certainly wasn't the case. My boys were very capable as well as (for the most part) responsible. I trusted them and often times relied on them for many things. With that in mind and the important fact that the world was a much different and safer place back then I felt confident in doing things the way we did. My sons not only ended up with a superior education academically but with life skills that have opened many doors for them later in life.

So it wasn't for lack of written information that has kept me from completing this book, it's from sheer procrastination; which leads me to my second huge regret. That is the fact that I didn't complete this book before the deaths of my parents.

I had started this work many years ago, but life got busy. I was working full time and quite frankly, putting off writing was just an easy thing to do. Then Dad passed away in 2006. I felt bad that I hadn't completed my book for him to read but I had relayed most of my stories to him and after all it was Mom who really wanted me to write the book.

Mom came to live with us in 2010, but that's a whole other adventure that I won't go into here. Anyway, she was doing great both physically and mentally. I loved her being with me and I kept on slowly working on this book. I was really busy though and the only time I really had to write was when we took a trip somewhere. Thus my progress was slow. Mom passed away on July 15, 2014 after a 3 month battle with colon cancer. She was 92. I mourned her loss and her friendship and also felt a huge amount of guilt at not having this book completed before she died. In her last days I told her I would complete my book and sit outside under the tree and read it to her out loud. I know she'll hear it.

I have tried to write this work for the many people who have never sailed. Because of that I try to describe the sailing terms in very simple language. To the experienced sailor this probably sounds ridiculous. To those folks, I'm sorry, but hope you will enjoy my story anyway.

PROLOGUE

After six days of Daryl laying in the bunk moaning we knew we had to get him down to Manzanillo where we would have a better chance of getting him some medical attention. He rejected the idea of taking him there by taxi. We pulled our anchor and headed south, Jerad taking over as the temporary captain.

By late afternoon we could see that we would not be able to make it into Manzanillo before nightfall. We were very nervous about going into an unfamiliar anchorage in the dark so at 4 pm we dropped our anchor in a place called Bahia Santiago. It was not a very good anchorage and so we weren't surprised to find that there were no other boats there. After making sure that our anchor was secure we stowed our sails and ate some dinner. Daryl remained in bed, unable to eat. We turned in early as we wanted to pull our hook and set sail for Manzanillo at first light in the morning.

Shortly after 10 pm Daryl said he was sick to his stomach. I got him a basin just in time for him to lean over the side of our bunk where he started to vomit. I was horrified when I saw that he had thrown up what appeared to be more than a pint of thick liver-colored blood. He glanced up at me as I was removing the basin, said, "Bye Baby", then slumped down motionless onto the bed. I thought for sure that he was dying and I'm sure he thought so too.

What was I to do? We were totally alone in a strange anchorage. It was a very dark night, the moon having not yet reached its first quarter. At that moment I was thinking of all of the good things Daryl had done and not of the many times that I was exasperated with him. I certainly didn't want him to die … or did I? This was awful.

I did the only thing I knew how to do at such a time as this; I prayed. Hard. Then I grabbed a flashlight and what cash I could find, ran up the steps from our aft cabin, crossed over the cockpit, and shoved my head down into the boys forward cabin.

"Jerad. Dustin. Wake up and get up here! I need your help!" I yelled down to them.

Within seconds they were both standing in their undershorts in the cockpit with me wondering what in the world I had awakened them for.

"Get some clothes on. I need you to row the dinghy to shore and find a doctor," I instructed. "Daryl has just vomited up lots of blood and I think he may be dying."

"Mom, it's totally dark out there, and besides when we get to shore we don't even know if there's a town there," Jerad reasoned.

"I know that. But you have to try. I don't know what else to do."

My two sons didn't argue with me. They quickly went below, got dressed, and took the money and flashlight I shoved into Jerad's hands. They then unlashed the inflatable dinghy and slid it down into the black water below. They took the oars and started rowing the long distance towards the shore. As I heard their oars slicing through the water I said another silent prayer and went down below to check on Daryl.

CHAPTER ONE

THE IDEA

He sat watching me. Without even looking up I could feel his eyes on me. It was unnerving trying to work like this. Why couldn't I just drive myself to work, do my job, and drive myself home like any normal person would do?

I'd married Daryl two years before this after divorcing Joe, my first husband of fifteen years and father to my four sons. The boys, who by now ranged in age from four to fifteen years, were well disciplined but still full of the youthful energy possessed by most boys of their ages. When we divorced, Joe told me that nobody would ever marry a woman strapped down with four young children. This was a pretty frightening thought for a young mother of four that had for the most part been a stay-at-home mom. So when Daryl came along and offered to fill the role as head of household I took the bait, hook, line, and sinker.

Now I'll be the first one to admit that I have done some foolish things in my life, mostly out of spite, and then, not wanting to admit to my foolishness I've tried to make the best of it. My first act of foolishness was getting married at age 18 to someone twenty-one years my senior. Of course I didn't know at the time that Joe was so much older. When he said he was 24 I believed him. And when he introduced his 20 year son as his kid brother, I believed that too. My father was most unhappy about this relationship. Unlike me, he saw right through Joe's lies. But I was actually upset with my father about another matter so my marrying Joe was just being spiteful.

The fact that Daryl was unemployed and had been for a prolonged period of time, was 19 years my senior, and had the appearance of an aged "hippy" didn't seem to faze me. His scraggly grey beard went weeks without trimming. His hair, too, was mostly grey but still showed some evidence of the blond color it had once been. It had some natural curl to it and was worn long and pulled back in a ponytail at the nape of his neck. He was over 200 pounds but his six foot four height gave him a lanky appearance. He towered over my petite five foot three inches making me look even smaller. We were an odd couple in every sense of the word, but he talked a real good line and besides, by marrying Daryl I would prove that Joe was wrong. That was my second act of foolishness.

Actually, Daryl did get a real job a short time after we were married and within two weeks time he had arranged for me to start working at the same place. The job was in a facility that manufactured aluminum windows located just outside Reno, Nevada. Daryl had originally founded the company and later sold it to a partner. I was the one and only female working in the entire plant. After exactly one year Daryl was told that his services were no longer needed there and he was let go. That was the end of my working there as well. Even though my job seemed secure enough, if Daryl wasn't there he wouldn't allow me to work there either. It was during this period of time that I realized that Daryl was a pothead. Daryl hated cigarettes and so I never suspected that all of times he would disappear and then reappear a little while later smelling of minty toothpaste that he had been smoking weed and would then brush his teeth to cover up the smell. I just thought he had good oral hygiene. After all, I had never been exposed to pot so how was I to know? I also didn't realize what he was going to do with all of the discarded mirrors he hauled home from the glass company during the time we worked there. He said he was going to use them on the walls of an exercise room he was building in a section of our basement. I later learned, quite by mistake, that he had actually built a pot hothouse in my basement. He kept the door to that room locked and only he had the key.

Daryl was undecided as to what he wanted to do. He was very talented and capable, just not motivated. He finally thought he might like to sell real estate so we invested in a complete real estate course that could be done at home. It arrived. Daryl looked it over and promptly decided he didn't want to do that. Daryl finally went to work for a company doing some local construction. Not wanting the money we had spent for the real estate course to go to waste I started to study the material, completed the real estate course and passed the test for my Nevada State Real Estate license. Four months into his new job Daryl had an accident at work which injured his back and knee. Although I couldn't prove it I always suspected that the accident had something to do with the fact that Daryl had been smoking pot just prior to the accident. Fortunately for Daryl, the injury never prevented him from doing anything he wanted to do except work, which he never wanted to do in the first place. Disability suited him just fine.

I had a job waiting for me as soon as I passed my real estate test and received my license. By now Daryl was officially 'disabled'. There was no type of employment that seemed suitable for him. From the first day I started working as a real estate agent, Daryl appointed himself as my shadow. He didn't want to study and get a real estate license himself but chose to follow me everywhere and critique my every move. I was becoming a bundle of nerves. This couldn't continue indefinitely, could it?

It did continue for several months. I was assigned to work in the sales office of a new subdivision my broker was representing. I really liked this job. My office desk was actually the dining room table in one of the furnished model homes we were selling. Everything was clean and new and it was fun getting to talk with new people, show them around, and try to help them buy the home of their dreams. It was perfect except for one thing; Daryl. He accompanied me to work every day, watched my every move, and felt free to tell me how I should or should not conduct my business.

So this day was no different than the others. As I sat doing some paperwork at my dining room table desk, I could feel Daryl watching me from where he sat on the couch in the adjoining living room. I knew he wasn't reading or looking out the window. I could feel his eyes on me. It was a creepy feeling. I'd had enough.

I pushed myself up from the table, walked over and planted myself squarely in front of him.

"If you could do whatever you wanted, anything at all, what would it be?" I questioned.

He gazed at me with a blank look for several seconds before responding. "I'd get a sailboat and go sailing."

"Okay, fine, we'll do it," I answered before returning to my seat at the dining room table. No more questions, and no more discussion. In those few short seconds my mind was made up. We would get a sailboat and go sailing!

Was this to be the solution to my problem? If Daryl was doing something he really wanted to do then he would stop following me around and telling me what to do all of the time. Right? And if we went sailing then he would no longer be able to smoke and grow pot in the basement. I really wanted to get him away from that. Sailing would be the perfect solution!

CHAPTER TWO

THE PLAN

Daryl, of course thought I was nuts. He dismissed what I had said thinking it was just a statement made without thought. He was wrong. He may have had three wives before me (although his wife just prior to me thought that she was number four so I may have been wife number five); in any event he had never dealt with the likes of a hardheaded, determined being such as me before. My mind was made up. I was willing to do anything in order to not fail at marriage again.

Live on a sailboat. I had never entertained an idea even remotely close to this. I could swim and water ski, but that was in a pool or a lake. I knew nothing of ocean water. I had grown up in the San Francisco Bay Area so I had lived only a short distance from the waters of the San Francisco Bay and the Pacific Ocean beyond that, but we never went to the beach there. I had been back and forth over the bridges connecting the East Bay to San Francisco and surrounding areas for as far back as I could remember. As a small child going over bridges frightened me. I remember "hiding" on the floor of the backseat of our 1950 Mercury during these bridge crossings. As

I got older I'd look down at the water. It looked grey and cold. Certainly not inviting to me. I could remember seeing many types of boats including those with sails but I never gave a thought about the people on those boats.

Where do you begin when you decide to make a total change in your life; and not just your own life but those of everyone that's nearest and dearest to you. I had sort of done that once before. Eight years earlier, in the late 70's, I decided that the Bay Area was getting too crowded and my sons, then eight, five, and one years in age and needed a better place to grow up. We sold our comfortable home in California and purchased ten acres of northern Nevada desert complete with an old single wide trailer and a root cellar. Without knowing a single sole in the entire state of Nevada we moved and started a new adventure. Friends and family members thought I was crazy then. This new idea would forever solidify that thought in their minds. Oh well!

"We need a plan," I stated several days later.

"A plan for what?" Daryl questioned in an offhand way not even looking up at me and trying not to lose the jest of the dialog of the sit com he was engrossed in.

"You know. To go sailing. We need to figure out how long it will take us to find a boat and get packed up and out of here." Dustin, now nine, flew through the length of the family room and up the four stairs towards the hallway leading to his room. Nathan was a short ways behind in hot pursuit. He would be turning five later this month. The falling November temperatures and biting wind was forcing the kids to play indoors today.

"Dustin, stop teasing you brother," I called out. "Someday he'll be bigger then you and then you'll be sorry!"

"Forget it. It'll never happen," Daryl said, still focused on the TV. "You and the boys will never be able to leave all this," he said sweeping his extended hand around the room, "and adjust to living in cramped quarters on a boat." Daryl obviously was not interested in this conversation.

By the time I married Daryl I no longer lived in the small single wide trailer sitting on our property and which was currently rented. Joe and I had built a huge home on our ten acres; the largest house in the entire rural community of Stagecoach. There were several out buildings, lots of farm animals, a seventy tree fruit orchard, and gardens. Our piece of the desert had blossomed. In looking back I was sure that it was this nice looking wrapper on the package that attracted Daryl more than the contents. After all, a woman with four sons was a lot to get used to when you hadn't been around small children in nearly 30 years. Daryl was positive that I and my sons wouldn't last a week leaving all of this behind for a life on the ocean. Actually, it was Daryl that didn't want to leave "all this" and was now dreading the thought of confinement with this odd crew. Besides that, even though he never spoke the words I knew he was thinking about all that pot he had growing down in my basement.

"It could take a long time to find the right boat," Daryl said once the commercial started. "Maybe I'll just build another boat."

"How long did it take you to build your last boat?"

"About three years from start to finish" he said, then added, "but I'm really not sure I want to work with that much epoxy again. It makes me sick."

"Three years is too long anyway. How about two years? Do you think we could find the right boat and be ready to go in two years?" I was excited. I'd been thinking about nothing else since my declarative statement several days before.

"Yeah, fine, two years. Whatever."

"Where are we going to find a boat? I mean there aren't any sailboats anywhere near here."

"Magazines. Sailing magazines have classified ads in the back. Look there." His program was coming back on and it was clear that he was finished with this conversation.

My mind was always going a hundred miles an hour. I'm sure he thought I'd forget this whole sailing thing by the end of the week and be on to something new.

I knew nothing about sailing so I headed for the library. I found several books about sailing, checked them out, and started to read. I didn't understand any of the sailing terms or technology. Quite frankly I didn't care about any of that stuff. I figured I'd learn that later if I had to. I was interested in the adventure.

I found a few accounts of other "crazy" people who had ventured out to sail the high seas. These stories would surely spark some excitement with the family.

"Okay, boys. Has everyone had their baths and got their pajamas on? Daryl, come on, I want you guys to hear this. Dustin, grab a tin of caramel corn out of the freezer and bring in with you." It wasn't always easy to get the whole group gathered to listen to the books I had begun to read out loud to the family.

"Mom, can't I please play *Frogger*? I can read the book on my own later. Please," Jerad pleaded. Jerad had just turned fourteen a couple of months back. He was small for his age but his dark brown hair, perfect straight teeth and large hazel eyes made up for his size. He was well on his way to becoming a handsome young man. Jerad was an avid reader. Exceptionally bright, overall. *Frogger*, the one and only game we could play on our 1985 Tandy TRS-80 computer was giving me competition.

"No, Son. Not tonight. We're all going to read together. You can play *Frogger* tomorrow after your schoolwork and chores are done."

"Man!"

"What?"

"Nothing. I'm coming."

"Alright. Here's the book I found at the library today. It's about a family from Australia that took a year off to go sailing. They had two boys, about your ages, Dustin and Nathan" ... and we would all lounge on our king size waterbed munching on homemade caramel corn still cold from the freezer and listen to the adventures of other sailors that had gone before us.

CHAPTER THREE

THE MONEY

Money. Now that could be an issue. I was doing okay selling real estate, but selling Nevada real estate wouldn't work on the ocean. Daryl had a disability check coming in every month. The disability would continue but how was I going to replace my commissions? Then something unusual happened.

"Hi, Kay. Daryl. How's it going? You getting much traffic through here today?" My broker, Bob, had stopped in at the subdivision sales office to check on some files. His office was in Carson City, about five miles west of the subdivision. Bob was about my age, single, good looking, and drove a cherry red Corvette Stingray. Daryl hovered over me even more when Bob was around.

"No. I think it's still too cold for most people to be out much. What's new in town? Anything?" I questioned.

"I've been busy working out a deal with Charlie. You know, that developer that's putting together those 40 acre land packages out past your place in Stagecoach. He's agreed to have our office market all that land but we've come up with a couple of snags."

"What kind of snags?" I was curious, as usual.

"We agreed that we could probably sell a lot more land if we offered it for 'nothing down', it being unimproved and so far out of town and all."

"So what's the problem?"

"Two things", Bob said, taking a deep breath and letting it out slowly. "First, if the buyer doesn't pay a down payment then Charlie will have to pay our sales commissions out of his pocket. He's not too thrilled about that."

"Understandable," I replied. "What's the second thing?"

"The distance and the terrain. It's so far out of town that none of my agents in Carson City want to drive that far. Plus you need 4-wheel drive to get to some of the parcels. No real roads yet."

That was when a light went off in my head. My brokers problem was about to become a solution to my problem.

"I have an idea," I said with a broad smile starting to spread across my face. "How about if 'I' market those 40 acre parcels?" Daryl shot me one of those 'Oh, brother, what now', looks. Bob said nothing for a minute.

"What about the subdivision? My other agents don't even like driving this far out of town."

"No. I mean in addition to working here at the subdivision. When you get calls for the 40 acres just give them my phone number. I can make an appointment to meet with them and show them the land. We've got the 4-wheel drive diesel and that land is only about five minutes from our house."

"Well, yeah. I guess that would work," he said slowly.

"And here's the rest." I was almost bouncing now. That happens when I think I have a really good idea. "Would you be willing, if it's okay with Charlie, to have the commissions deferred instead of paying them up front?"

"What would you want to do that for? Nobody likes waiting for their money."

"If I could get paid a little bit of the commission every month when the land payments are made then we would have money coming in each month when we leave to go sailing."

"I'll talk to Charlie but I'm sure he won't object to a deal like that. You still think you're going to do the sailing thing?" Bob, like everyone else, had his doubts.

"That's my plan," I answered brightly. There were no doubts in my mind even if Daryl was suffering from the 'be careful what you wish for' syndrome.

Funds to purchase a boat would come from a couple of different sources. I had a rental home just outside of Carson City that I had bought as an investment property before meeting Daryl. I had also purchased a gorgeous 2 ½ acres of lush, green land in Northern California not far from the Oregon border and about a mile inland from the ocean. It was dotted with tall redwood and ash trees, and during the still of the night you could hear the waves of the Pacific Ocean breaking along the shore. We had an 18 foot travel trailer parked on the upper end of the lot near what we considered to be the ideal spot to build a home someday. But that had been part of a different plan. By selling both of these properties we would have the money we needed to buy a boat free and clear. We also had money from Daryl's injury settlement in reserve.

"We are NOT selling the 10 acres." It was a statement, not a question. The tone of Daryl's voice told me there would be no debating this issue. We were driving home from the subdivision and I was babbling on about how all of our finances were falling into place in preparation for our sailing venture. Daryl still thought that my brain had turned to mush and that this crazy notion of mine would blow over. Daryl, being the unreformed hippie that he was, tried hard to keep the eyes of the world at large away from him and the lifestyle he tried so desperately to hide. Living out in the desert and having to drive to the nearest neighbor rather than walk really appealed to him.

"Okay. We can figure that out later," I replied.

"No, I mean it. If we do go then we will need a place to come back to, and it may be sooner than later."

"Yeah, I guess you're right." I sat silent for a minute or two. "Hey, I know!" My wheels were turning again. "We could store all of our furniture and stuff in the basement then seal off the basement door. We could rent the rest of the house. It's plenty big without the basement. Nobody would ever need to go down there anyway."

Little by little things were beginning to come together, but I still had one big hurdle to jump. I would need to find a way to educate my sons.

CHAPTER FOUR

THE SCHOOL

Today home schooling is widely accepted and there seems to be a lot of cooperation between the schools and the families of those who home school their children. Plus today we have the internet which we didn't have back then. During the mid 80's that was definitely not the case. Home schooling was almost unheard of and I had even read of cases where parents had been jailed for not having their children in the school system. I began to research educational options. Michael was in the 10th grade. (He would later decide not to sail with the family). Jerad was in junior high and would be able to complete the 8th grade in public school. Dustin would finish the 4th grade, and Nathan was still a pre-schooler. This was going to be a big spread for curriculum and lesson planning.

"Hey, I think I've finally found a school program for the boys. Well, for Dustin and Nathan, at least. I'm still not sure what to do about the other two." I would give Daryl updates as things came along whether he wanted to hear them or not. "It's the Calvert School in Baltimore, Maryland. I think they do correspondence stuff for kindergarten through the 8th grade. I'm going to write to them and see if they can send me more information."

The gathering of information before the days of the internet was time consuming. Sometimes we could get information by phone but mainly it was snail mail. It seemed okay at the time because we didn't know any different.

"How do you know this school's any good? Isn't there anything closer than Baltimore?" Daryl was forever the skeptic. His glass was always half empty while mine was always half full.

"Well, I don't know for sure, but I understand that Sandra Day O'Conner got her elementary education from Calvert and she's a Supreme Court Judge. It must have some degree of credibility. And, no, I didn't find anything closer. In fact, I didn't find anything else at all."

The packet from Calvert School arrived a couple of weeks later. I read and re-read the letter explaining about how their correspondence program worked and what we could expect if we chose to do business with them. The accompanying catalog listed all of the subjects for each grade and had a price sheet attached. An order blank had also been included.

"I'm not going to get the kindergarten or first grade courses for Nathan." I was looking at the expensive pricing in the Calvert catalog.

"What?" Daryl, as usual, was only half listening to me.

"The kindergarten and first grade courses. I can't see paying that much money to teach him how to color and learn numbers and letters. I can put together some workbooks for that. Besides, he knows most of that stuff already. I'll just start him off in the 2nd grade. The 5th grade material looks like it will be right on track for Dustin. They want an additional $195.00 each if we send them the assignments to grade and then issue a certificate of completion at the end of the year. I don't think we need that either. I can grade their papers. Does that sound reasonable?"

"Huh? Yeah, okay." It was obvious that education, too, was not high up on Daryl's list of interests.

I finally decided that I would use Calvert's program for Dustin's 5th grade year and Nathan would start on materials I would put together for kindergarten and 1st grade. I would buy the 2nd grade course from Calvert to have when Nathan was ready for that. Calvert did not offer any course of study above the 8th grade so my search for high school material continued.

"Someone at church today told me they think *Brigham Young University* has some sort of high school program. I haven't ever heard that before but I'm going to check it out," I reported while changing out of my church dress and panty hose. The boys and I attended church every Sunday. Daryl, however, never went. It was just as well though. Dressing in your Sunday best for Daryl meant finding a shirt with no buttons missing and kicking the horse dung off his boots.

I found that BYU in Utah actually had a full high school diploma program. Their catalog of courses was impressive and offered lots of choices. Both schools, although very expensive, would provide the means for a great education for each of my sons. Finding the schools and purchasing the materials turned out to be the easy part.

I pulled our light blue, four-door, Ford Fairmont into the parking lot of Dayton High School and parked in the nearest empty space I could see near the front entrance. Nathan scrambled down from the front seat and held tightly to my hand as we headed across the cracked asphalt toward the front door. Nathan at age five was shy until things became familiar to him. The light breeze rearranged the top of his light brown hair. His large hazel eyes were taking in everything around him. I was feeling good; excited that I was running an errand without Daryl's presence. As we entered the building the halls were empty. Class was in session. The large, glass door display case on the wall to our right contained the names of all the honor roll students for the year. Michael and Jerad's names would be among them. We headed for the main office two doors down on our left.

We entered the office and advanced as far as the 'L' shaped counter would allow. Two student aides on the other side of the counter were making an attempt at looking important as they worked on their assigned tasks. The secretary looked up.

"Hi, Kay," she greeted as I stood there. "What brings you in today?" The secretary, Jan, lived in my rural community of Stagecoach. It was an everybody knows everybody sort of place. I was no stranger here. I had always been an involved parent; always concerned with what my children were being taught at school.

"Nathan, stop that!" Nathan was trying to hide by burrowing his head under the backside of my tan car coat. "Maybe you can help me, Jan. I'm really not sure who I need to talk to or if I even need to talk to anyone. When this school year is out I will be taking my boys out of the school system. I just don't want anyone wondering what happened to them when they don't show up for school next fall."

"Wow. That's a new one. Nobody has ever asked me that before. I'm really not sure either. Let me go ask Mr. Dart. He's right here in his office," she said turning towards one of the offices behind the counter.

Mr. Dart was the principal of both the middle school and the high school. They both had classrooms in this building until bond money could be raised to build a separate middle school. Mr. Dart and I had locked horns in the past and I dreaded a meeting with him now.

"Come on back, Kay. He'll see you in his office," Jan called over to me.

"Thanks," I said quietly. I took a deep breath, reached down for Nathan's hand and together we walked to the far end of the counter then around the back to the office marked, 'Principal'.

"Good morning," I said, mentally commanding my face to smile.

"Have a seat. Jan tells me you want to take your sons out of our school system." This was going to be all business. No small talk here.

"That's right. But not until after this school year is over," I replied, still remembering to smile.

"So tell me. What is it we've done this time to ruffle your feathers?" he questioned.

"Not a thing. I mean I'm not upset about anything. It's just that our family is going to be doing some … traveling … and I'm going to have to teach my sons myself."

"I see. And where will you be traveling to?" Mr. Dart asked flatly.

"Um, I'm not really sure yet. We're going to buy a sailboat and just sail to different places. You know, other countries." This was not going well. My mouth was going dry and I tried to swallow.

"Have you heard of truancy laws?" He asked in a stern voice.

"Yes. That's why I'm here." My smile was gone now. "I don't want anyone thinking that my children are truants when the next school year starts. I just came in to let you know."

"Did you know that you need to get permission to take your kids out of school?" he asked.

"Well, not exactly," I said looking down at my hands. "So, may I have permission to take my kids out of school?" I said looking up at him once more.

"It's not up to me," he replied.

"Who, then?" I questioned.

"Permission has to come from the Superintendent of Schools for Lyon County." Now he was smiling.

I said a quick thank you and excused myself. Nathan and I walked back along the counter stopping only long enough to get the name and phone number of the Superintendent of Schools from Jan. I left not feeling quite as good as when I had arrived.

I scheduled an appointment with the Superintendent of Schools and explained my reasons for wanting to take my sons out of the public school system. Except for a serious health issue with a student in the past he had never had to deal with a parent wanting to home school their children. The meeting wasn't as 'smooth sailing' as I had hoped it would be. He concluded by telling me he would need the recommendation of the Lyon County School Board before he made his decision. I would be notified as to the date and time I would be put on their agenda.

I appeared before the five member school board at the appointed date and time. I felt like I was in a courtroom pleading my case. As I laid out my whole sailing plan I could tell from the looks on their faces that they, too, thought I was quite nuts. (Did nobody but Huckleberry Finn and I have any sense of adventure?)

"Okay, next on the agenda is Mrs. Olson," the chairman of the board read from the notes lying on the long table behind which sat the five member school board. I stood and walked to a spot in front of the long table facing the board members where a couple of others had previously stood, their issues having been discussed before mine.

"We understand you want to take your three sons out of the school system," the chairman stated.

"That's right," I replied. So far so good.

"Why?" His question was reasonable but I was sure someone must have already given them a heads up about my sailing plan. I gave them a condensed version anyway.

"And, how do you intend to have your children educated?" he asked, giving a slight rise to his eyebrows.

"They'll be home-schooled," I answered.

"Home schooled … Interesting … Who will be their teacher?" He asked in a patronizing voice.

"I will," I smiled brightly.

Up until now the other four board members had remained quiet, but now the plump mousy woman sitting to the chairman's right chimed in. "Do you have a teaching degree, Mrs. Olson?"

"No, I don't."

"Do you have a college degree other than teaching?" she continued.

"No. I've taken a couple of years worth of college courses but I never received a degree," I tried to explain.

"And you think you are qualified to teach three different grades of school, and all at the same time?" Mr. Chairman hadn't lost the patronizing tone in his voice.

"I know I can educate them at least as well as they are being educated now," I answered quickly before realizing I had just issued an insult to their schools.

"Where do you plan to get your text books?" asked the lady at the end of the table next to the plump woman.

"The fifth grade course will come from a school in Baltimore, Maryland called the Calvert School. Books for the older two will come from Brigham Young University. They have a high school program by mail that looks really good." I decided not to even mention Nathan. After all, he hadn't even started school yet so technically I wouldn't be removing him from school.

They all sat quiet for a moment. The chairman pursed his lips then wrote something on his notepad and passed it to the two board members on his right side then to the two on his left. "We are going to take a short recess," the chairman announced to the audience as a whole. "Mrs. Olson, you are welcome to take a seat while we are gone." The five board members filed from the room.

I took an empty seat in the front row. I folded my hands in my lap and tried not to show the nervousness I felt. The people in the room totaled maybe 25 or 30. I knew many of them were staring and me and I could hear low whispers throughout the group. I was beginning to feel like a circus attraction. I was grateful when after a very long five minutes the board members returned. I was once again invited to stand before them.

"Mrs. Olson," the chairman began. "I'm sure you understand that our main concern here is for the children in this county. Before allowing any students to be removed from the school system we need to feel confident that those students will receive an education equal to what they would receive by attending our schools. In order for us to grant your request we need for you to prepare and present to this board one year's worth of lesson plans for each subject for each of your children. In addition, we want to review each textbook you plan to use during that year".

Did they know how much work that would take? Of course they did. I'm sure they thought that was the last they would ever see of me. This was a real nut case taking up their time. Who in their right mind takes their young children from living in a rural Nevada desert community to live on a sailboat in the ocean?

Well, I did everything they requested and scheduled another appointment with the county school board. I presented them with an entire year's worth of lesson plans, (which to me was even crazier than my sailing plan) and in the end was given the blessing of both the School Board and the Superintendent to educate my sons on my own. Maybe they figured my craziness would come through in my sons so it would be best not having them in their schools after all.

Everything seemed to be falling into place. We still needed to sell off the animals and vehicles, store our furniture and other belongings in the basement, sell the rental home and property in California, and rent the big house. All of that wouldn't take us more than a few months to do. We arranged for our CPA to look after our property and finances once we had everything in order to leave. Now all we needed was a boat.

CHAPTER FIVE

THE SEARCH

Shopping for a boat isn't quite the same as shopping for a new car or even a house for that matter. There is no one location where you can go to see an inventory of the type of boat you need. We needed something that would accommodate our family, would not be excessively priced, and still be structurally sound.

By now my oldest son, Michael, had turned 16. He had a couple of years left before graduating from high school and according to the court Michael could choose which parent he wanted to live with. As he and Daryl didn't get along at all he decided to move to California where his father and my parents resided. Whereas Daryl was extremely strict and unbending, his father would let Michael do anything he pleased. Discipline, supervision, and setting a good example were totally foreign concepts to Joe. Plus Joe promised to buy Michael a nice truck if he went to live with him. He would complete high school there. The thought of being trapped on a boat with Daryl for prolonged periods of time was definitely not Michael's cup of tea. Anyway, this reduced our crew to five.

Daryl had a fairly good idea of what he wanted in a boat. He was sold on the ride and stability of multihulls over single hull boats. Sailors seem to have an ongoing controversy over these two types of boats. Conventional sailboats, mono hulls, have a single large hull with a keel extending downward several feet from the bottom of the boat to give them stability and to keep the boat from tipping over. If for some reason the keel were to be knocked off or the boat were to be filled with water in severe weather the boat would more than likely sink almost instantly. The general ride on a single hull sailboat is also much more pronounced than that of a multihull. At times you feel as if you are walking on the walls. Items within the boat as well as on the deck must be securely fastened down to keep them from becoming airborne or sliding when the boat heels.

On the other hand, multihulls have more of a tendency to flip over than single hull boats. The multihulls consist of either two hull catamarans or three hull trimarans. The two hull catamarans are joined together by long beams and generally have living space built between as well as within the hulls. Trimarans have a large center hull with smaller outrigger hulls on either side. The outrigger hulls are used solely for stability and have openings called hatches built into them where lightweight items can be stored. In very large trimarans these outrigger hulls, actually called ama hulls, may contain part of the living quarters. Multihulls don't heel over, or lean, to the same degree as monohulls do while sailing. If they did they would put an ama hull under the water and run the risk of the boat flipping over. The argument in favor of multihulls is that should this occur the vessel would stay afloat. Even if it were upside down in the water it would act as a big life raft. Also, the motion of the ride through the water is much more gentle since they don't sail on their side as monohulls do.

Of course I knew none of this monohull vs. multihill stuff back then. All I knew was that Daryl felt we should find something called a trimaran. We started buying sailing magazines such as *Sailing* and began to search the classified sections in the back for boats for sale. We also subscribed to a boat listing service that sent us monthly listings of boats for sale by private parties. The persons selling boats paid to have their boats advertised by the service but did not have to pay a brokerage fee if their boat sold. The service asked for some general information from us. They used our list of desires and requirements to compile an appropriate list of boats for us to review each month. The parameters we were asked about were things like monohull or multihull, size in length, number of berths, type of rigging, what the boat would be used for, and a price range.

"Mom!" Jerad yelled through the house tossing the days mail onto the kitchen table. He sounded a little winded after the brisk ride on his BMX bike down the long dirt driveway bordering the fruit orchard to the mailbox and back.

I closed the lid on the washing machine and started down the hall towards the sound of his voice. "Son, please don't yell. What's up?"

"I got the mail. You got another one of those boat list things. Can I ride my bike over to BJ's?" He asked, already heading towards the door.

"Okay, but don't stay too long. I'll be starting dinner soon. If you see Daryl when you go out tell him the boat list is here." I picked up the 8 ½ x 11 envelope with the boat listing service address in the top left corner and ran my finger under the seal being careful to avoid a paper cut. I removed the thick packet from the envelope.

It was exciting every month when our new list of available boats arrived. It included scores of boats from just about anywhere a body of water could be found.

"Jerad said the boat list came," Daryl stated, coming in from the garage and crossing the family room to the kitchen table where I was sitting. "See anything good?"

"I don't know," I said skimming down the page trying to appear like I knew what I was looking at. Actually the abbreviated information often confused me. "There were a couple on page two but it didn't look to me like they were live-a-boards." We would need a boat designed to live on full time rather than one designed for short day sails only.

"Oh, look at this one," I said pointing to one of the listings. "It sounds pretty good. Trimaran … live-a-board … sleeps six … inboard engine … Wow, it even has refrigeration … price isn't bad either … No, forget it … Too far," I said with the excitement falling from my voice.

"Why. Where is it?" Daryl wanted to know leaning over my shoulder for a closer look.

"The Mediterranean. It seems like all the good boats are either in Australia or the Mediterranean. There's no sense in even writing for more information and pictures for this one," I said, not even trying to hide my frustration. "I mean we can't go traipsing all over the globe looking at boats."

Each time we found a boat within the U.S. that looked like a possibility we would contact the owner by letter or phone if a phone number was included and request more information plus pictures of the boat. Daryl wanted to know about the materials and method of construction in building the boat. I just wanted to see what the boat looked like. I remember pictures we got of a boat that was located up in Alaska. The owner sent us several large glossy prints. It was named *Lizard of Oz*, was chartreuse in color, and looked like something from another planet. Just one look was enough for me to know I didn't want that as my new home.

One must be very careful not to offend the owners of multihull boats. Unlike monohulls which are often mass produced, most multihulls are built from a set of plans which the boat owner has purchased from the designer of the boat. The owner either builds the boat himself or hires someone to do it for him. Either way, by the time the project of completed the boat is very much a part of that person, almost like a child, and critical remarks, no matter how true can offend greatly. No reason to make someone feel bad. We found it was much better to lavish praise on the boat but decline its purchase because it was either not large enough for our family or it was just too big for our young crew to handle. It worked. Thus is was with the *Lizard of Oz*. We thanked the owner for sending the pictures of his beautiful craft but it was just more boat than we could handle. We left the "Yeah, right!" and, "You've got to be kidding," comments unsaid.

One boat looked particularly good on paper and sounded wonderful when speaking to the owner by phone. It was sitting in a harbor in Ft. Lauderdale, Florida. Taking a trip to Florida wasn't going to be cheap but Daryl and I decided it would be worth the trip if it were indeed 'the' boat. We made our travel plans, arranged for someone to come and stay with the boys, and scheduled an appointment with the owner to see his boat on the first day of our weeks stay in Florida.

I was really excited. Things were finally beginning to happen someplace besides in my head. Not only that, but I had never been to Florida before so this would be another new adventure for me. I love adventures. Florida was great. The boat, however, turned out to be a disappointment. I must give Daryl credit, though, for having the ability to look deeper than the surface. Upon close and thorough examination he concluded that although this boat would be great for day sailing off the coast, he was in no way convinced as to its sea worthiness in rough weather. Plus the stories the owner told us about the mountains of beer cans that accumulated around the boat during its construction made us wonder if the construction was something we wanted to stake our lives on. We didn't think so.

At the end of our week in Florida and after looking at dozens of boats along the coast and Florida Keys we still had made no headway in our boat search. We returned to Nevada no further along than when we started.

It was now April of 1987 and our search continued. Our next near success was a lot closer to home. We had contacted a multihull broker in Sausalito, California near San Francisco. They said they had two boats that might fit our needs. My parents still lived in the San Francisco Bay Area, just a five hour drive from our home in Nevada so a trip there would be a lot more convenient and less costly than our Florida venture. Besides, Michael had already moved to the Bay Area to live with his dad and we were always excited to get to see him.

"Come on guys, get a move on and get your things out to the truck. We want to be on the road by noon," I called down the long hall towards the boy's bedrooms. Short, spur of the moment trips had become the norm for us. We didn't require much time to prepare and pack. The single wide trailer we had once lived in on our ten acres was still there and had tenants that were always willing to watch the house and care for our animals. With no public school schedules to work around we were free to make these decisions to go as we wanted. We were spoiled.

"Mom, I'm only taking my ecology lessons with me. I'm way ahead on everything else," Jerad said passing by me in the hall. Jerad loved to learn; he was the epitome of self-motivation. Dustin was just the opposite. Although he learned quickly and was extremely bright he hated stopping anything long enough to do actual school work.

"I'm not taking any school stuff to Grandma's," Dustin informed me. "I'll do it when we get home."

"Sorry, Charlie," I countered. "You're taking reading and spelling. We can always work on those while we're driving."

"Man, that's not fair," Dustin muttered under his breath.

"What did you say?" I asked.

"I said that's not fair. Nathan never has to do any schoolwork," he complained.

"Nathan's six. Now get going before Daryl gets impatient and starts yelling." Daryl never required much of a reason to snarl at us.

We drove to Grandma and Grandpa's house, a trip of about 250 miles, and made arrangements for Daryl and me to look at the boats in Sausalito the next day.

We left the boys with Grandma and Grandpa and made the drive to Sausalito. This time as we crossed the bridge over the San Francisco Bay I actually looked down at the boats below and wondered how it was going to be living on one.

We found the broker's address and parked the truck. The spring day was cool but clear. As we walked towards the broker's office our light jackets felt good. Pulling open the front door a single ding sound announced our arrival. The room we entered contained two wooden desks with swivel chairs and a four draw metal filing cabinet which stood in the far corner. A waste basket and four additional chairs, two by each desk, completed the room's furnishings. The walls were randomly displayed with posters and old calendars of boats of every description. A large corkboard along one wall held dozens of snapshots of the boats they were currently trying to sell. Immediately a gentleman entered from an adjoining room.

"Hi. You must be the Olson's. I'm Ted Johnston. I see you found us okay. Here have a seat," he said smiling and pointing to the two chairs in front of the desk nearest to us. We exchanged pleasantries. "Daryl, you mentioned on the phone that you were looking for a Brown design. Have you ever sailed on a Brown before?"

"Actually, I built a Brown trimaran back in the 70's. A smaller one than we're looking for now but I know that Jim Brown designs strong boats and we need something strong if it's going to be our home," Daryl replied.

"Well, we currently have two Browns I can show you. But if it's a live-board you're after then the one probably won't work. It was built as a charter boat to take small groups of people on little tours around the bay so there are no actual berths built into it. More of a party atmosphere, if you know what I mean."

"What about the other one?" Daryl wanted to know.

"She's a dandy," Ted responded. "She was built in Hawaii a few years back and sailed over here last fall and put up for sale. She's been sitting out here on a mooring since that time so she's a bit dirty right now. She needs a little work done on her but nothing major. We could even arrange for the work to be done. We have lots of contacts." He was a typical salesman.

All this 'she' talk was weird. It was at this time that I learned that boats are referred to as feminine. I just wanted to see 'her'. "Can we go look at her?" I wanted to know.

Ted led us down the wooden dock not far from the office to where a small dinghy was tied. He pointed to some life jackets piled in the bow of the dinghy and indicated that we should put one on. We stepped into the small craft, donned our jackets and sat down sharing the bench type seat in the center of the boat. Ted untied the lines that secured the dinghy to the dock and stepped into the stern taking a seat next to the small outboard motor hanging over the rear of the dinghy. A couple of pulls on the starter cord and the engine jumped to life. We motored slowly away from the dock and out into the bay where the boat was moored. (That means it was tied up to a big buoy that was anchored out it the water). As we came closer we could see the name *Dream Chaser* in bold print along the side of the boat. I liked the name. That was a good start.

We looked the boat over inside and out and liked what we saw. "When can we take her out? You know, for a test ride ... er, sail, I mean?" I questioned, impatient with excitement, as usual.

"Oh," Ted replied, pausing to think for a moment. "It will take a couple of days for my guys to get her ready. She's been sitting here for quite awhile and we need to check the inboard over and get fuel and examine the rigging. We need to make sure that everything's in order before taking her out of the bay."

"We haven't even discussed the price yet. What's the owner asking for this boat, anyway," Daryl asked.

"He's asking $72,000.00. As you can see she's well built and fully equipped," Ted replied in his persuasive salesman voice.

"Seventy-two grand. That's more than we can handle," Daryl responded honestly, slowly shaking his head back and forth. My smile vanished and my shoulders fell. I was clearly disappointed.

"Well," Ted shot back, "that's what he's asking but I happen to know that he is very motivated to sell this boat. Why don't you make an offer?"

"We'll talk it over and let you know," Daryl answered back.

We finished going through the boat, took the dinghy back to the dock and drove back across the San Francisco Bay to my parent's house discussing what price we could afford to offer and what we hoped the owner of *Dream Chaser* would accept.

The following day was Palm Sunday and we were going to head back to Nevada. We left Jerad to spend a few days with his dad and Michael while Daryl, Dustin, Nathan, and I piled into the pick up for the drive home. We made a quick stop back in Sausalito to submit our offer on *Dream Chaser*. We wrote up an offer for $33,000.00 which Ted would submit to the owner. We wouldn't be able to handle much more than that. We knew that financing a boat was out of the question so we would have to come up with all the money up front. Financed boats required that the boat be insured and insurance companies refused to insure boats leaving U.S. waters. We would be returning to the Bay Area the following week to spend Easter with the family so arranged to take the boat out for sea trials the day after Easter.

On Tuesday we got a call from Ted. The owner countered our offer at $35,000. We agreed to this new price contingent with the boat passing a marine survey and performing well on sea trials. Daryl got busy making arrangements to have the boat hauled out of the water and surveyed after we did the sea trials. If the boat didn't sail well we didn't want to pay for a survey.

The day after Easter we once again drove over the bridge to Sausalito. This time we brought the boys along so that we could all get a feel for this sailing thing together. As we drove into the parking lot we could see that *Dream Chaser* was now tied up along the dock.

"There she is," I beamed, pointing at the boat. "What do you think?"

"Whoa, it's big!" Jerad exclaimed.

"'She's' big," I corrected. "You talk about boats like they are ladies." The boys weren't impressed with my newfound boat knowledge.

"Can we get on it now?" Dustin wanted to know.

"We had better find Ted first and make sure everything is ready to go," Daryl said. We waited for Daryl and Ted to return and tried to see as much of the boat as we could from our position on the dock. Seagulls circled randomly over the water and occasionally one would dive into the water capturing his midday meal. We were all taking in the new sounds and smells around us.

We didn't have long to wait before we were leaping from the dock to the deck of the boat being careful of our footing in order to avoid an unwanted dunking in the dirty harbor water. The inboard engine was started, the dock lines were released, and we started motoring slowly through the other boats in the anchorage. Daryl began pulling sails out of bags and laying out various ropes and hook type things. Ted was at the wheel. The boys and I didn't do much but sit back and enjoy the ride. It didn't take long before the men had the sails up and the motor off. Wow, this was fun! We sailed right out under the Golden Gate Bridge and into the open ocean. We sailed over something called the Potato Patch. I never did know why they called it that or how they knew we were even over it. The water all looked the same to me out there.

Our outing wasn't particularly lengthy but it was long enough for us to know that we had found 'the' boat. Daryl was impressed with the way she handled – 'responded' was the word he used. It had ample room both inside and out. It appeared to be in very good condition needing only some minor repairs. The price was within our reach. And, she was located on the west coast which is where we had talked most about departing from.

Now all that needed to be done was to have the boat hauled out of the water and examined by a marine surveyor. That was set up for the following week. If no dry rot or other structural problems were found we would write a check and *Dream Chaser* would be ours. It was at this point that Ted informed us of one more thing.

Although the price of $35,000.00 had been agreed to the owner wanted to be paid in all cash. We said as soon as we received a favorable survey report we would go to the bank and have a cashier's check made out, the present owner would sign off on the title, and the boat would be ours. No, Ted informed us. A cashier's check wouldn't do. The owner insisted on all cash. The green stuff with President's pictures on it. All of it.

The ride back to Nevada was one of mixed emotions. We were all fired up about finding the boat and how our plans were falling into place ahead of schedule and all. But on the other hand we had a funny feeling about this whole deal. Why in the world would anyone not accept a cashier's check? After all it was a lot safer than carrying thousands of dollars around in a bag. By the time we arrived home it was decided that first thing the next morning we would contact the department in Hawaii that handled boat registrations and see if we could get some answers.

That turned out to be a most revealing phone call. For starters there turned out to be more than one owner. Two friends who shared joint ownership, as we learned, had built the boat in Hawaii. It seems that the two parties were not getting along so one of the owners got mad and sailed the boat to San Francisco without the knowledge of the other owner. The owner who had sailed the boat to San Francisco hoped to get all cash for the sale, sign off both names on the title, and keep the lot for himself. The owner in Hawaii had no intention of selling the boat and was glad to finally find out where his boat had been taken. Needless to say, we backed out of that deal immediately.

We continued looking through the boats listed in the monthly listing service we received in the mail. It wasn't long after the San Francisco disappointment that Daryl made a phone call about another boat he saw listed. He didn't really think it was a boat that would work for us but he called anyway. During the course of that conversation, Daryl explained exactly what we were looking for. This man knew of just the boat. It was a Brown designed trimaran named *Lunar Glow* and was sitting on a ranch in the farming district of Camarillo in Southern California. He was pretty sure the owner would be willing to sell it.

With what information we had the owner was finally located, and yes, he would be interested in selling his boat. Within hours we had the kids ready, the pick-up packed, the animals arranged to be cared for, and we were heading down the highway towards Southern California.

Daryl had a nephew, Grant, who lived a short distance from Camarillo along with his wife Denise. We drove directly to their country home and arrived hot and tired after the nine hour trip. Grant was retired and Denise worked part time as a bee keeper. They were most gracious in putting us up for the night and in watching the kids the following day while we went in search of *Lunar Glow*. In fact, they proved to be extremely helpful to us in the weeks to follow.

Daryl and I took off after breakfast the next morning and drove to Camarillo following the directions given to us by the boat's owner. The boat was there all right. Sitting in the farmyard amidst an odd assortment of campers and travel trailers, *Lunar Glow* was perched high above the rest of the lot on stands consisting of 55 gallon drums and huge planks which had been tightly fitted under each of the outer hulls. She was dirty and had every indication of being abandoned and all but forgotten. Despite her name she was anything but glowing.

She may not have glowed at that moment but she was a good, strong boat and of the very size and design Daryl had been hoping to find. We sat down for a serious talk with Simon, *Lunar Glow's* owner and builder. We agreed to pay him $25,000.00; half down and the balance once we had completed the necessary work to get her ready for launching. This was conditioned upon two things. First, we would pay to have a marine surveyor do a thorough inspection of the boat. If the inspection unveiled any hidden problems the deal was off. And second, Simon would somehow get *Lunar Glow* transported from the Camarillo 'boat ranch' to the Channel Islands Harbor and launched once she was ready. This would include his obtaining the necessary insurance and permits required to transport the boat, and a trailer to move her on. No problem. Simon agreed. We had a deal. We had a boat!

CHAPTER SIX

THE BOAT RANCH

Lunar Glow was a home built boat. Simon had built her in Santa Barbara in the late 70's and he and his wife had sailed her for a couple of seasons in Mexico. A divorce not only ended his marriage and sailing days but nearly ended the life of *Lunar Glow* as well. There had been some bitter battles over the division of property during the divorce. While quite drunk one night Simon decided he would split the boat right down the middle, 50/50. Perhaps the fact that Simon was too drunk to start his chain saw was the only thing that saved the life of *Lunar Glow*. She had escaped the chain saw massacre but was left alone and neglected, a reminder of a happy, married life Simon no longer wanted to think about. So she sat now as she had for several years atop of the 55 gallon drums at the boat ranch more commonly referred to as Rancho Verde.

The boat ranch consisted of a large, old, faded green farmhouse. Nobody actually lived in the house. It was used more for a communal gathering place for the handful of residents living in an assortment of little old travel trailers and campers scattered in the farmyard around the house. Residents paid a small fee each month to reside there. Everyone shared the kitchen and bathroom facilities in the house. There was a TV, ping-pong table, pool table and it included the only pay phone I have ever seen installed inside a private house. Several boats had been built there over the years thus its nickname, the Boat Ranch. Ours was the only boat there during our stay. One resident was building an ultra light plane in the old barn. Everyone there had either owned a boat or worked as crew on sailboats at one time or another. There was plenty of interesting company, advise, opinions and stories at the ranch.

Lunar Glow, while structurally sound according to marine surveyor, Jack Maples, needed a lot of cosmetic work and re-fitting. Because the boat was a nine hour drive from our home in northern Nevada we decided to live on the boat at the boat ranch while we worked on her. Now that we were officially doing home schooling and our income was in place the move was easy. The boys thought this was great fun. They were each assigned duties according to their age and ability. The boat needed plenty of cleaning, scraping, and sanding that even a six year old could help with. I have always been a firm believer that everybody should have some sort of responsibility no matter how small or trivial the task. Each of the boys did his part.

Daryl concentrated on the structural part of the boat. It would need the mast refinished and all new rigging. Many areas would need to have new epoxy applied. The decks would need to be refinished and the entire boat would need new marine paint inside and out. Grant, happy to earn a few extra bucks, came out several days a week to work with Daryl on the areas that needed more skill then the boys and I could handle. This boat did not have an inboard engine so we would need to get an outboard motor. It was determined that a 25 HP Mariner with a long shaft would be sufficient for getting us in and out of port. The rest of the time we would just have to sail. Daryl built some sort of track on the back end (stern) of the boat to which the new motor was attached. This allowed the motor to be lowered down into the water when it was needed and then pulled back up the track again and locked into place when it wasn't being used. This would prolong the life of the propeller as well as cut down on the drag while we were sailing. He ran cables and controls so that once the motor was lowered it could be started and operated from the cockpit of the boat where the wheel was located.

I was more focused on the interior of *Lunar Glow*. I made new curtains for the windows and across the openings to the bunks. I varnished the wood in the kitchen and bathroom (which I learned was really the galley and head). I cleaned and painted and polished until it looked and felt like home. I found every little nook and cranny that could be used to store something.

We spread out each of the sails on the floor of the main room of the farmhouse one at a time and gave them a thorough examination. Some of them had rust spots where the hanks had laid against the sails while wet but the sails themselves were in excellent condition. There was even a huge and colorful spinnaker. The sail bags used to store the sails when not in use were worn; their once bright red color had faded and looked dull but they were still very functional. They would work just fine.

Redoing the decks was a joint effort we all worked on. There was a non-skid surface that was peeling with age and needed to be removed. Once the decks were chiseled, scraped and sanded smooth a new coat of epoxy was applied to the decks and crushed walnut shells were sprinkled evenly over the wet epoxy. When this dried the decks were given another coat of epoxy followed by several heavy coats of marine paint to keep the walnut shells glued down and to try to lessen their sharp feel. I had to admit that this type of non-skid deck worked well. We never slipped on the deck even when wet, however, it was a killer if you ever had to kneel down on it.

Jerad's biggest excitement during this time was the old surfboard he found down in one of the ama hulls. Jerad had never surfed but from the minute he found that board you would have thought he was a world class surfer. It was huge and heavy. When he stood it on end it dwarfed him, but he couldn't have cared less. All he could talk about was how he was going to surf on that board. Now 30 some years later, Jerad is, indeed, an excellent surfer although the boards he uses now are state of the art and much shorter.

Living on *Lunar Glow* during this time must have been much like the Swiss Family Robinson living in their tree house. Standing on our decks and the cabin top allowed us to look out over the tops of the trees growing along the property line of the farmyard and into the cornfields beyond. A tall ladder leaning against the side of the boat was used to climb on and off. It was a challenge hauling things up and down that steep ladder.

An entry in my journal reminded me of the day Dustin helped carry the groceries onto the boat. He somehow managed to drop a carton of eggs which landed squarely on Daryl's head as he stood on the ground below. We never did convince Daryl that it was an accident.

After nearly two months of hard work our time at the boat ranch was coming to an end. Michael had flown in on June 20th to spend some time with us during his summer break from school. It felt good having all four of my sons with me again even if only for a short time. He pitched in and painted the bottoms of all three hulls with thick red bottom paint with the finishing touch consisting of a two inch blue stripe sitting just above the red paint marking where our actual water line would be. We had all worked hard doing our share of the work according to our age and abilities, and it showed. The transformation of *Lunar Glow* over the past two months was amazing; we were now ready for the next chapter in our living adventure.

CHAPTER SEVEN

FROM LAND TO SEA

One of the most hair raising rides we ever had with *Lunar Glow* was before water even touched her hulls. Simon had agreed to get a trailer for the boat and transport her to the Channel Islands Harbor where she would once again be set afloat. This wasn't like hitching up your ski boat and towing it down to the lake for a day's outing. *Lunar Glow* was 37 feet long and 24 feet wide. The original design of the Brown 37 had a 22 foot beam, but before he built the boat Simon had another designer, Jay Kantola, modify the plans. He extended the width of the boat by two feet and added cut outs in each "wing deck" where nets were installed bring the beam to 24 feet. At any rate *Lunar Glow* was not the size of a typical vehicle traveling the public streets of Southern California. This was going to be more than a one man operation. As it turned out, in addition to our family, Grant, and Simon, nearly everyone from the boat ranch took part. After all, adventure ran through their veins too.

It was decided that the best time to move the boat would be about 3:30 AM after the local bars had closed, thus removing any drunks from the roads, and before the morning commuters started for work. We actually started preparing for the night's journey early the day before when Simon delivered the huge boat trailer. Because *Lunar Glow* had been sitting at the boat ranch for so many years things just seemed to grow up around her. There was no longer a clear path between where the boat sat and the road as there had been once upon a time. Piles of debris had to be cleared away and shrubbery cut back. A big job. We discovered that the trailer Simon brought did not have any wiring for tail, brake, or back-up lights. This would be a problem, but not for long. We headed for the local variety store where we purchased several flashlights and red cellophane paper. By covering the end of the flashlights with the red paper we created our own rear lighting. Nobody needed to know we had live bodies riding on the boat to operate the running lights. In addition we would have two cars in the lead and two more following which would also have a set of our home crafted signal lights. We felt sure it would work great.

The distance from the ranch to Channel Islands Harbor is only about 12 miles. It was the longest 12 miles we would ever travel. We would have to go over the roads belonging to Camarillo, Oxnard, and the City of Ventura. Each of these cities required a single use permit to transport something of this size on their streets. Camarillo and the City of Ventura was just a matter of completing some paperwork. Oxnard, however, was also requiring a short term insurance policy in case we damaged any property on the way. This was nearly impossible as there wasn't an insurance company to be found that would issue the required policy. In any event all of this paperwork was to be part of what Simon agreed to as a condition of the sale. We had paid him half of his money after the boat had passed the survey and we had a cashier's check for the balance which would be given to him as soon as the boat was moved safely to the water.

"Come on, boys. It's time to get up and get ready to go." I was standing in the cockpit leaning down through the open hatch of the forward cabin as I called in to wake my sleeping sons. Michael and Jerad were sharing the double bunk while Dustin and Nathan squeezed into the single bunk on the opposite side of the boat. "Dustin, reach over and shake Nathan. He'll need to get up and dressed too." The time was 2:45 AM. The night was dark and cool; a light dew had dampened the decks and cabin top.

Although the night sky was covered in a blanket of stars the new moon of the night before left the sky void of moonlight. This would be the last night we would look out over the cornfields and the state mental hospital beyond that on down Lewis Road. Bodies on both sides of the cabin started to stir. The two inch foam pads that served as mattresses on the bunks didn't offer enough comfort to entice them to lounge there any longer.

"Mom, are we going now?" Nathan yawned, rubbing the sleep from his eyes.

"Pretty soon. They've got the trailer hooked to the truck. Now they've got to jack the boat up a little to loosen the planks and barrels and I want you off the boat before they do that. Get dressed and be careful when you step outside. The decks are wet."

The boys dressed and carefully descended the ladder for the last time. Jerad was especially cautious. His leg was still healing form a wound he received a couple of weeks back when he had lost his footing at the top end of the free standing ladder. It had been frightening and none of us wanted a repeat of that event.

"Where's Simon's truck?" Michael questioned looking at our diesel pick up now hitched to the big boat trailer.

"I don't know. He drove up in that about 30 minutes ago," I answered jerking my head towards the shiny black Porsche parked at the front end of the dirt drive. I was a little irritated that Simon was not following through with the launching plan as it had been agreed to.

"Oh, cool," Jerad said brightly heading towards the sports car illuminated by the yard lights.

"Get back here. All of you, go into the kitchen. There's juice and milk in the frig and a box of donuts on the counter. Hurry and get something to eat before we take off."

When Simon arrived with the trailer we asked if he had all of the permits. He said he did and had handed over a sealed envelope which I put on the front seat of the truck. Okay, so we were set to go. We had a total of four pilot cars. A couple of people were on the boat with the make-shift running lights; the rest would ride in one of the pilot cars. Everyone had their assignments.

We pulled slowly out of the farmyard and onto the road. Daryl ended up driving our truck that pulled the boat as Simon had some excuse for not wanting to do so himself. We were so wide, 24 feet on the beam, that we took up the entire roadway. Jerad rode in the lead car, the shiny black Porsche, along with Simon. We hoped his excitement about the car wouldn't make him forget his job with the colored flashlights Daryl had pressed into his hands as we were leaving. His job would be to signal and warn any oncoming cars about the very wide load coming up behind them. The rear cars would do the same. Michael would be positioned inside the stern castle of *Lunar Glow* working his colored lights out the back window of the boat. We hoped that none of these signal lights would even be needed.

Jerad spotted the first set of oncoming headlights about two miles into the trip. As he leaned out the side window of the Porsche madly clicking his colored flashlights, Simon gunned the car ahead to meet the on comer. The oncoming car didn't even slow down but kept barreling towards *Lunar Glow* now only several hundred yards ahead. Simon pulled to the side of the road and both he and Jerad turned and watched as the car narrowed the distance between him and the boat. Daryl had come to a complete stop hitting his high beams on and off in an attempt to warn the unsuspecting driver. Then suddenly Simon and Jerad saw the brake lights come to life and the car swerve onto the shoulder of the road. He missed the port ama hull by inches. If that driver had been drinking I'm certain that that encounter sobered him up real fast. As for the rest of us, our hearts were pounding and the adrenalin was pumping fast.

Our next encounter wasn't with a vehicle but with a diamond shaped road sign. Daryl, concentrating on the roadway ahead watching for more cars hadn't seen the yellow sign on our right side. It wasn't until we heard the horrible scraping noise that we knew something was wrong. Daryl braked to a sudden stop as we jumped out to investigate.

"What the heck was that?" Michael questioned in a voice of panic, his head now popping out of the stern castle as he entered the cockpit. "It sounded like this dang boat was being torn in half."

"It's okay. We just got a bit too close to this here road sign," I said pointing to the yellow diamond shaped sign that was now bent back from its normally upright position and still firmly pushing into our boat. There was a deep gouge in the fresh paint of our starboard ama hull about five feet long. Although it was ugly it was just cosmetic. Thank goodness the gouge had missed the beautiful large lettering announcing the name *Lunar Glow* which had been painted on each ama haul in blue to match the waterline stripe below. By now both lead cars had turned around to find out what the trouble was. After a couple of minutes of Daryl cursing the sign and making excuses for hitting it he swung back towards the center of the road and we were on our way again leaving the sign at its new bent angle.

Our worst moment came while going through Oxnard. We had one tight turn to make onto the main street of town. Although the roads were deserted except for our entourage, Daryl didn't make the turn wide enough to clear the traffic signal post planted on the corner. I had my head out the window looking back at the boat and yelled in time to stop Daryl before wrapping *Lunar Glow* around the signal post. Again, more cursing from the driver's seat. He backed up and tried again. Again I hollered for him to stop. My stomach was in knots and then I was almost physically sick when I looked up and read the sign on the building right in front of where we were doing this circus act. It read "Oxnard Police Department". Oh crap! I prayed that no one would look out the window or receive a call to exit the building. On the third try he managed to clear the post and make the turn. That was just one of dozens of times I would experience over the next five years that I knew my Heavenly Father was looking over me. The remainder of the trek, thankfully, was short and uneventful.

Normally a trip of this distance with no traffic to deal with would take maybe twenty minutes. This night it took nearly two hours. The sun was just beginning to light the morning sky as we pulled into the harbor. We made a wide circle above the boat ramp where *Lunar Glow* would be lowered down into the water. Everyone was exiting the boat and vehicles, smiling, laughing, and retelling the close calls we had just passed through. I was still in the cab of the truck. On the seat lay Simon's envelope with the transport permits for the three cities we had just drove through. I was curious. I knew about the insurance policy the City of Oxnard required before they would issue their permit. I opened the envelope. There was a permit from the county covering the roads we traveled in Camarillo. There was a permit from the City of Ventura covering their area. That was it. Not a single thing from the City of Oxnard. Nothing. Nada. No wonder Simon didn't want to be the one to actually tow *Lunar Glow* to the water. A quick flashback of the turn in front of the Oxnard Police Department reminded me to offer a quick prayer of thanks for our safe if not totally legal arrival at the water's edge.

CHAPTER EIGHT

STEPPING THE MAST

The actual launching of the boat was smooth and uneventful. *Lunar Glow* was a shallow draft boat which meant she only required about 34 inches of water to float freely in. Even so we would need to wait another hour for high tide in order to safely back her down the boat ramp, off the trailer, and into the harbor water. We gave Simon his final payment and thanked all of our new boat ranch friends for their help. Grant would stay until we had the boat in the water then return the trailer to the ranch. Daryl, Michael, and Grant busied themselves attaching safety chains to the trailer and tying dock lines to the cleats on the deck to help guide the boat off the trailer and secure it to the dock. I did my best to keep the younger boys out of the way. There was no lack of things to see and explore in this new environment.

When the tide was right *Lunar Glow* was backed down the ramp and put afloat for the first time in years. She still wasn't looking much like a sailboat at the moment as the mast, instead of standing upright, was laying alongside the cabin top where it had been strapped down to the bow and stern rails during transport. Channel Islands Harbor is large and well equipped for handling the many needs of the yachting community so 'stepping the mast' wouldn't be a problem.

With the boat afloat Daryl lowered the 25 HP Mariner down the stern track and into the water. He hit the starter and the motor roared to life for the first time in something other than a 55 gallon barrel of water.

"Okay, you guys. Get over here and jump onboard. We're ready to go!" Daryl was excited. He was at the helm once again and loving it. It was evident from the look on his face that he was finally in his element.

"Are we going sailing now," Nathan questioned.

"No, Dummy, we don't even have the mast up yet," Dustin shot back.

"Dustin, don't call you brother names. He was just asking." I sometimes felt I had a full time job just to keep the peace.

"We're just motoring the boat over to the crane dock," Daryl explained. "That big crane over there," he said pointing to a crane in the distance, "will lift up our mast here and stand it up on the deck."

We pulled up alongside the crane dock. Michael and Jerad hung our new, still unscuffed bumpers over the side of the boat and jumped onto the dock feeling important as they tightened the bow and stern lines to the dock cleats.

"Does anyone have a penny," Daryl asked.

"Is that all it costs to step the mast?" Michael had a puzzled look on his face.

"No. It cost a lot more than a penny but good sailors know that if you put a coin under the mast before it's set in place that its good luck and the mast will never blow down." Daryl seemed to be calm and patient as he explained this superstition to all of us. Maybe this sailing thing really would be a good idea.

"I think we should put a penny and a nickel under the mast," Jerad piped in. "We need all the help we can get."

"I agree," I laughed while digging into my purse for the coins.

There was still a lot to do before actually hoisting our sails which would not happen for a couple of days yet. Our coins were set in place and the mast stepped and secured. We were dead tired from our all night ordeal and all we wanted to do now was tie up to the guest dock, go below, and catch a few hours sleep. Time was no longer of the essence. Our adventure had begun and we were free to do things on our own time frame.

CHAPTER NINE

READY - SET - GO

We didn't accomplish a great deal that first day in the water. We tied the boat up to the guest dock there in the harbor and after a short nap the boys were off to explore. Dustin took his fishing pole and actually caught his first three fish right there in the harbor. Over the years he would prove to be our most able fisherman. Nathan found loads of little frogs in the shallow water near the boat ramp and spent his time trying to catch them. Michael and Jerad went to "check out the area". Michael found a pay phone and made a call to his new girlfriend in the Bay Area. Jerad was fascinated by the names painted on the scores of boats throughout the harbor. He said later that he was glad we didn't end up with the *Lizard of Oz*. I attempted to organize the interior of the boat along with chasing after things for Daryl as he worked on getting the boat rigged.

Our second day in the harbor went much the same as the first except that the older boys worked along with Daryl getting the rigging finished and the boat ready to sail. Jerad made his first trip up the mast. We had purchased a boson's chair for hoisting someone up the mast but that couldn't be used until halyards were run through the pulleys at the top of the mast. The steps which Daryl had previously mounted along both sides of the mast worked well as Jerad made his climb to the top and followed the directions that Daryl called up to him from the deck below.

We were all getting used to the sounds, smells, and feel of our new floating home. Although we were still sitting alongside a dock we experienced some motion as other boats slowly motored by or the wind blew. The smell of salt air was inviting. Sounds were more noticeable at night. Laying in our bunks we listened to the sound of halyards slapping against the masts of the boats in our vicinity. This would eventually become as familiar and comforting as a lullaby.

By the third day we were finally ready to take *Lunar Glow* out of the harbor and sail her in open water. Grant had driven down from Piru to join the family on this maiden voyage. We would be making a day sail out to Anacapa Island and back. Anacapa was one of the Channel Islands off the coast of Southern California where we would learn to sail. Daryl had, of course, sailed before but except for the short ride on *Dream Chaser* up in Sausalito this was a first time experience for the boys and me.

Daryl lowered the outboard down into the murky brown harbor water and started the motor. We were all feeling quite full of ourselves as we motored past the other boats at anchor in the harbor.

"Here, put these on," I instructed, handing each of the boys a safety harness and tether. "I don't want anyone falling off the boat."

The day was warm and the water calm as we motored slowly through the anchorage. There was no chance of them being swept off the deck and they must have looked silly to the experienced sailors as we motored on by. Michael, Jerad, and Dustin sat side by side along the port wing deck with their legs hanging down over the front end of the boat.

"I want to sit out there too," Nathan pleaded from where he was standing in the cockpit.

"No, Son. You're not old enough."

"That's not fair. I never get to do anything", Nathan protested.

"Don't worry, you'll get to things later," I reassured him.

We were moving closer to the channel heading out to open water. As Daryl turned the boat between the long lines of buoys marking the deeper water of the channel I noticed that the water was choppier out here and *Lunar Glow* was making a slight rocking horse motion. Daryl began barking orders.

"Boys, get back into the cockpit now. We're going to hank this sail to the forestay and be ready to hoist it once we reach the end of the channel. Kay, go down below and get the sheets."

Knowing Daryl's unpleasant side would surface if he had to ask something more than once, I hurried through the cockpit and down the wooden steps into the forward cabin. Once there I stopped, realizing I didn't fully understand my mission. The forward cabin was divided into three sections. As you entered the cabin there was a double bunk on the right hand side and a single bunk to the left. These were about four feet up from the cabin floor; a set of drawers had been built in beneath the double bunk. Each bunk was like slipping back into a cave under the cabin top. The top half of each foam bunk mattress had enough headroom for a person to sit upright if they weren't too tall. The bottom half of the bunks where your feet went had no more than two feet of clearance with a cubby hole built over this area. This is where the boys stowed their belongings. Maybe three feet beyond the stairs there was a bulkhead which was like a wall with a big oval area cut out of its middle. Stepping through this cut out opening brought you into a very tiny area with a little sink, mirror, more drawers, and another cubbyhole back behind the sink where all of our linens were stored. Forward of that and through still another bulkhead with another oval cutout to step through was the toilet, or head. Directly above the head was a hatch that opened up onto the center front deck of the boat. On either side of the head there were numerous hooks with all sorts of ropes hanging from them.

I stood down there for a couple of minutes or so wondering if I had heard my orders correctly. The front hatch over the head opened just then and Daryl called down. "Hurry up and get those sheets up here. We're going to be to the end of the channel soon."

The hatch closed again with a bang. Okay, but I'm not sure what he needs them for, I thought, as I gathered up an armload of bed sheets from the cubby hole behind the tiny sink and headed back up the stairs. I dutifully carried the sheets through the cockpit and up onto the foredeck where Daryl stood waiting with Grant. I extended the armload of sheets towards him.

"Here you go," I beamed. The motion of the boat was starting to affect my stomach but I was still excited.

"What did you bring those up here for?" Daryl was obviously irritated. "I want the sheets!"

"These are the sheets." My stomach was feeling worse.

"Not those sheets. I want the sheets up forward in the head," he grumbled.

"There's nothing in the head but a bunch of ropes," I said feeling rather irritated myself. That was when I learned that there is more than one type of sheets and the ones used in sailing a boat were definitely not the ones we sleep between.

The remainder of that first day's day sail went smoothly and once out of the channel *Lunar Glow* sailed like a swan. The one and only time I was ever seasick was on this day. I learned real fast from then on to never go down below for sheets or anything else for about an hour after leaving port. Fresh air and looking out at the horizon did wonders for keeping the stomach in its rightful place.

We returned to the harbor after an enjoyable sail and spent another night at the guest dock. The following morning Michael made another call to his girlfriend then informed us that he wanted to get back home. Now! We had thought he would be staying longer so had not made arrangements for a return flight as yet. He was adamant. At age 17 girls took top preference over almost anything else. We took him to the local bus station and got him a seat on a bus going to Oakland.

We needed to learn how to sail and there was no time like the present. After seeing Michael off at the bus station we headed back out of the harbor. This time the sheets (ropes used to adjust the sails), were all laid out on the deck before we left the dock and I made sure not to go down into the cabin until I had adjusted to the motion of the boat. Grant had helped Daryl sail the boat the day before but today it would be all up to us. Daryl gave us instructions and explained the techniques of sailing to us as we went along. Nathan was really too young to do many things at this point but was allowed to hold the wheel at a given compass heading if the rest of us were busy and the winds were light. He felt very important steering the boat. Dustin was restricted to things that could be done from within the cockpit. Jerad and I were given jobs out on deck.

Our destination was Smugglers Cove on Santa Cruz Island, another one of the Channel Islands off the coast of Southern California. We had taken the black canvas sail cover off the mainsail attached to our boom and had it folded and stowed. This was one of the things we would learn to routinely do each time before leaving a port or anchorage.

"Dustin, you untie the mainsail and be ready to start hoisting the main once we shut the motor off. Jerad, come up here with your mom. You need to learn how to get this sail hanked on." Daryl was pulling a large white sail out of one of the faded red sail bags. Along one edge of the sail brass hooks and been attached. "These are the hanks," Daryl said. "Start at the top of the sail and attach this short cable to this halyard. Good. Now attach each of these hanks to this forestay", he instructed, showing us the cable that ran from the bow of the boat to the top of the mast. "Make sure you keep your harnesses tethered to the bow rail or the Jack stay while you're working up here. Okay, are all of the hanks hooked on? Good. Now, see this big grommet in the corner of the sail here. We'll hook one of the sheets to this and run the other end through that snatch block over there, then around that wench and then fasten it down in that lock there on the cabin top." Maybe Jerad followed what he was telling us but I was totally confused. I just did the best I could to follow his instructions.

I figured we must have done something right because before long the engine was turned off and pulled up the stern track and secured, the sails were filled with the light sea breeze, and we were headed out to the islands. We sailed along for a ways just enjoying the day. Then the wind started to pick up. It was about this time that I realized we had sailed very close to an oil rig off the coast. Daryl saw it too and started barking more orders.

"Turn to port. Jerad, port. Left. Turn the wheel to the left. We're way too close to that oil rig. We've got to sheet in." Daryl was talking faster and louder; his voice was starting to sound panicky.

"I don't know how to sheet in." I was feeling helpless. The wind was blowing harder, and we were getting really close to that stupid oil rig. It really didn't matter if I knew how to sheet in or not because at that moment the cleat with the snatch block connected to it tore right out of the deck. The sheet that had been run through it started flailing through the air like a huge bull whip with the snatch block and cleat still somehow attached to it, the sail was snapping, and we all started running around in complete chaos trying to catch the whipping sheet before it hit us in the face.

Somehow we missed the oil rig, but if any of us had been of a mind to I've no doubt that we could have jumped from our deck to the rig's platform. Daryl was furious that we had looked like the derelict sailors we were to the men on the oil rig. Actually, I think they thoroughly enjoyed the show we put on for them and it was probably the highlight of their day. I offered another silent prayer of thanks and once our heart rates came back down and the sail was back up we sailed on to Santa Cruz Island without further problems.

Daryl had his first of many repair jobs to do that afternoon fixing the deck where the cleat had been torn out. The boys and I learned a couple of very important things that day. At least they were important if you were going to be living on a sailboat. First, we learned the correct way to run the sheets so that strong winds wouldn't cause them to damage the boat again. The second thing we learned was the difference between port and starboard. When facing forward in the boat port was on your left and the right side was starboard. The color of the running lights at night also let us know the direction other vessels were traveling. I later learned an easy way to remember this was by association. By my remembering the phrase, "the boat *left port*", and "*port* wine is *red*", I could always remember that left and red equaled port; therefore right and green must equal starboard, the other side of the boat.

CHAPTER TEN

FINISHING UP BUSINESS

That first night anchored out at Smuggler's Cove was exciting for us. It was our first time learning to set an anchor, stow the sails, and make entries in our new log book. It was also the first time we had been confined to the boat. Up until now we could step off the deck onto a dock but we were now surrounded by the waters of the Pacific. We had charts of the Channel Islands and the Southern California coastline which we were learning to interpret. The boys fished, Daryl made repairs, and I tried to figure out our evening meal from the canned goods stored in the bilge. Everything was new and fun.

We sailed back to the Channel Islands Harbor late the following day and spent another night at the guest dock. In the morning we got everything buttoned down on the boat and motored her over to the Vintage Marina where we paid for one months dock rent as we would be driving back to Nevada to get our business there finished up.

"How come we can't stay here?" Nathan had been having fun and didn't understand why we would drive all the way back to our home in the desert if we were going to live on the boat.

"We have a lot of things left to do at our house before we leave on *Lunar Glow.*"

"What kind of things," he questioned.

"Well, we need to move all of our furniture out of our house into the basement. We still need to sell the horses and you need to make sure you didn't forget to bring something along that you might need on the boat." There was actually a long list of things we needed to wrap up but a six year old wouldn't understand about any of that.

We left the marina at noon and drove back to Stagecoach arriving at 9:45pm. It was July 1, 1987. Our next five weeks would be our last in Nevada for several years. There was so much work to do it was frightening. What was I thinking, anyway, mouthing off with my hair-brain ideas. No wonder everyone thought I was nuts.

Besides our own properties that I was trying to sell I had some other real estate deals in the works that needed to be finished up. I put ads in the paper to sell our horses and rent our house. The rental property in Nevada and the land in Northern California were already listed for sale and we were seeing some interest in both of them. Our diesel truck had developed some problems and needed to be taken in for repairs. Daryl wasn't feeling well and made a trip to the local clinic. He moved slow for several days but still managed to get the garage cleaned out and the property trimmed and watered. Our house was big, but room by room we sorted through and stored what we wanted to keep in the basement and boxed the rest for the Salvation Army. We were able to take very little with us because we not only would not have room but also had to keep our weight light.

Our house soon began to echo as the rooms emptied out and the thousand square foot basement got fuller and fuller. On July 15th we found a family to lease our house. Three days later we received an offer on our Ft. Dick property in California. We went out to dinner in town that night to celebrate.

Each day we thought of yet another thing that needed to be done. We had wills drawn up at the attorney's office. We got a safety deposit box at the bank. We met with the banker to arrange for transfers of money as we might need it from time to time. We met with our accountant who would be receiving all of our mail and paying our bills in our absence. We redid the insurance on the house and arranged for our tenants renting our mobile home to give the rent to the accountant. I met with my broker so that he would know where to send my monthly commission checks I had earned from the sale of the 40 acre parcels I had sold. I gave the boys haircuts and we got our passports. We shampooed carpets and went to the dumps. I wrote an offer and opened an escrow for the sale of the general store in Stagecoach. Life was busy.

Through all of this Jerad continued with his schoolwork. He actually took his finals in both typing and ecology. Although he did very well with those first two courses I discovered that BYU had a very strict policy for giving tests that wasn't going to work for us once we were on the boat and traveling. They had a list of certain people who could give the tests. The list did not include a parent. It had to be someone like a public librarian or a school principle. We had to arrange with the librarian to agree to give the test. Then we sent her name and address to BYU who in turn sent the test materials to the librarian. She then contacted us to take Jerad in so that she could give him the test. Once he finished it she then mailed it back to BYU for grading. BYU then sent the librarian the test results which she passed on to us. I knew at once that we would never be in any one place long enough to make this process work. I would have to look elsewhere for a high school program. I didn't even bother with school for the younger two. It was, after all, summer vacation.

At 12:20pm on Tuesday August 4th we left Stagecoach. We finished up some last minute business in Carson City then headed west to my parent's home in the Bay Area for the night. Daryl and Dustin went in the truck while Jerad, Nathan, and I followed in the car. This would just be a quick overnight stop but I didn't know when I would be seeing my parents again and we couldn't take off without some last good-byes. This was probably harder than the past five weeks had been.

CHAPTER ELEVEN

NO TURNING BACK

I
t was just after noon when we arrived at the harbor. We moved *Lunar Glow* from Vintage Marina to the guest dock and paid for three nights stay. We were tired from the mornings drive but still had a lot of work to do on board. Even though we tried to "keep it light" we were bringing more and more boxes and armloads of belongings onto the boat. I had emptied my pantry at home and now my newly varnished bilges were being lined with canned goods. Daryl was fretting as our blue water line sunk further down into the murky harbor water. Didn't he know that all those tools he brought along weighed more than my canned goods and we couldn't even eat the tools!

The next couple of days were rather laid back. The weather was foggy but didn't stop the boys from having fun playing on the dock. I was trying to help Daryl work on projects on the boat. On Friday we drove out to Piru for dinner at Grant and Denise's and picked up a port o potty from them. The pump on our head wasn't working properly and I didn't want to use a five gallon bucket until Daryl got the repairs done. We would sail back out to Smuggler's Cove in the morning to continue on with our sailing instructions. Besides, Daryl said he would rather work on the boat out there for free rather than pay a nightly fee to tie up to the guest dock.

Our sail to Smuggler's Cove was smooth and uneventful ... the way sailing should be. We still had so much to learn but it would be mainly a learn as you go program. Dustin couldn't wait to get a line in the water which he did as soon as the boat was anchored and the sails were stuffed back into their bags and stowed. His catch of the day was one small ray. He was excited with it but ended up throwing it back as at that point I had no idea what to do with it. We settled instead for a dinner of onion soup and a chocolate cake for dessert.

"Okay, crew. All hands on deck," Daryl called down into the forward cabin where the boys were still in their bunks feeling the gentle roll of the boat as she sat at anchor. Daryl had risen early and started hooking up the new wind speed indicator while I got breakfast started in the galley. The day was beautiful. We were alone in the anchorage with Santa Cruz Island just a short distance off our bow. "Today," he announced, "you will get your first rowing lesson."

"Me too? Do I get to row too?" Nathan hated getting left out just because he was the youngest.

"Yep, mate, you too. But first we need to eat. Hurry and get dressed. Your mom should have breakfast ready in just a minute."

The boys dressed in record time and before we knew it breakfast was eaten and the galley cleaned. We had purchased a new Avon inflatable dinghy while still living at the boat ranch. Daryl had never let the boys inflate it despite all of their pleading and it sat now still folded tightly in its original bag. Together the boys pulled the boat from its bag and unfolded it on the deck. The three wooden floorboard sections were set off to one side. The connection at the end of the foot pump hose was attached to the fill valve on the dinghy and Jerad started stepping hard on the foot peddle forcing air into the chambers of the dinghy.

"Let me pump now. Come on Jerad, you've pumped long enough. Let me have a turn," Dustin begged as Jerad continued pushing his foot up and down on the foot pump.

"Mom, I want to pump it," Nathan said looking up at me.

"Jerad, let your brothers have a turn." Jerad continued pumping.

"Jerad! Now." My tone of voice made it clear it was time for his brothers to take a turn. "Let Nathan try it while the sides are still soft and it's not so hard to pump." Nathan stepped up to the pump as Jerad backed away. He stepped with all his might on the foot peddle but not much happened. At six he just didn't have enough size or weight behind him to make much impact. I watched him for two or three minutes before telling him he did a great job but now it was Dustin's turn.

Dustin pumped for a few minutes until we could see he was getting tired. He was pumping slower and slower but he didn't want to give up. "He's going to take all day. Here Dust, let me finish so we can get this thing in the water." Jerad didn't like delays when he wanted to do something and soon convinced Dustin that he should get the oars out of the ama hull while he finished inflating the dinghy. Daryl gave a couple of last pumps on the peddle just to make sure the chambers were firm. The floorboards were fitted into place and the Avon was ready to go.

Daryl tied a long line of rope to the ring attached to the front of the dinghy and wound the other end around a deck cleat on the stern of our starboard ama. Jerad was a pretty good swimmer but the other two weren't. None of them had ever rowed a boat before. They were each told to put on their life jackets, which Jerad did under protest, and to take turns rowing the dinghy. They could row the dinghy out only as far as the rope tether would allow. We were, after all in the Pacific Ocean and didn't want them drifting away from us. There is a knack to rowing but they all did amazingly well. They seemed to have a natural rhythm or feel for it. When they had each had several turns at the oars they came back and climbed aboard using the built in steps at the back of the boat.

Next it was our turn. Daryl and I lowered ourselves down the steps and into the dinghy. This was fun. I could tell my arms would get tired after a short while but it was still fun. We didn't have any sort of motor for the dinghy at this time so if we were ever going to get from *Lunar Glow* to the shore it was imperative that we learn to row. We finished our "lesson" in rowing and returned to the boat. I was seated on the center seat in the dinghy which was actually like a long round inflated pillow wedged into place between the sides of the dinghy. Daryl was sitting on the back end. As we came up alongside the rear steps Daryl grabbed hold of the rail and pulled himself up the steps first. I stood up to follow him but made the huge mistake of stepping first onto the inflated side of the dinghy. With nobody else in the dinghy to balance things out my weight off set the whole thing and I took my first and very unplanned dunk in the Pacific. My sons thought it was hilarious.

The boys spent the rest of the day fishing off the boat. They caught lots of small mackerel which I cooked up for dinner. The next day was spent in much the same way except that I didn't fall into the water again. I did laundry instead. The boys were going through clothes like mad and I didn't want them to run out of things to wear. Doing laundry in a five gallon bucket with a washboard is truly an experience. Not only did I learn that clothes washed in salt water don't dry very well and retain a tacky feel to them but I quickly gained a lot of respect for my pioneer ancestors.

My fishing crew came through for us a second day in a row. We discarded the small ray and little crab Jerad caught but had a feast with the mackerel and halibut. Life was great.

The one and only time in the entire five years at sea that we were ever boarded and searched was at Smuggler's Cove by our own Coast Guard. They announced themselves with a bullhorn then came aboard and started looking around. I don't know if this is a routine thing that they do or what they were looking for but it was a little frightening. They said it was a safety inspection and that we passed. We pulled the anchor a short time later and sailed a short distance to a place called Albert's Anchorage. It was here that the boys made their first untethered trip in the dinghy. They rowed to shore and did some exploring while I did chores and Daryl tried to figure out how to operate the Loran, our new piece of navigational equipment.

We stayed only one night at Albert's Anchorage then returned to Smuggler's Cove for two more nights before heading back to the Channel Island Harbor and our familiar spot at the guest dock. We had been gone for six nights and for the most part had a great time. Daryl's feet and ankles were swollen from being sunburned and the lights on top of the mast kept going out so that would be added to the list of things he needed to repair. The day was foggy and there was a light drizzle so we mostly had to stay below in the cabin. The guest dock included hot showers which we all welcomed.

The following day I used the laundry facilities to get caught up on the washing without having to use a bucket. We did some shopping at a nearby supermarket then took both the car and the truck and headed out to Grant and Denise's place. Instead of selling the car we decided to give it to Grant as payment for all the help he had given us on the boat. He seemed happy with that.

We stayed six nights tied alongside the guest dock trying to get as many things checked off our "to do" list as possible. Daryl got the mast lights fixed and was finally figuring out how the Loran worked. We drove to San Pedro to pick up the remainder of our rigging material and then on to the boat ranch to work on it. Escrow papers for the sale of my rental house in Nevada were there waiting so I got those signed and returned. Our California property had also closed. The many strings holding us to land were being clipped one by one.

I went shopping and did the laundry one last time at the guest dock in preparation for setting out again the next day. Daryl finished working on the new rigging and the boys did a first rate job of washing the boat. I also did a thorough inventory of all of the food we had onboard and where each item was located. I put it on a handmade spreadsheet which I kept updated for the remainder of our sailing days.

Our sail back out to Smuggler's Cove proved once again how green we were as sailors. We had wind gusts up to 35 knots and we were having trouble knowing how much sail to have up and our sail changes were anything but smooth. We got whipped with a sheet but no damage to the boat. We did discover a small leak in our main water tank and the new rigging was in need of tightening. We all breathed a sigh of relief when the sails were dropped and the anchor caught in the sandy bottom of the cove. We wouldn't even think of pulling it up again for several days.

CHAPTER TWELVE

NEW FRIENDS

We met our first ever friends at sea there in Smuggler's Cove the next day. The *Martha Rose* motored into the anchorage and dropped anchor not far from where we sat. Dean and Coppy were a nice couple traveling with their only son, Fritz, age 11. I'm not sure what kind of boat *Martha Rose* was but it certainly wasn't a sailboat. It was some sort of power boat that reminded me of a tug boat. It had been their home for several years. Like my boys, Fritz was being home schooled so right away I had something to talk about with Coppy. She even knew of a high school correspondence program that several other boat kids used through the University of Nebraska-Lincoln which gave me hope that I would be able to find something better for Jerad. The kids were happy to have a new friend and eager to see Fritz's boat and show him theirs as well. Dean ran a floating handyman business. He was quite willing to check out Daryl's list of repairs and give his input.

The boys were getting into a routine on the boat. We did schoolwork first thing of a morning. They knew that they had certain assignments to finish before being turned loose to play and explore. Fritz was doing the same on *Martha Rose* so that worked out great. After school the boys all got together to play or fish while Coppy and I visited and exchanged recipes. I was learning what a great resource other yacht people could be. Daryl always seemed to have some project to keep him busy and if not he was always happy for an afternoon nap.

After four days *Martha Rose* pulled out. We were preparing to head for Catalina Island but because there was no wind we changed our minds and stayed on another night. We left the following morning just before 8:00am and sailed to Santa Barbara Island arriving at 4:15pm to a crowded anchorage of about 20 boats.

Our batteries were failing so we were trying hard to conserve our power. This meant keeping our lights to a minimum as well as our radio. We had a kerosene lantern that hung over the table in our settee which gave us the light we needed in the evenings to eat, read, and play games. Daryl and the boys did some fishing off the boat after anchoring and caught some nice perch which I fried up for dinner. We were all tired after the days sail so we turned in early.

The following morning we all got into the dinghy to row to shore. Santa Barbara Island is one of the several Channel Islands and this one looked like it could be interesting. We rowed towards the shore and got close but we never landed the dinghy. As we neared the shore the water was full of sea lions swimming close to our little dinghy. Dustin and Nathan were both scared so instead of landing the dinghy we slowly rowed back out to *Lunar Glow*. The day was nice and the winds were good so we got ready to head out for Catalina Island. The boys worked on their schoolwork once we were under way. I baked bread, which I had been doing every two to three days since moving onto the boat but today's baking emptied our propane tank. Lucky for us we would be able to refill it in Catalina.

Catalina Island is a popular vacation spot sitting 27 miles off the coast of Southern California. The main town is Avalon where ferry boats come and go on a daily basis taking passengers back and forth from the mainland. The anchorage there is usually congested and there is a charge to hook up to one of their moorings. We chose to sail into the backside of the island and anchored in Cat Harbor. The anchorage there is huge and well protected. The scenery was beautiful. There were already several other boats but it was not crowed by any means. We anchored a ways off shore where we figured no other boats could swing around and hit us.

The boys had finished their schoolwork the following morning and were washing the boat when we saw *Martha Rose* arrive. They anchored close by and the boys were glad to see their friend, Fritz, again. It was the 28th of August and as we were soon to learn hundreds of people come to Catalina for Labor Day, mostly on private boats. We were there for twelve days and loved every minute of it.

The town of Cat Harbor was small but very friendly to the boating community. We went to shore often for hot showers, water and ice, and to make phone calls. There was a children's festival going on with free drinks and food and lots of fun stuff for the kids to do. The island was also a great place to hike which we did often. We would follow the wild goat trails up to the highest peaks of the island to take pictures of the unbelievable number of boats arriving in the anchorage below. We met Dave and Kathy on *Easy Glider* and finally learned how to cook the rays or skates that we had been catching and throwing back. The only part that could be eaten was the wings. They were cut into about 1" pieces, breaded, and fried and tasted just like scallops. We watched sea planes come in and each day as it got closer to Labor Day the anchorage continued to fill. What originally had felt like a comfortable distance around our boat was closing in fast.

Daryl finally got our head working properly. No more port o potty. Hurray! Dean also helped him redo our steering. A self steering system was connected which would allow us to steer the boat without one of us actually holding onto the wheel all the time. We name the self-steering "Mike". That way each one of the four brothers would be able to help with the steering even if Michael wasn't physically with us.

From where we were anchored the row into shore was long and hard. We were one of the very few boats that did not have a small outboard motor for their dinghy, but what we did have was sons with great imaginations and ideas. They decided that it was easier to sail than to row so they turned our inflatable Avon into a little sailboat. They found an old man overboard pole in one of the ama hulls and used that for their mast. A bed sheet became their sail. One of the boys would sit on the back of the dinghy with an oar held down into the water at the stern for a rudder to help steer their vessel. The other boys would sit in front of the sheet and yell back which way to steer as the rudder operator couldn't see past the bed sheet. It was the silliest boat I had ever seen but it sailed great ... in one direction. It all depended upon which way the wind was blowing.

The best part of the celebrations in the harbor was a dinghy parade through the anchorage. Those that participated obviously knew in advance about this event as they came all prepared to deck their mini vessels out for the occasion. For us it was fun just watching. Programs onshore also continued throughout the week.

By Monday, September 7th Cat Harbor began to empty out as the weekend sailors returned home. Jerad got his first surfboard ride being pulled in and out around the remaining boats in the harbor behind Dave's dinghy from *Easy Glider*. We left just after 8:00am the following morning for a 12 hour sail back to Channel Islands Harbor.

CHAPTER THIRTEEN

LAST WEEK ASHORE

We still had a couple of pieces of remaining business holding us to the land. We realized that we would need a small generator as an emergency backup in case our batteries failed, and we still needed to sell our diesel pickup truck. We hoped this wouldn't take too long as we were anxious to start working our way south towards San Diego where we would make our final preparation to sail on down into Mexico as soon as the hurricane season was over. We also knew we needed more experience with the boat before doing any serious sailing.

We spent a couple of days shopping for groceries and bought a small generator. We caught up on the laundry, washed the boat, stayed on tract with the schoolwork, and placed an ad in the local paper to sell the truck. We used the phone number from the boat ranch as the contact number. The ad would run over the coming weekend and I would sit at the boat ranch hoping for some calls on the pay phone in the main house.

We went out to Grant and Denise's house one last time for dinner. Our head was working great now so we were happy to return their port o potty. We related all the fun we had had out at Cat Harbor and told them our plans to return there for awhile once our truck was sold. They decided they would try to take the ferry over and stay with us for a couple of days once we were back out there again.

I stayed all of Saturday and Sunday at the boat ranch. It was fun being with our friends there but there were very few calls for the truck. I had mailed off a letter to the University of Nebraska-Lincoln while at Cat Harbor giving the boat ranch address in Camarillo as our address. There was a packet of information including their catalog of courses waiting for me when I arrived. I had plenty of time to comb through the pages and see what courses I could order for Jerad. There were suggested classes for a college prep program and the number of credits needed for science, math, English, and so on. There were a lot of choices and none of them were cheap. Their testing process, however, was quite simple. Upon completion of each course I would administer the enclosed exam and send it on to the university for grading. That worked for me. I mailed off an order using a marine store in San Diego as a shipping address. Everyone at the ranch assured us that Downwind Marine would be quite willing to receive mail and packages and would be a valuable resource for us in getting ready to leave for Mexico in a few week's time. They were correct.

By Sunday evening I was getting worried. What if the truck didn't sell right away? I couldn't just sit here forever. I had a family to take care of and an adventure to get on with. Then something wonderful happened. Billie came by the ranch. Billie was another long time yachtie and avid surfer who had lived at the ranch at one time but was now living elsewhere in the area. It just so happened that Billie was in the market for a pickup truck and he really liked ours. Over the next two days we negotiated a price with him, did the paperwork, and Billie had himself a new truck. As for us the last string holding us to the land had just been cut.

CHAPTER FOURTEEN

OFF AT LAST

Billie picked up the truck the morning of Tuesday September 15, 1987 and at 1:15 that afternoon we untied the dock lines from the Channel Island guest dock for the last time. We sailed 14 hours straight arriving at Cat Harbor in the wee early morning to a quiet, dark, and nearly empty anchorage. We dropped our hook and went below for a few hours sleep.

Jerad seemed to have some sort of radar that attracted him to nice boats with fun toys. He spotted one the next morning and as soon as his schoolwork was finished he was rowing the dinghy over to meet our neighbor. Before long we saw him out in the harbor trying to wind surf for the first time. What a great life for a kid! I baked cookies and Daryl worked on the motor.

Our days were laid back but yet there was always something to do. When we bought *Lunar Glow* there were no life lines on the sides of the boat and Daryl said that life lines would spoil her looks. By now, however, he could see that going to sea with young children on board life lines would be a necessity regardless of how they looked. Without them it was just too easy to fall off the boat. He had bought the life line scansions during our last week on shore and spent two days here in Cat Harbor installing them. Even with the new lifelines I still thought *Lunar Glow* was a fine looking craft.

Daryl helped Dustin re-rig the dinghy for sailing so that it was a little easier for the boys to sail to shore. They fished, they snorkeled, they hiked and they swam. And with each passing day the color of their skin was growing darker. Daryl took them night fishing after dark and then we would all sit around the kerosene lamp at our table and drink hot chocolate while I read aloud to the family. We had finished *Robinson Cruiso* and had now started Henry Dana's, *Two Years Before the Mast.* I baked almost every day; cookies, bread, cakes, banana bread. We were never without good things to eat.

Jerad continued meeting people on other boats and learned to trade labor for the first time. A man named Jim needed some sanding done on his boat which Jerad was happy to do. His pay was a wet suit that Jerad loved. He was, after all, intending to become a surfer and the wet suit was just what he needed. A few days later he traded Jim more of his labor for a wallet and a chess set. *Easy Glider* was still anchored here, never having left after Labor Day. Dave and Kathy came to visit us often and brought me some shorts and a load of books they had finished reading. We learned that books are constantly being rotated amongst all of the boats. This worked out great for everyone and there was never a shortage of reading materials.

Journeyman, a beautiful monohull with lots of teak, pulled into the anchorage a few days after we did and Dustin at age 10 was suddenly in love. Sarah was a pretty little 10 year old blond who loved the water and swam like a fish. The only other child aboard was Sarah's infant sister who was nearly blind. She had been born the year before while the family was living aboard *Journyman.* Sarah was always trying to get Dustin to go swimming with her but he flatly refused no matter how much he liked her.

"Dustin. What's the matter with you? Sarah's been after you all morning to go swimming with her. Why won't you go?" I questioned.

"I'll only go if I don't have to wear my life jacket," he answered me back. "Sarah doesn't have to wear a life jacket."

"You know the rules. No swimming without a life jacket until you pass your swimming test." I wasn't about to negotiate on this one.

"You won't even let me go in the dinghy without my life jacket. That's not fair." Dustin was getting mad.

"Sorry, Son. Once you pass your swimming test you can swim and row to shore without your life jacket on. Do you want to take your test now?" I knew he felt like a baby wearing a life jacket when Sarah didn't have to and I felt bad for him but I wasn't taking any chances. If he wasn't a strong enough swimmer to pass the test then the life jacket stayed.

"No. I don't want to take that dumb test now."

I knew that Dustin would pout for awhile but it wouldn't last too long.

The *Lunar Glow* swim test consisted of jumping into the water without a life jacket and swimming twice around the boat without stopping or touching the boat. I would walk around the outer edge of the boat's deck and watch from above. The boat was 37 feet in length and 24 feet across making twice around the boat a total of 244 feet. Jerad had passed this test weeks before but Dustin and Nathan were still required to wear their life jackets. The two boys did attempt this test a few days later when Dustin knew that Sarah had gone into town with her parents but neither of them passed.

We had been at anchor for two weeks before Grant and Denise took the ferry out to the island to visit us. We had moved *Lunar Glow* closed to shore so that our company wouldn't have such a long dinghy ride to the boat with their luggage. They stayed with us for two nights which was a lot of fun for all of us.

The day before Jerad's 15th birthday we moved the boat around the island to the other side and picked up a mooring in Avalon. As always that anchorage was crowded and maneuvering our wide boat around was no easy feat. Avalon was also expensive but we knew we wouldn't be here for many nights. It would be a much easier place for us to top off our gas jugs and refill the propane bottles. We could also fill our water tank and spare water containers.

We celebrated Jerad's birthday on October 5th with breakfast at a restaurant on shore. We gave him a Hawaiian sling for his birthday. This was a type of spear for spearing fish and lobsters which we hoped he would be able to put to some good use. He was excited to have it so we felt good.

We left Avalon on October 7th and sailed down the California coast to Dana Point. We anchored in a free anchorage right by the *Pilgram*. This was a lot of fun for us as Dana Point was named after Henry Dana, the author of the book I was currently reading to the family, *Two Years Before the Mast*. The *Pilgram* was the tall masted sailing ship that Dana had crewed on back in the 1800's. The ship here next to us was actually a replica of the original. We went on one of their daily tours and found it to be most interesting.

We bought a lot of groceries while we were anchored at Dana Point. The super markets were a long walk from the boat and we were, of course, without any sort of land transportation. We all went together as a family, each of us wearing an empty back pack and after asking some directions started our walk through town. The walk back was much harder and seemed a lot longer. Each of our backpacks were filled, the younger boys carrying the lighter items. In addition we each had double lined plastic bags to carry. We must have looked quite a sight but at least we got our stores replenished.

It rained several days while we were in Dana Point so we were pretty much confined to our cabins. Dustin did pass his swimming test while we were sitting at anchor there which was truly a happy occasion. We were quite certain we would be seeing *Journyman* again and this time Dustin would be ready and eager to go swimming with Sarah.

After six nights in Dana Point we decided to move on. We left shortly after first light and sailed south again this time stopping at Mission Bay. We sailed through a very large school of dolphins for the first time which was really exciting. We didn't do much the two days we were anchored at Mission Bay but we were able to go to shore and make lots of phone calls. We called our accountant and learned that everything was right on track there. We called a neighbor in Stagecoach as well as my folks. We also called and talked to Michael. He and his dad, Joe, were going to make a trip down to San Diego later in the month to see us before we departed for Mexico. That would be fun.

CHAPTER FIFTEEN

SAN DIEGO

We arrived in San Diego on October 15, 1987, my 38th birthday. My journal entry notes that I received a flashlight from Dustin. We anchored in a place called Shelter Island and saw that *Martha Rose* was also anchored a short distance away. The Navy fleet is stationed there in San Diego so we felt quite small amid all of the huge Navy vessels. Dean had caught some bonita that day which they shared with us for our dinner that night. We learned that by cutting the dark red strip off the fillets that they no longer had a strong fishy taste. They were really quite good.

The following morning we moved the boat around to a special anchorage called La Playa. Daryl and I went shopping while the boys spent the day at a local recreation center. We found Downwind Marine and learned that they had a truck they loaned to the yachties. We would borrow it the next day to haul some rather large purchases back to the boat. They would be most happy to watch for the shipment of text books I was expecting.

For some reason the boats sailing into San Diego were not permitted to stay more than a few nights in any one place. Because of this there was a continuous parade of boats moving between the three main anchorages. Shelter Island was nicknamed, Rock 'n Roll, because of all the large Navy boats churning up the water there. The small boats bounced around constantly. Then there was La Playa which was the most convenient for getting into town. Glorietta Bay was clear over in front of Coronado which was a fair ways off. The anchorage there was right in front of a very nice golf course and the boys thought that gathering golf balls out of the water traps was great fun. It didn't matter how many times you stayed in each anchorage as long as each stay didn't exceed a certain amount of time.

On our first stay in Glorietta Bay I went ashore and found the local library. Jerad had one more final to take with his BYU studies and I arranged with the head librarian to do his test there. Twice from Glorietta Bay we took the ferry back over to San Diego to do shopping and take care of business. We got all of our Mexico paperwork done which was really quite easy. We bought a pressure cooker which we figured would save us a lot of propane. We also bought some solar panels for the boat which we hoped would keep our batteries charged and thus our running lights and electronics working. Daryl bought a foot pump for our fresh water tank in the galley which worked great.

Schoolwork was a lot of work for me. In order for me to teach each of the lessons I first had to read the lessons and all of the accompanying assignments, then teach it, then grade the work once the boys had completed it. Dustin was doing his 5th grade course and Jerad was doing 9th grade. I spent countless hours reading and preparing. At that point, however, it was actually Nathan that was the biggest challenge. Both of the other boys were already good readers so I could give them an assignment to read and they were fine. Nathan, however, never having been to school didn't know how to read yet. I spent hours with him. We had done all of the phonics but when it came to putting the sounds together it was just that … a bunch of sounds strung together in slow motion that didn't seem to translate into any type of words. I was so frustrated some days I could scream. I would even try to get Daryl to sit and listen to him making all of those sounds that translated into nothing. Maybe the school board was right after all. Then one day it was like a light bulb went on in Nathan's head. He finally got it. If he put the sounds together fast enough they turned into words and if he said the words fast enough they turned into sentences. From that point on it was pretty much smooth sailing.

Michael and Joe came down and spent a weekend with us. I was always happy to get to see Michael and this would more than likely be the last time the boys would see their dad for awhile too. Grant showed up and brought us a few things we had left with them in Piru but just stayed for the day.

We continued to have a great time no matter which of the three anchorages we were in. We were meeting lots of other cruisers that would be heading down the coast to Mexico about the same time we were. I couldn't believe how many of the boats had kids aboard. Michael and Anne of the *Michaelanne* had a son, Brian, who was Dustin's age. Don and Brenda on *Willow* had two sons, Denny age 8 and Steve was 11. The kids all became fast friends and none of us parents could ever keep track of which boys were sleeping on which boat every night. There were several others but this group was especially close.

A section of non-skid had worked itself loose on part of the deck so Daryl was able to get that repaired. We had our compass adjusted and I repaired a tear in dodger. The new solar panels were secured into place ready to soak up the rays of the sun. Jerad took his final exam at the Coronado Library and his new text books finally arrived at Downwind Marine. Our departure time was drawing closer all the time.

Michaelanne was the first of our group to depart. They headed out on November 8th and *Martha Rose* followed them two days later. We decided to buy one more solar panel which Daryl installed in such a way that it could be rotated to follow the sun depending upon the time of day. Grant and Denise came down for one final night aboard *Lunar Glow* before we, too, said adios to the US and headed south.

CHAPTER SIXTEEN

SOUTH OF THE BOARDER
... DOWN MEXICO WAY

he next months travels are taken word for word from my personal journal and letters that I had written home:

We finally left San Diego at 4:40pm on Thursday, November 12, 1987 after what seemed like forever to get ready. Our friends on 'Willow', Don and Brenda Plantz and sons Steve and Denis, were planning to sail out at the same time so we were happy to get to hear friendly voices on the VHF as we departed.

Captain and crew of 'Lunar Glow' were all excited as we headed for Ensenada, Mexico on our first ever all night sail. We had a nice sail and the trip was uneventful. We arrived in Ensenada Harbor at 12:30 pm on Friday afternoon and dropped anchor near 'Willow'. Before the hook had even reached bottom we were greeted by Manuel of Tito's Barbieto Water Taxi service and before he knew what was happening Daryl had contracted two round trip rides to shore. We soon learned that that was an expensive error which we didn't make again!

Jerad, Dustin, and Nathan remained on the boat while Daryl and I went ashore to "check in". This being our first time with the check in procedure we did pretty good. This is something that all the boat people are required to do at most of the major ports. We have pads of forms (all in Spanish) called crew lists. We need four (sometimes five) copies of these in each port. We also need our tourist cards and some papers form the Mexican Consulate we got in San Diego. We take all of these to the Port Captain's office. He does something with them then gives part of them back and sends us to the Immigration Office. They do something with them then send us back to the Port Captain's office again. Sometimes that's the end and sometimes you must go to customs. These offices are <u>never</u> in one place; always spread out across town. What's more, the procedure in each town is different. Sometimes it's Immigration first and so on. And we have found that some offices aren't even marked. (In Cabo San Lucas the Immigration is a small whitewashed wooden shack. No sign – no nothing). At any rate it's interesting. This procedure is also repeated when you leave. Daryl's theory is that by making you walk all over town you end up spending more money.

Our only scare came from the immigration office. They didn't know if they should allow the boys to stay in Mexico without a letter of approval from their father. Finally they decided that they could stay because they had valid passports. Our stay in Ensenada was short, two nights, but enjoyable. The harbor there is real dirty as is the town but still a fun place.

There was only one other notable happening in Ensenada. It was on Saturday when Daryl and I took Nathan into town along with Don, Brenda and Denny. It didn't look like a good place to go off and leave the boats alone so Jerad, Dustin, and Steve all stayed behind on 'Lunar Glow' to watch the boats. While we were gone our anchor slipped due to some strong winds that came up. The boys pulled the anchor, started the motor, and spent two hours trying to re-anchor in a very crowded anchorage. Dustin steered, Jerad handled the anchor and Steve ran around fending off the other boats. They did a super job (only hitting one boat – no damage). When I think of the tight places Dustin maneuvered that big boat in and out of I still can't believe it. By the time we returned they had set two anchors and were fine; just shook up a bit. (At least Jerad was. Dustin thought it was great fun)!

We left Ensenada at noon on Sunday just behind 'Willow'. We were delayed a few minutes while we untangled our anchor line from around a dinghy moored near us. We had fairly good wind as we left Ensenada and took with us some fun memories plus an anchor full of thick Ensenada Harbor mud – yuck!

Our passage from Ensenada to Bahia Santa Maria was our longest so far and took five nights and days to cover nearly 600 miles. We became extremely tired but the weather was good and we had no problems. During the day there was hardly any wind so we didn't make much distance but during the nights we'd scream. We decided not to use our motor during that leg of the trip so during the day when 'Willow' would start their motor they would pull ahead. But at night with the wind we'd pass them until their lights were only a dot behind us. We always had good radio contact. At first night watches were a little scary but they got better. There was a lot of traffic at night as we were in the shipping lanes. We have learned to recognize the light patterns on the other vessels so we can tell which direction they are going. Only a couple of times did we have to alter course. Jerad took his night watches, and we used "Mike" our tiller master a good deal of the time which helped greatly.

Daryl practiced taking noon sights with the sextant and I struggled to do the sight reductions. Even the very simple teach yourself to navigate books were extremely confusing. Our Loran (navigation system) was great for about two days but then we were out of range so we had to rely on dead reckoning. We were never very far from 'Willow' who ran their engine a great deal. We sailed the entire time until just before entering Bahia Santa Maria.

We anchored in a beautiful spot in Bahia Santa Maria along with six other boats. The water was so clear we could see the anchor touch down. There is no town; only about half a dozen small fisherman shacks. Besides ourselves and 'Willow' there was also 'Michaelanne' whom we had met in San Diego. Although we had never seen the other boats that pulled into Santa Maria that day we had heard their voices on the radio quite often over the previous few hours so it was interesting to put the faces and voices together.

We had our first experience with lobster trading here. The local fishermen came alongside our boat in their ponga and traded us four big lobsters for one can of outboard motor oil. Boy, were they good. The only problem was that with no refrigeration we had to cook and eat the lobsters right then. By the time we were halfway through dinner I was so exhausted I laid down on my bunk *and fell sound asleep. I didn't wake until the following morning and found I still had lobster in my mouth.*

The surf in Bahia Santa Maria was more than we could handle. Each time we attempted to row to shore we flipped the dinghy. The water felt warm so we didn't mind. We swam, collected shells, and hiked on the sand dunes. Jerad did his first surfing and was quite good. He stayed so long in the water he shriveled up like a prune. We remained for two nights in Bahia Santa Maria. Dustin stayed for only one night then went on to Bahia Magdelina with 'Michaelanne' who left along with 'Willow'.

We had a nice eight hour sail from there to Bahia Magdelina. We anchored in a place called Man-O-War Cove among the other boats in front of a small fishing village. There was a large wrecked ship on the shore; a reminder of the last hurricane that had passed through. The village had a generator which was started each evening to light the houses.

Landing the dinghy here was easy as there was no surf. It was even more pleasant because of the many children in the village that ran to meet us as we rowed towards shore and helped to pull the dinghy in. I took a bag of clothes for the children and they seemed happy to have them.

We attended a four boat pot luck on the night of our arrival. It was held on 'Martha Rose'. The food was good and the music and singing was fun. We did have a scare upon leaving. Jerad had used the dinghy earlier and had tied it up in a hurry to 'Martha Rose' and it had come loose and disappeared. Lucky for Jerad another boat had spotted it floating by and rescued it before it went out to sea.

The following day was check-in and check-out time for Bahia Magdelina. The bay there was nearly as big as San Francisco Bay and the check in place was in San Carlos which was on the other side of the bay. Everyone went together to do the paperwork. The crews of 'Willow' and 'Martha Rose' rode with us on 'Lunar Glow' while 'Michaelanne' followed in their boat. It was a long day and I spent most of it in the galley. I made pancakes for everyone for breakfast, toast and tea later for a snack, and soup for lunch. I also baked two cakes as it was Nathan's 7th birthday and we would be having a party later that night. It was a long but enjoyable ride to San Carols with pilot whales swimming alongside us for a long ways.

San Carols had no paved roads and few sidewalks. Everything was dirt and sand. The people were helpful but nobody spoke English and our Spanish was very limited. There were no street signs. We just wandered around and hoped for the best. Everyone had brought along their gas and water jugs as this was a place to refill them. We must have been quite a sight all walking through town with all those jugs but it was a fun day.

Nathan's birthday party was nice but boy was it crowded. The weather had turned cool so we all squeezed down into our aft cabin — all four boatloads of us.

We remained only five days in Bahia Magdelina then left for another all night passage, this time to Cabo San Lucas. This was a delightfully fun passage for us. The weather was warm, the water calm, and the dolphins were numerous. We sat and laid on the ama hull bows for a long time playing with the dolphins as they swam along with us. We tried to photograph them but some things just cannot be captured on film.

CHAPTER SEVENTEEN

SO THIS IS CABO

W e arrived in Cabo on Thanksgiving Day. The anchorage was very crowded and terribly inconvenient for getting into town. This was definitely not a place we would want to stay for long. We postponed going into town as well as our Thanksgiving dinner until our second day. We had to anchor a long ways from the dock. We were fairly close to the beach but there was a big surf (the kind that swamps the dinghy) so after I ended up swimming in my long skirt that first day there I decided against beach landings in Cabo San Lucas. The check-in process was no problem, just a good walk in between offices. We made the mistake of not checking out at the same time we checked in and it ended up costing us $15.00 in overtime fees later ... another mistake we wouldn't repeat. Daryl got together with Don on *Willow* in the afternoon and drank so much rum he ended up missing Thanksgiving dinner.

Cabo San Lucas was an expensive place to be. We walked around a lot but did little else. We made several phone calls. One was to Michael to confirm his plans to meet us in La Paz on December 16th. Dustin spent some time down on the docks and met some people on a big, fancy fishing boat. When Dustin told them how much he loved to fish they invited Dustin, Steve, and Brian to go out on a deep sea fishing trip. He was so excited. They hooked four and landed two marlin. Each boy brought back about fifteen pounds of marlin. It was good white meat though not the best eating fish around.

Dustin would still rather fish than do most anything else. When he's not fishing he's making lures. Some of them are really good. He caught a nice bass on one he made out of sequins and drinking straws.

We stayed five days in Cabo mainly waiting for a new Sat Nav to arrive. This was a navigational instrument that Daryl had ordered with the help of a Ham radio operator on one of the boats in Magdelina Bay. It was to be shipped from Downwind Marine in San Diego to a place called Papi's in Cabo San Lucas. When it still hadn't arrived after five days we decided to press on.

We checked out and left Cabo late in the afternoon. It had started to rain but we were hoping it would clear. An hour later the weather was looking worse so we returned to the anchorage to wait until the next day.

Our next stop was in Los Fralies. We traveled with *Willow* although they mainly motored along shore while we tacked out quite a ways. We beat them in by about an hour even though we logged many more miles than they did. *Lunar Glow* really was a fast boat.

Los Fralies was lovely. The first thing Jerad spotted upon entering the anchorage was a large power yacht named *Sumdum* with two windsurfers on board. Our hook wasn't down long before Jerad was in our Avon rowing against about 20 knots of wind over to *Sumdum*. He struck up a conversation with the crew members aboard and in no time at all was out windsurfing. He was given the grand tour of the boat as well as an invitation to return that evening with his brothers and friends to watch videos. The owners of the yacht were out of the country and had left their crew members to take care of their two million dollar boat. Jerad was quite impressed. It had huge staterooms, a frig, freezer, microwave, dishwasher, and a washer and dryer. (No washing clothes in a five gallon bucket with a toilet plunger on that boat)!

There was a small mountain on the east side of the anchorage. We spent one afternoon hiking a good ways up it. Dustin and Nathan made the climb barefooted. From up there we could see a cove on the other side of the mountain. The next day Don, Brenda, Daryl, and I decided to hike over to the cove. It proved to be a most interesting hike. We walked through graze land and along an arroyo until we came to the ocean. We explored the seashore which included some low caves. At one place the entire shore was piled with smooth round boulders from the size of basketballs on up. Our return trip was via a different and much more difficult route. We ended up almost crawling through a cactus filled wood. We went for what seemed like forever before reaching the road.

It was on this hike that I collected a piece of cactus wood which would shortly become our Christmas tree and later still a bird perch.

Although Los Fralies was a fun and pretty place we only stayed three nights. Our next stop was to be Ensenada de Muertos which means Bay of the Dead. The name sounded horrible but we loved it there. Again we had to make some long offshore tacks due to the fact that we were going to weather (sailing into the wind) and we had high seas. It was after dark when we made the anchorage. It was difficult trying to enter after dark because the contour of the land is very deceiving there. To make matters worse our motor had taken on some water in the high seas so didn't want to start when we wanted to motor into the anchorage. Jerad spent a few minutes in a panic while Daryl went back to work on the motor in the dark. He got the spark plugs changed and the motor started but he dropped the plug wrench overboard in the process. At least the motor was running and we were soon safe inside the anchorage.

Los Muertos has no town; just a few fishing huts along the beach. It's a popular winter camping spot for a few American campers, several of which had set up camp there. The water was real clear and not too cold. There was a wonderful coral reef inside part of the bay and we spent two afternoons snorkeling. Jerad found a lobster and speared it with his Hawaiian sling. It tasted great but we told Jerad that in the future he was to keep quiet about such catches. Americans are not allowed to take lobster, so when Jerad surfaced waving this lobster on the end of his spear and shouting, "I got a lobster", at the top of his lungs we had to shut him up fast then hurry and eat the evidence!

Daryl and I took a long walk up the beach one morning while the boys played around the boat. We had gone about a mile and a half when we saw a Mexican woman out on some rocks. She was carrying a five gallon bucket and had something on her head. When we got close enough we could see that she had a net filled with twenty or so lobsters on her head. Her husband was in the water diving for them. We finally asked if we could buy some and we ended up paying $2.00 US for five nice sized lobsters. As we had no bucket to carry live lobsters in I put them in a spare blouse I had along and plopped them up on my head as I'd seen the woman do for the walk back to *Lunar Glow*. Except for wiggling around once in awhile they rode there quite well.

A strong north wind kicked up while we were in Los Muertos. Several boats pulled in to escape the strong wind and rough seas. Our water was running low as was our propane. (Between our main water tank and all the jerry jugs combined we held a total of 91 gallons of water. We had two five gallon propane tanks). I was anxious to reach La Paz before Michael was due to arrive. After five nights we finally left heading north up into the Sea of Cortez and beating into the wind once again. Eleven of the fourteen boats in the anchorage left that night. We were the only one who chose not to go through the channel but to tack out and around the large island of Ceralvos instead. We were hoping for some good wind and found it. Our sail was beautiful save for one mishap. We tore a fair sized hole at one of our second reef points in the mainsail so had to complete our sail into La Paz reefed down twice.

(As a side note here for those not familiar with sailing: The main sail is a sail attached to a boom or long beam which is connected to and sticks out perpendicular from the mast. This large sail is connected to the boom and then pulled up along the mast with a line called a halyard. By using a type of pulley system attached to the top of the mast the sail is pulled up along the mast thus forming a large triangle. About every three feet up from the bottom of the sail there are straight rows, our sail had three such rows, with several short ropes attached to the sail with a piece of the rope extending out on either side of the sail. If the wind became too strong and the mainsail needed to be made smaller you could lower the sail part way down the mast and by using the short dangling ropes tie the ends from both sides of the sail under the boom thus shortening the sail. You could shorten the sail up to three times depending upon how much wind there was).

We caught our first dorado (otherwise known as mahi mahi) during this run. They weren't real big but enough for a nice meal which we shared later that evening after anchoring in Lobos which was just before La Paz. We stayed just one night in Lobos and didn't even go ashore. We were all tired after a hard sail the night before and just needed a good night's sleep.

CHAPTER EIGHTEEN

FINALLY ... LA PAZ

A s we left the little cove at Lobos Dustin caught a small bonita which I cooked and gave to Daryl for breakfast. It was only a short sail into LaPaz. The large number of boats anchored there was quite overwhelming. After a few minutes of "checking out the neighborhood" we finally found a place to squeeze into. We dropped our hook in front of the Los Arcos Hotel. As Rafael's Dinghy Beach was also here it was a good place to leave the dinghy while going to shore. Rafael or his nephew, Abel, were almost always there on the beach to watch the dinghies. We usually paid them a few hundred pesos for this service.

After changing into our "go to town" clothes we went into town along with *Willow* to do our check in routine. Offices here were really spread out so we got to (or had to) see a lot of the town just checking in.

Our first impressions of La Paz were very good ones. The town was quite large with many interesting sights. Walking down the sidewalks was a challenge, just as it had been in Cabo San Lucas. You had to be constantly aware of holes in the street, pieces of rebar sticking up, curbs that could vary between a few inches and several feet, and yes, dog pooh. There were dogs everywhere. Some were healthy looking but more often they were thin and mangy looking. Not the kind you want to scratch behind the ears or let lick your kid's nose. And another strange thing about the dogs – they were all, or mostly all – long and rather short; like maybe a male basset hound had had a hay day in La Paz.

We found the market place to be quite delightful. The fresh produce was very nice and inexpensive. The bakery was right in the market place and had wonderful breads and pastries. There were also fresh fish and meat stands.

The food was dirt cheap and we ate at lots of little stands along the streets. Sometimes we weren't really sure what it was we were eating and it was probably better that way. We stopped for a meat taco at one of the little stands and looked up while we were eating and tried to translate what the sign said. We recognized the words "head of" but not the rest. We decided to finish eating before looking up the last word. Whatever it was it tasted good.

Just about anything you needed could be found somewhere in La Paz. The morning "net" on our single sideband radio was a good source of information. Through it we were able to find a woman who did sail repair and she mended our mainsail.

We phoned Michael so that he'd know we had arrived in La Paz. It was Friday, December 11. We learned that he would be one day later in arriving and we could expect him on December 17th. We had a nice surprise the following day to find that Billie, Laurie, and Sport, three of our boat ranch friends were in La Paz. We met for lunch on shore and had a nice visit.

Thanks once again to the morning "net" we got a message that our Sat Nav had finally arrived in Cabo San Lucas, and here we were in La Paz! Russ and Shirley on a boat named *Wanderlust* heard that call come through. They had a car in La Paz and were planning to make a trip to Cabo the next day and did we want to go along? What luck. Daryl and I rode with them to Cabo and had a great day.

There were laundry facilities in La Paz which was much easier than trying to wash clothes on the boat. Although the amount of laundry I had to wash now was less than when we first moved onto the boat it was still a big job. Shortly after leaving Cat Harbor I had to initiate the "you wear it, you wash it" rule. The boys had been changing clothes so often that I just couldn't keep up with them. Once they found out that they had to wash their own clothes it was almost impossible to get them to put on a clean outfit. I still did the personal laundry for Daryl and myself as well as all the towels, bed linens, etc., but even that was a huge amount of work. Towels and sheets were especially hard. Leaning over a five gallon bucket with a toilet plunger for the agitator or spreading the clothes on the deck to scrub out tough spots with a scrub brush was back breaking work. And trying to get all the soap out wasn't easy either. Then everything had to be wrung out. Small articles weren't too bad but try wringing out a full size bed sheet or bath towel. I found that if I looped the large articles around the metal forestays or other rigging on the boat and started twisting the ends around each other that I could get most of the water wrung out. I then used the life lines that Daryl had installed back in Cat Harbor as clothes lines. This irritated Daryl to no end. He said it made us look like a bunch of Gypsies but I didn't know how else I was supposed to get the laundry dried.

CHAPTER NINETEEN

A VISIT FROM MICHAEL

Michael's plane was late in arriving but we were told to expect that. When he did arrive there was a bit of a problem. Michael had neglected to follow my instructions and had come into Mexico without obtaining a tourist visa, a passport, or an original birth certificate. After a shaky fifteen to twenty minutes with the immigration officer who was saying that Michael must return to the US we were finally able to buy his way in for $10.00.

The boys all enjoyed seeing each other again and couldn't wait to show Michael around town. We still had Christmas shopping to get done and for me that was a big job. We decorated a Christmas tree on *Lunar Glow*. The cactus branch I had picked up in Las Fralies was just the right size. Daryl made a wooden base so that it stood well. We covered the base of it with cotton from the vitamin jars. I had brought a handful of ornaments along so we hung those on the tree as well as several cookies. Jerad topped it off with a stale pancake instead of a star. It really looked quite festive. I had told the boys we would get a piñata for part of our Christmas celebration.

Nathan chose a large Santa Clause. Between Santa, the Christmas tree, and the six of us the stern cabin was quite crowded.

December 20th was a new moon and the lowest tide of the year. In the afternoon we took the boys to a Mexican festival in town where they were able to participate in the breaking of a piñata. It was a fun time except for Nathan getting clobbered by a wild swing of the bat from a local boy taking his turn at the piñata. Later that day we joined with friends from lots of the other boats for a clam bake and picnic at a place called El Magoti. This was a fair dinghy ride across the anchorage from La Paz. It was also a gold mine for shell collecting.

A couple of days before Christmas we decided to spend a few days along with *Willow* out at the islands to the northeast of La Paz. Both boats sailed out to Isla Partida and after anchoring we all took a long walk across to back side of the island and along the rocky shoreline. The boys had fun exploring the tide pools there.

Christmas Day was very pleasant. We opened our gifts and then had breakfast. The boys all got new snorkeling equipment which they had to try out.

They left for another hike, this time exploring some caves while Daryl repaired another piece of our walnut shell deck. I was busy preparing our Christmas dinner which we shared with *Willow* later in the day. Dustin returned from their hike with a new treasure ... a bone that we were sure was from a man's leg. After one night of having it on the boat we made him get rid of it. It gave us the willies; (and Daryl thought all the shells and driftwood I always brought back were bad)! Later that evening a red tide came in. This is caused when the algae bloom, or some such thing. Anyway, we didn't want to get into the water at that time.

The next two days were cold and windy. I kept the boys on the boat to get caught up on some schoolwork. Michael had brought several school assignments with him but it was like pulling teeth trying to get him to actually do it. The other three boys knew the routine so for them it wasn't nearly as bad. We were strict parents. We had certain rules and we expected them to be followed. Michael, having been away from my discipline for so long now resented being told what to do. He was often belligerent and mouthy. When he was with his dad he could do as he pleased and it showed.

There were no good beaches at Isla Partita so we had to put our Santa piñata on hold for a few days. We did finally get to break him open when we stopped at Lobos on our return to La Paz. Daryl kept telling the kids they were terrible to want to hit Santa Clause and break him into little pieces. I think the boys were even starting to feel bad about hitting him. I told Daryl we wouldn't break Santa if that was what he wanted. We would just continue to carry this very large piñata with us forever and ever. Daryl changed his mind!

Our remaining two weeks on the Baja were rather uneventful. Two things did take place the day we sailed back into La Paz from Lobos, though. First, we went into town and bought a new family pet; a little Conure parrot. We had seen a street vendor with some young ones on an earlier trip to town and had decided this might be a fun pet. We got a cage that would fit in our stern castle where the Santa piñata had been residing. We named our bird Sweetie Pie. The second thing that happened that day was personally recorded in my journal by Michael. He wrote, "Mike met mui bonita chickita Chantel".

The kids were meeting new friends daily and were constantly busy. Michael was suddenly "in love" so we had that to deal with. Jerad would take the younger kids to the park, and Michael would be off with Chantel. Jerad, Dustin, and Nathan would go to play games on another boat, and Michael would be off with Chantel. Jerad was getting upset that his brother came to visit but now was more interested in spending time with a girl than with him. I felt like I had lost the Michael I had once been so close to and it made me sad.

On January 3rd there was to be a big disco and pizza party in town and all the boys were going. Michael (and Chantel) did go into town to do the laundry for me to help get ready. We bought Jerad a new outfit as he had nothing suitable for a party. Greg and Maria from *Tao* came over for a visit. Their three kids had also gone to the party on shore. Don and Brenda joined us as well and we all enjoyed a nice dinner without any kids.

I couldn't help thinking back and laughing to myself. I couldn't even count the number of people that told me if I took my sons out of the school system that they would have no social life. This was the most socially interactive group I had ever seen. They were having experiences far superior to those kids back home in the public schools. I was only sorry that Michael had moved to California the year before and not been with us the whole time.

Under protests from Michael we went back out to the islands for another three nights. He was most unhappy to have to leave his new girlfriend so soon. We all enjoyed the trip though. There was lots of snorkeling during the days and we played games around the table in the evenings. We took long walks along the shore and had scones and hot chocolate when we returned to the boat. Life didn't get much better than this.

There was plenty to get done when we returned to La Paz. We had to provision for our passage across to the mainland and make sure our water, gasoline, and propane tanks were filled. We went out for Chinese food as a last family dinner together. We also took hot showers on shore. Nathan somehow broke an oar while rowing the dinghy so Daryl had one more last minute repair to do. We made copies of some school work and made the long trek through town as we did our check out process. We would be ready to set sail as soon as Michael's flight departed for California.

CHAPTER TWENTY

HEADED FOR THE MAINLAND

It was always exciting to be going back out to sea, especially when we would be exploring new places. The only one of us that ever experienced seasickness on a regular basis was Nathan. Almost without fail the first few hours out after being on shore or sitting at anchor for a prolonged period of time he would be sick. In all our years of sailing I don't recall even once of him complaining about this though. When he felt sick he would walk to the stern of the boat, lean over the railing, and puke. He sometimes did this more than once, usually whistling in between his bouts of nausea.

We stayed just one night in beautiful Ballandra where we took a walk and dug for clams before moving further south to Muertos for yet another night. We left Muertos at 11:30 am with good winds headed for Isla Isabella. This is an uninhabited island (with the exception of a few fishing huts), a bird sanctuary actually, off the west coast of mainland Mexico. The wind remained good throughout our first day and our sailing was great but Daryl and I had both developed bad colds and didn't feel real well.

Jerad hooked a big fish with the new "hukie" lure he had just gotten for Christmas but forgot to put a wire leader on his line so lost both the fish and the lure. Next he caught a fifteen pound tuna which he landed but broke about eighteen inches off the end of one of our two deep sea rods in the process. Needless to say, Jerad felt pretty bad so decided to have Daryl land the next fish which was another fifteen pound tuna.

We started to lose our wind the second day out. Our colds were no better and to make matters worse we lost two rigs and landed no fish. We were starting to feel better by our third day but the weather had turned very hot and we had lost our wind altogether. Daryl landed another fifteen pound tuna before we decided to lower our engine and motor the last remaining miles to the island.

The anchorage at Isla Isabella was crowded. We were the eighteenth boat in that day and not the last. There were frigates, pelicans, and booby birds everywhere flying overhead and diving into the water for a yummy lunch of fresh fish. We cleaned up the boat and stowed our sails and gear then took the dinghy to shore. The hike across the island was a lot of fun and we were careful not to disturb the many species of birds and other marine creatures that nest there. We especially liked the nests with baby booby's. They were white and fluffy and I'm sure very soft although we never touched them. There were lizards and iguanas but that was about all save some little shacks used from time to time by the fishermen from the mainland. So much to see. To me these kinds of outings were every bit as important for the boys education as were their textbook lessons. The water was warm and the boys spent lots of time swimming in an area well away from the fishing shacks as well as catching a load of fish.

We must have been living right as we set sail for San Blas, our first stop on mainland Mexico. The wind was with us and we were able to make our best and fastest sail yet averaging eight knots over the water and catching two nice bluefin tuna on the way.

Upon entering the channel into the inner harbor, Daryl took one look at the fishing shacks and pongas lining the bank of this fast running tidal estuary and said, "This is awful. We'll just check in and go shopping then move out to the bay," which was about five miles south. I liked the place at once. To me it looked like real Mexico. Within a short time we had all fallen in love with San Blas and ended up staying a long time there.

San Blas was not a tourist town nor was it a place that many of the folks in the cruising community chose to visit. Because the anchorage was in a tidal estuary the water was either running swiftly past our hulls in one direction when the tide came in and then we swung around and the water rushed past us going the other direction as the tide went back out. So basically our scenery changed twice a day depending upon the tides. There were only two other boats at anchor when we arrived, but we were followed a short time later by *Duet* whom had passed close enough to us as we sailed past them coming from Isla Isabella that they snapped a picture of us under sail. Jerad was glad to have Wade, a boy his age from *Duet*, to hang out with and before long they headed for the beach to check out the surf.

The youngest two boys came into town the next morning with Daryl and me to check in. This was a very old town and as was typical of so many towns in Mexico, very dirty. There was a lot of trash, and stray dogs wandered the streets aimlessly looking for any discarded tidbit of food they could find. There were no paved streets and few cars. Most people walked to where they wanted to go. The walk into town was a short one and the shopping was good and very inexpensive. But best of all were the people. They were friendly and welcoming. We struggled with they could. Later that afternoon Dustin and Jerad went off with their boogie boards and returned later with four Mexican boys. They all went and filled our water jugs then just came back to the boat to visit.

The following morning the Mexican boys were back. It was early and we hadn't even had breakfast yet. Before we knew it more and more kids were arriving. Some of the kids took Jerad to collect coconuts but the others just stayed.

Seven hours later we were still entertaining our little guests. The fact that they spoke no English and we spoke very little Spanish didn't seem to matter. Kids don't need words to laugh and have a good time. This routine went on for three days until we finally learned the magic words: "No entrada in yate hoy". Peace and quiet at last!

CHAPTER TWENTY-ONE

A LETTER TO MICHAEL

A letter I wrote home to Michael on February 8, 1988 reads in part:

Dear Michael,

Well here it is into February already. Hard to believe you have been gone almost a month already. Time goes by so quickly. I am writing this while traveling by bus from San Blas to Tepic (the capital of this state) then on to Puerto Vallarta. Anyway if it's messy that's why. At least we were lucky and got seats. Half the people must stand. The bus holds as many people as can squeeze in – a lot! Me, Daryl, and Nathan are taking this trip. Dustin and Jerad are staying with 'Lunar Glow'. We also have a couple from Oregon staying there with them. We are staying in San Blas longer than we had originally planned. We should have mail in Puerto Vallarta which is why this trip.

This bus from San Blas to Tepic will take about 1 ½ hours. Then we get another bus to Puerto Vallarta which is another 3 ½ hours. This is an agricultural state so we are going by many farms and orchards. We are also going inland up into the mountains. I wish you were able to see this. The mainland is <u>very</u> different than the Baja. Everything is green here and real warm. About 80 degrees usually. The only thing we don't like are the "no-see-ums", tiny bugs that bite like mosquitoes. We all have many bites. We like San Blas very much. It is a very poor town of about 10,000. It is so sad to see how most of the people must live but they always smile and give you friendly greetings. The "plaza" in the center of town is the central meeting place and always full of people each night. The people here have many fiestas. Probably the only thing to bring some gaiety into their lives.

There are no tourist shops here. You don't see any of the stereos, TV's, watches, etc. that you saw in La Paz. The people sell their produce, etc. in donkey-drawn carts along the streets. The streets are all dirt and some dirt and stone. They are littered with coconut husks and chewed up sugar cane. (Your brothers are very fond of sugar cane). You can buy a bag of sugar cane in bite size pieces for 400 pesos (about 18 cents). The bakeries here don't have that good fresh bread we got in La Paz so I bake all the bread again. We can get good French rolls though. Everything we eat is fresh as there are very few canned goods here. I've learned to make my own re-fried beans as well as some other Mexican dishes.

We are finally learning to speak Spanish. A 15 year old boy named Elicio comes to the boat each day from 3 to 5:00 and gives us lessons. We have a lot to learn yet but we are getting better. Elicio takes English in school and brings his school materials with him. He is a good teacher. He is also a good friend to Jerad. They go surfing sometimes. One day he took Jerad and Dustin to collect snails. (The kind on rocks in the water about 1" high). They came back with a bag of them which he showed us how to fix and eat. They were pretty good but it takes awhile after they are boiled to pull them out of their shells.

We also can get all the coconuts we want. The green ones are for drinking but the meat hasn't set up yet so those must be scraped out and eaten with a spoon like pudding. The native kids showed Jerad how to open the brown cocos and get the meat out in one piece. (He isn't very good at it yet)!

'Lunar Glow' is anchored in a tidal estuary right at the edge of town. There are only two other yachts anchored here. Not many boats come in as the channel is very shallow. Most boats anchor in a bay about five miles further up the coast. Where we are is very close to town. There is also an ice plant on the shore near us so we have treated ourselves to using the ice chest. A 100 lb block of ice is less than $1.00. We usually get ¼ or ½ block at a time.

We had a nice sail from La Paz to the mainland. After we left you at the airport we sailed over to Ballandra. That's just past Lobos where we broke the Santa piñata. It was very beautiful there. We all went to shore and took a walk and dug for clams. We even took our pictures by that rock you always see on postcards that looks like a huge mushroom. We left Ballandra the next morning and had a nice sail into Los Muertos. We met up with "Duet" there and were glad to get to know Wade and his parents pretty well over the next 7 – 10 days. We only stayed in Los Muertos one night as we had good wind and didn't want to waste it. From there to Isla Isabella was a 1 ½ day sail. We had good luck fishing – or I should say we had fresh fish for lunch and dinner each day. Jerad's luck wasn't too good. He was landing a large tuna and broke about 18" off the end of one of our two deep sea poles. Then awhile later he hooked up something real big and worked at getting it in for quite awhile then it cut the line on the prop and Jerad lost his new big lure he got for Christmas. Then Dustin had a nice dorado almost on the deck and gave it one final big tug and pulled the hook out of its mouth. Oh well.

Isla Isabella was a very interesting place. It's a sanctuary for sea birds. There are <u>everywhere</u>. The harbor was small and crowded - 18 boats when we were there. We stayed 4 or 5 days, I can't remember. Nobody actually lives on the island but there are some huts used by the fisherman who fish for shark around the island. They live in San Blas. The fishermen brought in ponga loads of hammerhead sharks and would slaughter them on the shore. The water was full of shark jaws and it was a job to miss them while landing the dinghy at low tide. The smell at such times was beyond description. We hiked across the island which was fun. Large sea birds – frigates and boobies nested in almost every tree. We got some pictures of some baby boobies. There were dozens of whales spouting all around the island. We left Isla Isabella along with 4 other boats and made one of our fastest ever sails into San Blas (Yes, we beat all the other boats)!

We have now changed buses in Tepic and are on the bus to Puerto Vallarta all seated again. Tepic is a very large and quite modern town (for Mexico). Bigger by far than La Paz. We are now at a high elevation. Don't know how high but my ears have popped. The landscape is rolling hills and mountains further back. There are green fields of sugar cane and papaya and banana *plantations. The road is almost fair – two lane and I'm finding it best not to watch as we pass on the curves! Saddled horses are tied to trees quite often.*

Well, it appears that our bus is now taking a little break. We have been on this bus for 2 hours and have gone through numerous towns although I don't know their names. Now for some strange reason they pull over and start working on the assembly that opens and closes the door of the bus. This is truly an interesting trip. I wish all of you up north could experience it with us!

Well, here it is February 11th and we are back in San Blas again. Both Puerto Vallarta and Tepic were so large I never did find the post office in either place. We only stayed one night in Puerto Vallarta. It was pretty enough there I guess but very expensive. We saw more rich Americans than Mexican people there. It's more like a winter resort for wealthy Americans who can afford to spend the winter vacationing in a warm climate. For folks like us trying to live a somewhat routine life on a limited budget it is an impossible place.

We did have some mail there for us but still not the stuff from our attorney we have been waiting 2 months for. We will try to reach him by phone today. When we do go south from here it will only be a short stop in P.V. just to check our mail once more.

Dustin and Jerad did just fine here. They want to take the tent and go camping on the beach for a few days. It's not far from here.

Let me tell you a little more about San Blas. The town runs along one side of the estuary here then there is a strip of jungle on the other side with the ocean beyond that. Quite often an old man in a ponga goes across the estuary along with his horse and 5 dogs which all swim after the ponga. We have also seen a herd of cows swim across here with cowboys on horseback swimming also. Pigs are taken across in the pongas. We get visitors in pongas quite often. They never can speak any English except for the word "candy" which the children know well. Fishing is good here. There is a never ending school of small tasty fish around the boat. They go after a plain small hook – no bait. Dustin and Nathan can pull in 15 – 20 of them in about 10 minutes time; sometimes two at a time. After several meals of them we have to request that they don't fish for a couple of days.

There is a farm in the jungle across the estuary. They speak no English, of course, but we have become friends. We visit there and they come to the boat. We do the best we can with our Spanish, and we laugh a lot. One day when

Nathan and I were visiting at the farm the old grandma gave Nathan a tiny baby chick whose mother had died. They put it in a box with feathers. Nathan loved to hold it and give it drinks of water. It lived for 3 days but we couldn't seem to keep it warm enough and it finally died. Nathan was so sad. He still won't let me throw away the box of feathers ...

CHAPTER TWENTY-TWO

A NOTE TO MOM AND DAD

ere is part of a letter I sent off to my mom and dad on February 12, 1988:

Dear Mom and Dad,

I started writing four days ago so will finish this now. The first 10 pages I have sent to Michael and he is to pass them on to you. I couldn't see writing the same thing twice.

I just took an apple cake out of the oven so the galley smells good. It's quiet here tonight. The boys are having their 2 day camp out at the beach. Our friends from Oregon are camped next to them so they have supervision. They have so much fun. They have made lots of friends here which is helping their Spanish a lot. Dustin came home from the beach yesterday with a funny story. A Canadian man saw him riding his boogie board in the surf and thought he was a little Mexican boy. (The boys are very tan). When Dustin got out of the water the man attempted in very poor Spanish to ask Dustin if he could use his boogie board and he would give Dustin 1,000 pesos. Dustin kept quiet until the poor man had finished trying to make himself understood, then Dustin said, "Do you speak English?"

We have finally (I think)! decided to remain in Mexico through the summer and fall. We will stay right here until hurricane season then go up into the Sea of Cortez. We would like very much if you could come and visit us here. Everyday I see things and think I sure wish Mom and Dad were here to see this, too. San Blas is not a tourist town which is probably why we like it so well. When I look around it's like something you'd read about in a book or maybe see in a movie. More interesting things and people here then I could ever write about. I try taking pictures but I know they can't come close to the real thing. This is an inexpensive place to be. We went and checked at the hotel. It is very Mexico — again like out of a movie — but neat. Its $10.00 a night for two. Or, of course, you could stay on the boat — best rate in town! Both March and April should be fun months here. We are told that that's when thousands of parrots migrate here …

We will walk to the beach in the morning to see how the boys are doing and watch Jerad surf. He is becoming a master at that as in all things he attempts to do. We are lucky to have such good boys …

CHAPTER TWENTY-THREE

MORE ADVENTURES
IN SAN BLAS

O ur time in San Blas was busy yet relaxing. There was always something to do, sometimes together and at other times we were all going in different directions. The boys were all social animals and were forever making new friends on shore and often bringing them back to the boat. Huban was a favorite friend from a large family. His father was a shark fisherman. Huban's mother and one of his sisters had come out to the boat with Huban and Dustin one day for a visit. I'm sure Huban's mother wanted to find out more about his new friends. They, of course, spoke no English and my Spanish was extremely limited but that didn't seem to matter much.

"Mom! Mom! Can we spend the night at Huban's house? His mom says it's okay. We're caught up on our schoolwork. Can we?" Dustin and Nathan were so excited.

"Pleeease," they begged when I didn't answered right away. After all, how did they know that Huban's mom said it was okay?

"Oh, I guess so. Just make sure you behave." After all, I had met Huban's mother.

"All right! Thanks, Mom," Dustin shot back, giving me a hug.

"Yeah, thanks, Mom," Nathan echoed. Another hug.

"Where's Huban's house, anyway?" I questioned. They gave me directions, stuffed a few belongings into a backpack, and were ready in a flash for me to row them to shore.

By early afternoon the following day the boys still hadn't returned to the boat. I was beginning to be a little concerned so got Daryl to go with me into town to find Huban's house. It wasn't hard to find. Dustin's directions had been spot on.

This family, as we found to be typical of most of the people we met there, were friendly and hospitable. When we arrived my boys were sitting around a large table with the mother and several other children eating a meal.

"Hi, Mom," Dustin greeted me. "Look. No silverware."

"Yeah, Nathan piped up. We eat our silverware," and they both proceeded to demonstrate how they had learned to tear off a piece of a tortilla, pinch some food into it, and stuff the whole thing into their mouths. "Only I've eaten so much silverware I'm getting full."

This was certainly a lesson in culture they would never receive out of a text book. I looked around the room. The house consisted of one large room with a double bed in one corner. Several pillows and blankets were pilled on top. A faded and torn cloth curtain that could be pulled across that corner of the room for some privacy hung close to the ceiling from a piece of clothesline that had been tied off to hooks nailed into the two adjacent walls. This was most likely where the parents slept. I had seen another small room off from the kitchen as we had come in; no doubt sleeping quarters for the children. In another corner were a stove and a very basic kitchen setup. No cupboards. Just some board shelves and a narrow table covered with oilcloth which served as a work area. Next to that was the table where everyone now sat. There was also an area with a couple of chairs and a side table with some Mexican pottery on it. The floors were all dirt with no floor covering except for a mat in the center of the sitting area.

A picture of Christ hung on the wall as well as a crucifix. Also adorning the walls were several sets of shark jaws.

I was doing a mental inventory of the Spanish words I knew to try to make conversation. I knew the words for "shark" and "big" and "where" so attempted to start my conversation using those words. Huban's mother laughed at my bad Spanish as did we. I understood her to say that her husband was a shark fisherman and these jaws were from some of the sharks he had caught. I guess I pointed and said mui grande one too many times because before I knew what was happening she had removed the biggest set of jaws off the wall and presented them to me as a gift. The boys were having a great time there and at the mother's invitation they stayed over for a second night.

A set of shark jaws was not a practical piece of décor on a cramped sailboat. I hung them on the wall of our little charting area. I thought they would be out of the way there but one day Daryl reached back to the shelf behind them and got a nasty cut on his hand from one of the teeth. We teased him after that about being bit by a shark.

As boats came and went from the estuary we would get together for meals, games, hikes, or just visit and swap stories. It was always fun to meet up again with boats we had met in other ports but now and then a new boat would pull in.

It was here that we met Patty and Gary on *Neried* for the first time. They were a nice couple who actually got married on their boat while they were in San Blas and had a big wedding fiesta on shore at Roberto's casa. A couple of days before their wedding they had to make a trip to Tepec and asked Jerad if he would watch their boat for them while they were gone. Jerad dropped Patty and Gary off on shore then motored their dinghy back to Neried where he spent the night.

The following morning after their school assignments were done Dustin and Nathan rowed our Avon to shore. A short time later Jerad motored over to *Lunar Glow* in *Neried's* dinghy. The three of us were sitting at the table in the aft cabin when we heard screaming from somewhere outside. Jerad looked out the cabin window and saw that something was wrong further out in the water near a boat called *Good Looking*. Before we know what had happened he had run out and jumped into *Neried's* dinghy, started the motor and was racing through the water. All Daryl and I could do was stand out on deck yelling for help.

The tide was running strong and the water was always a murky brown color there and impossible to see through. *Good Looking* had anchored in the estuary a few days before but seemed to want to keep to themselves so we had never met them. The boats owners, Ron and Melissa, were a bi-racial couple from California where she worked as a lawyer. Melissa had lost her balance when attempting to get into their dinghy and had fallen into the dirty, swift moving water. Ron was hysterical. Melissa was afraid of water and didn't know how to swim. Jerad killed the motor on the dinghy and dove into the water near where Melissa had gone in. He surfaced two times and re-dove before feeling her below the water. He brought her limp form to the surface. By now other boats had heard our screaming and another dinghy was pulling up alongside Jerad. I can't remember the man's name but together he and Jerad got Melissa into his dinghy. By now Ron was in *Neried's* dinghy and picked up Jerad. Together both dinghies raced to the shore where they pulled Melissa, still unconscious, onto solid ground. The man immediately started CPR while a large crowd gathered round. None of the Mexican people would touch her. I don't know if it was because she was black or because they thought she was dead. There were a tense few minutes before Melissa flickered back to life.

I have thought about this event many times and can see clearly God's hand in saving Melissa. Had Jerad not had *Neried's* dinghy with the big motor tied to our boat at that particular time there would have been no way of getting to Melissa soon enough to save her. Even if our Avon had been available we wouldn't have been able to row against the strong current to reach her in time. In the six months we had been sailing this was the first time we had had the use of a power dinghy.

Many evenings were spent in town around the plaza where there always seemed to be a celebration of some sort going on. Families went there together, the ladies always wearing a nice dress and the children were clean and well behaved. During the day school work continued for the boys as did our Spanish lessons.

Elicio, our Spanish teacher, was 15; a nice boy whom Dustin had met on one of his trips to the beach. He took Jerad to school with him one day which was fun for Jerad. We found out that Elicio had never traveled more than 43 miles from San Blas so invited him to go on a five night trip with us out to Isla Isabella which his parents gave him permission to do. We stopped first in Chacala for the night. The fishing was really good there but poor Elicio was feeling sick. We sailed on out to Isla Isabella the following day with whales fluking in the water around us. The fishing was good again but now Daryl was starting to get sick too. We were the only boat in the anchorage; quite a change from our stay five weeks earlier.

After the second night Elicio was feeling better and enjoyed being on the boat and playing with the kids. *Neried* arrived the next day and by the time we were ready to leave Isla Isabella the anchorage was up to six boats. Daryl hurt his back on the sail back to San Blas. This seemed to be an ongoing thing. He spent an awful lot of time either sick or in pain from his back, knee, or some other body part hurting. Most of the time he kept going though.

The day after returning with Elicio we started to prepare to leave San Blas. As much as we liked it there we knew there were other places we wanted to see as well. We checked out with the Port Captain and made phone calls back to the states. We filled our gas and water jugs, stocked up on food, and got a block of ice. Early in the day we had a last visit from our friends that had the little ranch down the way. They had given Nathan the baby chick some weeks before and because it had died they wanted to replace it. In my poor Spanish and lots of hand gestures I tried to tell them that we had no way to keep such a little chick warm and I was afraid that another one would also die. "No", I told them. "El pollo es muy, muy, chicita y frio y muerto". I figured that was good enough along with my charades to get my point across. Anyway, we told our friends we were going to be leaving the next morning and would be gone for several weeks. They got back in their ponga and left but returned a short while later with a parting gift for Nathan. This time they brought him a much bigger chicken! Nathan was ecstatic. I nearly died. We had already learned that it is very rude to decline a gift that is given to you so I tried hard to smile as I said, "Muchos gracias". Nathan took his new "chicken of the sea" down below where it flew around the cabin and pooped on everything and finally ended up taking safe refuge in the cubbyhole behind my stove where the pots and pans were stored. Nathan was trying to think of a name for it … I was thinking of stewing it for dinner!

Later that afternoon, the chicken having been cooped inside a cardboard box, we received an invitation to visit Ron and Melissa on *Good Looking*. We had been gone for several days and hadn't really seen them since the day Melissa nearly drowned. They presented Jerad with a beautiful machete they saw him admire hanging on their cabin wall. They were a very nice couple but were thinking about bringing their sailing days to a close after the horrible scare they'd had. I felt really bad for them.

Later that evening Jerad went out on his first "date". He had met Bertha (pronounced Bear-Tah) at the wedding fiesta for Patty and Gary and had made sure he accidentally crossed paths again with her since that time. He took her to the movies in town. It was probably a good thing that we were planning to leave the next day, however, as Bertha's father was not pleased to have a gringo from one of the boats courting his daughter.

We had been in San Blas for over five weeks and it was time to move on. The five of us along with our parrot, Sweetie Pie, and Nathan's chicken, pulled anchor, waved farewell to our friends on shore and headed south. We would return another day.

CHAPTER TWENTY-FOUR

BANDERAS BAY

We didn't go far that first day out of San Blas. Nathan and I weren't feeling well that day but nothing that would keep us down. As we entered the anchorage at Chacala we dropped our hook near the shore of what looked to be a small farm. A path leading up from the water's edge wound its way up a dirt trail to several make-shift enclosures containing a few farm animals. Chickens wandered the yard freely in search of unsuspecting bugs. A couple of small children played just outside the very modest house which had once been a brilliant turquoise color but had long since faded in the hot Mexican sun.

I was busy with my everyday chores and not paying much attention to what the rest of the family was doing. Nathan had been real quiet but I knew he wasn't feeling well so I assumed he had climbed up on his bunk to lie down. I realized my assumption was wrong when I came up out of the aft cabin where I had been doing up the morning dishes. We had towed our Avon dinghy behind the boat on our short sail from San Blas to Chacala. Without a word to anyone, Nathan had taken his chicken in its makeshift cardboard box pen, gotten into the dinghy, and was rowing it to shore. I watched from the deck as he reached the shore and laid the oars inside the dinghy, got out and pulled the little boat up onto the sandy shore. Even at age seven and only after one night of having his new pet chicken Nathan could see that a chicken and a boat just don't go together. He was taking his chicken to a new home.

We learned later that the little farm actually belonged to the Port Captain there in Chacala. He was happy to receive Nathan's "gift", although he probably wondered how we had acquired a chicken in the first place.

I was surprised to find a "model home" the next day as we took a walk through town. A small home with a plot of land could be purchased for $7,000. It sounds like such a meager amount of money yet that was the same amount that we were living on per year during our years on the boat. Later that night we were awakened by sounds at the stern of the boat. We got up to investigate and found that an unwelcomed visitor was attempting to "borrow" our motor. We were much more careful in securing and stowing our belongings after that. Two days later we left Chacala in the rain heading further south to Banderas Bay.

We stayed for the night in the anchorage at Punta de Mita. Our friends on *Duet* were there and Jerad was happy to see Grant again and catch up on the latest adventures. He ended up staying a second night there with *Duet* while the rest of us sailed on to Nuevo Vallarta where we actually tied up to the dock. Jerad would catch up with us the next day.

Being alongside the dock was a real treat for us. There was power, water, and best of all, public showers! Showers on the boat were generally a lot of work. First of all we had to haul all of our fresh water to the boat in five gallon jugs. We could hold a total of about ninety-one gallons between our water tanks and the jugs. We had a solar shower which we would hang in the rigging for showers. This was a vinyl bag that held about three gallons of water. It was black on one side and clear on the other. The top of the bag had a fill hole and a hook for hanging and the bottom had a short clear hose with a little shower head and a little device for controlling the water coming out of the bag. A couple of hours before taking a shower we would fill the bag and lay it on the deck with the black side up so that the sun could heat the water. When it was hot enough we would hang the bag in the rigging behind a large towel for privacy and take our shower. We had to use very little water as that one bag had to do all of our showers. When a fellow boater told me there were real showers just down from the dock I was excited!

After stowing our sailing gear I grabbed my towel, soap, and shampoo and headed off to find the shower. A friend had pointed out a two story structure just a short walk from where the boats were docked and said the showers even had hot water. I couldn't wait. As I got to the building I noticed there were several doors but no signs of any kind. I tried several doors on the lower level but found them to be locked. Finally the last door was open. I looked inside and saw that it was, indeed, a huge shower room and completely unoccupied. There was a very large cement bench in the center of the room where one could leave their clothes, etc. while showering. Half a dozen shower stalls lined one wall. None of them had any sort of door or shower curtain except for the one at the far end.

I undressed, left all my clothes along with my towel on the cement bench, took my shampoo and soap and entered the last stall pulling the shower curtain closed behind me. I was enjoying my shower when I heard the shower room door open and someone enter. I could tell that person was starting to undress. A minute later the door opened again and someone else entered. Now the two people started to talk … in real deep voices. I peeked out of my shower curtain to see two Mexican men stripping down to their birthday suits. Oh great. I was in the men's shower room and my towel and clothes were out in the middle of the room about ten feet from my shower.

I had a very long shower that day as I waited for what seemed like forever for several men to come and go before I dared to exit from my shower stall to grab up my belonging and return behind my shower curtain to dress and leave that place. I learned later that the ladies showers were upstairs but all of the signs had been removed to paint the building.

We spent the next three weeks in and around Nuevo Vallarta. A letter I wrote to my parents on March 17, 1988 says:

… I received the two letters you sent to Puerto Vallarta and also the one to Dustin. He was delighted to receive the check and we shall take him to town

shopping soon. We had his birthday in a little place called La Cruz which is just about ten miles north of P. V. He had a fun time. We had chocolate birthday cake on the boat then went into the little town for triple scoop ice cream cones.

I was hoping to give you a call when we reached Manzanillo but plans changed — again!!!-and we didn't go that far south. We have been staying in and around Nuevo Vallarta which is about 5 miles from P.V. At present we are tied up to a dock. Quite a change from always being anchored offshore. We have fresh water to the boat plus hot showers. Real luxury!

We have met some really neat people in our travels. Most of the people out sailing around are retired couples, but a lot of families as well. People from all walks of life; doctors, lawyers, school teachers, pilots. You name it — they're here.

Our days are always busy. C.P.R. classes two days last week. Pot luck dinners, chili cook-offs, dinghy races, fishing. Always something. Oh yes — always school work and boat maintenance. Never ends. Everyone we meet has either already met or heard about our boys. We never get anything but the very best reports and compliments on them which, of course, makes us proud. They are good — all in all. Oh, they have their moments but don't we all. I think some days Jerad's hormones are out of balance (his 15 year old hormones!) as he gets real moody. But we just give him some space then he's fine. Other days he's so "up" we can hardly stand it. Anyway, everyone loves Jerad.

The fishing has been quite good out here. Sometimes we eat fish three times a day. When we get into the Sea of Cortez I'm hoping to make fish jerky. We are all getting very tan. Look like natives — almost! I managed to sunburn my lips the other day. Boy is my bottom lip sore!

Daryl bought the boys a used Sabot sailing dinghy last week. It needed some work so he spent three days re-fiberglassing it and it turned out real well. The kids are having so much fun with it. Plus we needed a second dinghy. (It was hard with five people to be a one dinghy family!) …

We will remain here at the dock for maybe another week while we redo our decks then head back up to San Blas where we will stay probably until the middle of April. We will then head north to La Paz where Daryl will take a bus to San Diego to renew our visas. At least that's the plan right now. Anyway we can pick up mail in La Paz …

CHAPTER TWENTY-FIVE

THE JABAMA – S

We had some great times in Bandaras Bay but on March 25th it was time to cast off our lines and sail back towards San Blas once again. Jerad stayed behind as he had taken on a boat sitting job on *Mithril* for a week. We missed him as one of our main crew members but Dustin and Nathan were taking on more and more of the sailing duties and so we managed just fine. We took three days getting back to San Blas stopping along the way to snorkel and play in the surf. After all, physical education needed to be a part of the boy's school curriculum.

We dropped our anchor in our same old spot in the San Blas estuary. Except for the bugs we were glad to be back in San Blas. We had made lots of friends here. It was Monday March 28, 1988. We missed Jerad but he would be back in a week's time and I knew how much he liked to pick up boat sitting jobs.

We woke early on Tuesday morning. Dustin and Nathan wanted to get their school work done early so they could go to shore and look for their local friends. We were just finishing a breakfast of sourdough pancakes when we heard a knocking sound on the stern of the boat.

"Now who can that be coming by this early in the morning?" I said to nobody in particular.

"I'll look," said Dustin who was sitting closest to the open window at the rear of our table area. He stuck his head out the opening to get a look around then quickly pulled his head back in with a puzzled look on his face.

"Well, who is it?" I questioned.

"It's an old man in a dingy. He has a big white beard with an orange ring around his mouth."

Daryl and I looked at each other then both headed for the stairs leading up to the cockpit. We stepped out of the cockpit and onto the deck to see what this man wanted. Sure enough, there sitting in an aluminum dingy was an old, white bearded man with an orange ring around his mouth.

"Hey there," Daryl called out. "How can we help you?"

"My boat sank about 20 miles off shore but I was able to save my dingy and outboard. Yours is the first boat I've come across. My name's Settler. Gerald Settler."

"Well, Mr. Settler, throw me a line. I'll tie up your dingy and you can climb aboard." Daryl instructed. "Twenty miles. Wow, that's a long dingy ride."

Mr. Settler did just that, bringing with him a small satchel and a gallon size plastic jug which was about a quarter full of orange liquid. We directed him down into the rear cabin and gave him a seat at the table. He gratefully accepted a drink of water but declined breakfast. Dustin and Nathan now seemed more interested in finding out about our strange guest than about getting their school work done and going into town. After a few minutes of small talk Mr. Settler, Gerald, started to tell us his story.

Gerald had been happily married to a lady named Jane. They had two daughters, Barbie and Marcy, both grown now. Life had been good until Gerald got the notion that they should get a boat and go sailing. Gerald actually spent several years building his boat but Jane could never share in his enthusiasm. (Apparently Jane did not share my sense of adventure). The closer Gerald came to completing the boat the further Jane and his daughters drifted away from him. By the time the boat was completed Jane had filed for divorce and their happy marriage was over. All that Gerald had left was his boat which he named after the three ladies he loved most. Jane, Barbie, and Marcy. He took the first two letters from each of their names, JA, BA, and MA and added an S at the end for Settler and came up with the boat's name, *Jabama-S*. Gerald launched his vessel and ventured out into the Sea of Cortez. About 25 miles from the west coast of the Mexico mainland he started drinking. Drinking and thinking of the family he had lost. Lost because of this boat he had built for his family. The more he thought of his family the more he disliked the boat he had built. And the more he drank. He drank until he came up with a plan. He would burn his boat and once the boat was gone he could get his family back. So Gerald gathered his money, some paperwork, and a few belongings putting everything into a small satchel. He doused his vessel with gasoline. He grabbed a half full jug of orange juice and topped it off with a bottle of vodka. The satchel and jug were lowered into his 14 foot aluminum dingy. Gerald threw a match into the gasoline soaked galley and backed out of the boat. He stepped into the dingy, untied the line, and motored far enough away from the *Jabama-S* to stay safe while he watched her burn and finally sink down out of sight. He then started his long dinghy ride to the nearest shore, drinking his orange juice and vodka as he went, thus the orange ring dyed around his mouth by the time he reached *Lunar Glow*.

Gerald had finished his story but what do you say to such a sad tale. We all just sat there; none of us talking. Not even the boys who always had something to say. I firmly believe that things happen for a reason and once again I could see God's hand directing this play. *Lunar Glow* had sleeping accommodations for five. Normally we would not be able to have an overnight guest unless someone slept in a sleeping bag on the deck, but Jerad had stayed behind in Nuevo Vallarta to boat sit so his single bunk would be empty.

"You are welcome to stay here with us for the night," I finally blurted out. Daryl shot me one of those 'are you crazy' looks. "Our son Jerad is away for a few days so you can sleep in his bunk." Dustin and Nathan were happy to share their forward cabin with our new friend.

We finished out the morning as normally as we could manage. Mr. Settler went forward to take a nap. He was tired from his night at sea. The boys worked on their school assignments then rowed the Avon to shore and went into town. Later that afternoon Gerald also ventured into town. He said he needed to see the Port Captain.

Apparently Gerald wasn't able to conclude his business with the Port Captain as easily as he had hoped as he was asked to return to their office again the next morning. When he returned to *Lunar Glow* he informed us that the Port Captain wanted him to remain in San Blas until Monday ... and he was instructed to stay with us! Oh dear. What had I gotten us into?

We got hold of Jerad later that day on the VHF radio. We told him all about our new boat guest and that he would be using Jerad's bunk until Monday. Jerad said that would work out just right because he didn't think he would be returning until Monday anyway. What I wasn't thinking about at the time was that our single sideband (VHF) conversation with Jerad was heard by not only Jerad but by every other boat who happened to be tuned in to that frequency at the time.

Dustin and Nathan spent the second and third nights of Gerald's stay in town at their friend Huban's house. Daryl, Gerald, and I took the dingy up the estuary gathering clams for dinner. Gerald treated us to dinner in town on Thursday night. We stopped by Huban's house to check on the boys then walked over to the plaza where some sort of fiesta was starting.

The next couple of days were uneventful. After schoolwork the boys would head for the beach. I worked on repairing the edges of our mainsail with leather. Daryl went out on Sunday with one of the local guys named Roberto to collect oysters. Daryl ate so many oysters and drank so much mescal that he was sick for the next three days.

Gerald left on Monday morning for Tepic. He gave us his 14' dingy and 4 H.P. Suzuki outboard motor for our hospitality. After all these months of rowing our dingy we would finally have an outboard. We gave Gerald's dingy to a local fisherman, Humberto. He was extremely grateful and we knew he would put it to good use. We never saw Mr. Gerald Settler again. He was gone but not forgotten.

CHAPTER TWENTY-SIX

AND LIFE GOES ON

J erad returned from Nuevo Vallarta that same day. I had taken Nathan and Dustin up the estuary gathering clams while Daryl remained on the boat still sick from the overdose of oysters and mescal. We hadn't been back to the boat long when we heard someone calling to us from the shore. Jerad volunteered to go see why this guy was calling us for. He was excited to use the dingy now that it had a motor on it. He wasn't gone long before returning with a Mr. Mick Highwater in tow. Mr. Highwater was a reporter from a magazine called <u>Santana</u>. It seems that our VHF conversation with Jerad in Nuevo Vallarta several days before had been overheard by someone from the magazine and Mr. Highwater had come for an interview. We explained that Mr. Settler of the *Jabama-S* had already departed but at his request we told him the whole story anyway. He actually came back the next day to take pictures. I never did see a copy of the magazine so I have no idea if the story was ever published.

The next week passed by rather uneventfully. Daryl's head and stomach got to feeling better but his back hurt. That was an ongoing event, however. We found an anchor in the estuary. Jerad went surfing. Petri, the fisherman's wife, brought us over two sharks. We sailed out to Mantachan for a two nights stay in order to collect some mail that *Windsong* had picked up for us in Puerto Vallarta. We met a couple from Tepic, Arturo and Florencia, and they came on board for a BBQ shark dinner. A booby bird landed on our deck and wouldn't leave. And, of course, the boys did their schoolwork each day.

We returned to San Blas on Sunday and took our laundry to shore and worked as a family washing our clothes at a fresh water faucet next to the ice house. The boys then went on into town to see a movie, Superman IV.

Monday was busy as we got the boat ready to leave San Blas. We stopped by to visit Petri and made a phone call to my mom and dad to let them know we were fine and give them an update on our travel plans which tended to change often. We would be leaving San Blas on Tuesday morning and sailing back out to Isla Isabella before heading south to Mazatlan then west again across the Sea of Cortez.

Isla Isabella was peaceful and relaxing. The boys swam and fished. Daryl worked on some minor repairs that were needed on the little sabot sailing dingy we had bought in Nuevo Vallarta. We had dinner on *Mithril*. The boys snorkeled and fished some more. And, yes, did schoolwork! I kept busy preparing lesson plans as well as meals. Our three nights stay passed quickly.

It was an overnight sail to Mazatlan. After the first couple of nights at sea months before when I had been scared half to death I had come to enjoy sailing at night. The sky this night was incredible, huge and moonless but covered with a blanket of stars. Standing at the wheel in the cockpit, the only light except for the stars was the light inside the compass mounted just behind the wheel and the running lights high up on the mast. The sails were full and the water running along the hulls was like music to my ears. What a magnificent world God had created. Life was good.

Back then Daryl, Jerad, and I took turns doing the night watches in four hour shifts. Dustin had turned eleven back in March and was old enough to do some time at the wheel during the day but not at night. Nathan at seven did very short watches during the day when someone was there with him. His attention span wasn't very long. Daryl had taken the 8pm to midnight shift followed by Jerad from midnight to 4 am. My watch would end at 8am in time to get breakfast for the family.

As the sun was just coming up over the horizon I was treated to one of the most amazing water shows I had ever seen. Just off the starboard side of the boat huge manta rays shot up out of the water turning summersaults in the air before entering the water again. One ray actually seemed to walk on top of the water standing tall on its tail with its wings flapping back and forth. I could see the face on the ray and was sure it was smiling at me. That was one of the several shows of nature I would witness over the next few years that will be forever engraved in my mind. I only wished I had had someone else on deck to share the moment with.

We sailed into Mazatlan early in the day. The harbor was dirty and smelly. I had been to Mazatlan ten years earlier when the boy's dad, Joe, and I took Michael on a week's vacation. Michael had been seven at the time and was going through a stage where he complained about everything. I thought that if he could see the many poor children in Mexico and how they lived that he might appreciate all that he had. It didn't work. Michael still complained but the trip for the most part was fun.

Because it was Saturday the check in process would have to wait until Monday. We used the weekend to fill our gas and water jugs and do some shopping. We all accompanied Jerad with his big surfboard down to the beach to watch him surf. The surfing beach was quite a distance from the boat harbor so we had to take a bus part way and then a long walk after that.

We went through the check in process on Monday. Nathan came along with Daryl and I while Jerad went to babysit the kids on *Mithril*. Dustin went into town with Jack and Sylvia, a retired couple from a boat called *Windancer*.

The boating community is a very tight knit group. Whenever someone needed help there were always plenty of hands willing to pitch in. We were always having folks over for games or dinner or going to their boats for the same. A guitar player in the group could keep us entertained for hours. Tug-o-wars on the beach or a game of volleyball in the sand were common. It was always fun to see friends from boats we had met in other anchorages. We would swap sailing stories and discuss the routes we were planning to sail. Our paths were constantly criss crossing each other. Although we had come from different backgrounds and walks of life and our vessels ranged from luxury to extremely modest our life on the water gave us a commonality that overrode everything else. For the most part we trusted each other and so if my sons were with someone from another boat I didn't worry.

After five days in Mazatlan we were ready to press on. We went to the bank, topped off our water jugs, and did our cross town check out with the Port Captain and such. By 8:30pm on Wednesday April 20th we were ready to head back across the Sea of Cortez once again to the Baja.

We always trolled a fishing line behind the boat when we were out at sea. We attached a bungee cord to one of the aft cleats and had a heavy fishing line with a large lure tied onto that which trailed about 20 feet or so behind *Lunar Glow*. In that way if a fish took our lure the bungee would absorb the shock and keep our line from breaking. We caught countless fish in this manner.

Thursday turned out to be a great sailing day. We caught a large albacore which was a very good fish but best of all we were treated to two more sea life shows.

First, another school of sting rays surfaced by the boat. They were so playful as they jumped out of the water and waved their wings. We waved back at them. Seeing these huge fish perform at such close range was amazing.

The second show started about 11pm that night. It was so breathtaking we got everyone up and onto the deck to watch. A huge school of dolphins came up and was swimming with the boat. What made it so spectacular were the phosphorescent lights that seemed to cover the dolphins. It was like thousands of tiny lights attached to the bodies of the dolphins shooting back and forth through the black water. We all put on our harnesses and clipped our tether lines to the forestays so that we could safely lay down on the ama bows to get as close to the dolphins as possible. They swam with us for several miles then just disappeared as suddenly as they had come. It was times like these that made me know that the decision to go sailing was a good one. There was no way in the world my sons could have ever experienced this from reading a text book in Dayton, Nevada.

On Friday a strong wind kicked up right on our nose and the seas were rough. It was early afternoon by the time we dropped our hook in the anchorage at Los Muertos. We were very tired. Although we had a lot of wind there it was still an enjoyable five days. We fished and went exploring in the dingy. We had a picnic on the beach. The boys went free boarding with a boat named *Breanna*. Daryl greased the motor and worked on the fishing reels and apparently wasn't watching his step because he also fell off the boat!

It was a fairly short sail from Los Muertos to Ballandra. April 27th was a beautiful day so we dropped the anchor and took the dinghy to shore. There were sand hills back off the beach and we spent the afternoon sliding down them. It was loads of fun but by the time we were done we were all a sandy mess. I guess we tracked a lot of that sand onto the boat as we had to give *Lunar Glow* a good wash job the next morning before sailing on up to La Paz.

We anchored close to the shore in La Paz. We had spent time here months before so knew where we wanted to be. We took the dinghy to shore and left it on Rafael's Dinghy Beach. It was good to see him again and find that he remembered us. It was too late in the day to do our check in so we just found a pay phone and called my mom. It was her 66th birthday today and we all wanted to wish her well.

Because our stay in La Paz would be a short one this time we checked in and out at the same time saving ourselves lots of leg work in a few days. We also did some shopping while we were in town.

CHAPTER TWENTY-SEVEN

DID I MENTION SHOPPING??

S hopping for groceries was always an interesting experience. Except for the short period of time that we had a car available on the Mexican Baja and again in American Samoa, we had to walk or take a bus. One time while in Mexico we even picked up a ride in the back of a dump truck.

When possible we would all go together to shop; this way there were more hands and backs to carry the groceries back. Having lived my entire life with access to large, well stocked grocery stores and a vehicle to transport my purchases in, this was a real eye opener. I would soon realize how very fortunate and in some cases just plain spoiled the majority of American people are.

We would all set off wearing empty backpacks. After a dinghy ride to shore we would start walking into town or to the nearest open air market. (I might add here that on occasion *Lunar Glow* would be anchored someplace where there was a large surf near the shore. This required great skill getting the dinghy safely through the surf without flipping it over in the process. As this was a skill that we learned over time and only after some mishaps we trudged into town in wet clothes more than once). These markets usually consisted of a group of locals trying to sell their produce. A blanket would be spread out on the ground upon which their goods were displayed. Some items were familiar and easy to identify but there were many items, fruits and vegetables, that we had never seen before and thus had no idea how they were to be prepared and eaten. I was usually up for trying new things so would try, despite a language barrier, to learn what to do with a new item. Friends from other boats also proved to be a good resource for some new recipes.

Eggs were a particular challenge. I thought eggs were always sold in egg cartons. Not so. The eggs we found in the markets were piled high in baskets. There were usually, lucky for us, small plastic bags there to put the eggs in. You would just bag as many eggs as you wanted. Getting them back to the boat inside a backpack filled with other food items without breaking any was the fun part, especially if the trip included a bus ride or a less than smooth dinghy ride. On the first trip I made north to the United States I made sure I acquired some egg cartons. I kept and protected those cartons for the remainder of our sailing days as if they were gold. I also learned that eggs do not need to be refrigerated. As long as you turn the eggs daily they will last a long time at room temperature.

Bread was different, too. It was not sold in a bag and it was not sliced; just nice loaves of bread in a pile. We didn't buy much bread, however, as I baked our bread every couple of days or so. The exception to this was during our time in French Polynesia.

Beans and rice were sold in bulk and we ate lots of each. There were always lots of little rocks and sometimes even little bugs with the beans and rice so as soon as we got back to the boat we had to empty the beans or rice onto large cookie sheets and sort the whole lot before storing it in airtight containers.

I remember one market in Mexico well. It was quite large and included an outdoor area for buying chickens. There was a small pen where several live chickens walked around pecking at bugs in the dirt. On the back wall hung three large funnels. Three or four inches below the lower open end of the funnels was a metal trough running the length of the funnels. It had no ends on it and was also nailed to the wall. We watched as a customer wanting a fresh chicken for supper pointed to the chicken of choice in the pen. The owner of the chickens grabbed the chosen bird by the neck, gave it a quick swing through the air, laid its neck on a stump, and with one swing of the hatchet beheaded the unlucky fowl. He then took the headless bird by the feet and stuck it neck first into one of the metal funnels hanging on the wall. Chicken blood flowed out the severed neck of the bird and through the funnel onto the metal trough then just ran off both open ends pooling up on the dirt below. When the blood flow had slowed to a trickle the chicken was removed from the funnel and handed to the customer. We all decided we did not want chicken for dinner!

Inside that same market were rows of vendors selling fish. Not packages of fish fillets like we usually see in our markets but the whole fish. Flies were everywhere and the smell was quite unappetizing. We passed on buying any fish.

The perimeter or the building which resembled a large warehouse, had actual meat cases with all kinds of meat; beef, goat, pork, lamb. Every part of these animals was for sale from the hoof to the tongue and everything in between. We walked around looking into the glass meat cases watching the flies light all over the fresh meat. Then we came to the vendor selling pork. On top of the meat case was the head of a big pig. It sat there staring down at us with blood running out from the head down the front of the glass meat case. We all looked at each other and decided that beans and rice would be just great for dinner that night.

CHAPTER TWENTY-EIGHT

LA PAZ TO ESCONDIDO

Having our check in and out process in La Paz completed and the shopping done we were able to spend time relaxing, playing, and visiting with friends from other boats. One of the most interesting individuals we met at that time was a man by the name of Caden from a sleek looking trimaran named *In-Flight*. Caden was a disabled Vietnam vet who had survived that war with a multitude of injuries. He had lost the sight of one eye, a ruptured eardrum had left him deaf in one ear, and one foot had been blown off just above the ankle. One hand had been severely damaged as well but after years of determination he was able to open his fingers from a closed fist position to an open handed position with only a slight curling in of his fingers. Caden had long, blond, stringy hair and was very much a "hippy" held over from the 60's and 70's. I think it was his shaggy appearance that caused Daryl to gravitate towards this unusual sailor. We couldn't help but notice him as he single-handedly, and with a very exaggerated, lopsided gait, sailed into La Paz and dropped his anchor a short distance from *Lunar Glow*.

"Hey, Mate." Daryl called out to him. "Come on over when you get yourself settled." This was out of character for Daryl who didn't usually warm up to new people easily. It was generally the boys that "found new friends" and brought them to meet the family.

As Caden pulled his dinghy up alongside *Lunar Glow*, Daryl took his line and tied it to a cleat on our deck as Nathan and Dustin stood close by. "Welcome aboard," Daryl beaconed. This was definitely someone he could relate to. Caden stepped aboard and our two youngest crew members stood there with their mouths and eyes open wide.

"Wow! That's cool," Dustin exclaimed as Caden removed his artificial foot when stepping onto the boat and laid it on the deck. "Where did you get that?"

"Can I wear your foot?" Nothing shy about Nathan. No "Hi, how are you, glad to meet you," type greeting. Just "can I wear your foot."

"Sure, go for it," Caden replied. He was a good sport and really liked kids. I tried to apologize for my son's rudeness as Dustin grabbed for the artificial appendage stuffing his own bare foot into the hollow opening and taking a few steps.

"Mom, I asked first and Dustin just took it," Nathan complained. "That's not fair."

"Dustin, get over here and let Nathan have a turn. He was the one that asked," I scolded, "and be careful with it. I don't want you breaking this man's foot."

"Oh, don't worry," Caden laughed, "they can't hurt it. I always take it off when I'm on board. Just easier for me to move around more quickly without it." And with that Dustin relinquished the foot and passed it off to Nathan who immediately stuck his own foot inside. He looked quite silly. The calf portion which fit Caden just up past the ankle went clear up to Nathan's knee.

Caden had sailed his boat south from San Diego. He had no crew but did an excellent job of maneuvering his vessel without help. We would become good friends over the coming weeks and months in Mexico.

We left La Paz on Tuesday May 3rd and spent the next five days working our way north to Escondido. We hiked on Isla San Francisco and in Puerto Los Gatos we explored inland and looked for geodes and combed the beaches. We spent the night in a cove just south of Puerto Escondido and built a fire on the beach. We heard on the VHF that our friends from *Willow* had already arrived in Escondido and the boys were excited to meet up with their friends again.

We had never bought any new sails for *Lunar Glow*. It came with several sails which we had inspected and found them to be in good condition. We had tried them all out except for the big colorful spinnaker. This was a huge sail made of lightweight nylon rip stop material. It's the kind of sail you might see on a postcard or the front of a calendar. Anyway, the sail billows out at the front of the boat and holds a lot of wind and can pull the boat along at a pretty good clip. When Daryl heard that *Willow* as well as other boats we knew were already at anchor in Escondido he decided that we should make a grand entrance into the anchorage flying our spinnaker. The wind was coming from our back which Daryl said was the right condition for this sail.

We were all given our stations on the boat and instructions. While still a ways out we dropped our genoa and got the spinnaker pulled out of the sail bag and hooked in place. It went up fairly smoothly and we were moving quickly towards Escondido. As we sailed towards the entrance to the anchorage we could see that there were lots of boats already at anchor. Daryl scoped out what he felt would be a good spot for us to anchor in and got his "crew" into position. Dustin and Jerad were harnessed in and each stationed on the front of each ama bow. I was at the center bow. Nathan had to stay in the cockpit so he was given the job of letting out on the halyard connected to the top of the sail and which was wrapped around a winch on the mast. Daryl was at the wheel steering the boat.

"Okay. Everyone in position," Daryl barked. "I want this to look good." We were coming in really fast.

"Nathan, when I give the word you are too slowly let out on that halyard and at the same time Dustin, Jerad, and your mom are going to start pulling the sail down and getting it ready to bag. Got it?"

"Uh huh," came Nathan's reply.

"Okay. NOW! Nathan, NOW! You guys up front. Pull that sail down."

"We're trying. It won't come down," Dustin yelled.

"Nathan, take a wrap off that winch."

"Keep it under control."

"Hurry you guys. We're going way too fast."

"Pull harder on that sail. Get it in. NOW!" Daryl was in a panic. The boys and I pulled down on the sail as hard as we could, but each time we pulled down on the sail the halyard pulled up through Nathan's little hands burning them in the process. Finally it just burned too badly so he just let go of the whole thing. The loose halyard flew up the mast, through the pulley at the top of the mast and the whole huge spinnaker flew over the bow of the boat landing in the water in front of us.

It was a hysterical comedy routine for the other boats in the anchorage watching us try to pull that huge, wet sail up out of the water. Daryl yelled at us crew for embarrassing him and was so humiliated that it would be a very long time before he allowed the spinnaker to be flown again.

CHAPTER TWENTY-NINE

ON THE ROAD AGAIN

O ur friends on *Willow,* Don and Brenda, had sailed south from the Seattle area and were only planning to sail into Mexico for a season and then return to Washington state again. They had purchased an old van before leaving the states so that they could travel up and down the Baja between LaPaz and San Diego.

Two days after our grand entrance into Puerto Escondido we left on a road trip with Don and Brenda. They were heading up to San Diego to pick up supplies and asked if we would like to go along. Jerad and Dustin stayed on *Lunar Glow* while Nathan, Daryl, and I joined Don, Brenda, and their two sons, Steve and Denny for the trip.

The van had been a real low budget deal. It had two bucket seats up front but that was it. We took along blankets and sleeping bags so we did the best we could sitting and laying on those in the back. We didn't dare travel after dark as the roads were bad and you never knew when the free range cattle might wander onto the road.

That first night we all slept, or I should say tried to sleep, in the van.

Four adults and three kids. No matter how we tried to arrange ourselves there was always a foot, elbow, or something hitting you. Both Don and Daryl were well over six feet so that didn't help much either.

We arrived in San Diego safe and sound and spent most of the first day taking care of business. Our tourist visas were about to expire so we got those renewed and made a stop at a bank to get some cash wired to us. We saw *Misty Sea* sitting at the dock. It was always fun to run across friends on other boats that we had met it the past and swap stories of our adventures. When we told them about our sleeping arrangement the night before they invited us to spend the night on their boat with them that night which we were happy to do.

We completed our shopping the next day and made phone calls home. By the time we completed our shopping it was too late to start our drive back to Escondido so we actually got a motel and slept the night in a real bed.

We left San Diego for Mexico on Friday morning. If we thought the ride north in "the van" was uncomfortable it was nothing compared to the ride home. We now had loads of supplies for two boats not to mention the 5 h.p. outboard motor that Don and Brenda had purchased for their dinghy. And our three young boys were getting cranky and tired of this adventure in cramped quarters. When nightfall came there was no way we could lay down and sleep on the crowded van floor. We hauled our sleeping bags and pillows outside and tried to sleep the night away under the stars.

There were no restaurant stops on this trip. Just finger foods and whatever we could find in the cooler. We had a flat tire on that last day. It slowed us down a bit but we still arrived back at the boat just before dark. Jerad and Dustin were just fine as were both boats so all in all it was a real nice trip.

We spent another week in Escondido before Daryl announced that the anchorage was getting too crowded and wanted to move on. It was a fun week, however. We had pot luck dinners with the other boats and went to shore to explore. We celebrated our fourth anniversary on May 18th by taking a hike and searching for crystals. We all took another trip in the van; this time just a day trip to a mission in San Javier. We also drove into Loreto where we did our check out process from Escondido. What a treat not to have to walk all over town.

CHAPTER THIRTY

LIFE IN THE SEA OF CORTEZ

The Sea of Cortez is the long body of water running north and south between the Baja and mainland Mexico. We spent about a year, all totaled, in the sea bouncing from place to place. It has so many anchorages and small islands; always something new to explore. The fishing was great and some of the best snorkeling we ever found was in the Sea of Cortez.

Most days were pretty routine. Schoolwork in the morning for the boys and myself. Daryl usually had some project or boat repair to work on. Jerad has always been a self motivated individual. He did his school assignments without prompting and loved to soar on ahead of where he needed to be. I often tried to slow him down a bit. As the "teacher" onboard I had three different grade levels to prepare and present followed by three levels to read through and grade at the end of the day. Jerad's enthusiasm for learning was exhausting for me!

Schoolwork always seemed to go quicker when there were boats with the boy's friends anchored nearby. The sooner they finished their assignments and chores the sooner they were free to meet up with friends and have fun.

A few of my journal entries while we were in the Sea of Cortez say: Jerad went freeboarding behind a Mexican ponga; milk jug race in the anchorage; pot luck on shore; boys went snorkeling; explored water caves; rafted *Lunar Glow* and *Stickwitch* together for big party – BBQ'd 50 lbs of fish; bonfire and games on the beach; sat in hot springs near the boat; went swimming in anchorage; speared fish for dinner; boys went freeboarding behind *Stichwitches* dinghy; gathered clams and scallops for dinner; sailed the sabot; speared an octopus – ate it for dinner; made wind chimes with shells and drift wood. With three boys and plenty of imagination there was always something to do.

By now Jerad was four months shy of turning seventeen and Dustin had celebrated his eleventh birthday a couple of months back. Growing up Jerad had been very close to his older brother, Michael, and felt abandoned when Michael chose not to sail and travel with us. Dustin had filled that void and the two of them became very close. They were very much alike in so many ways; bright, personable, quick witted, imaginative, hard working, and excellent sailors. However, they were very different, too. Where Jerad loved schoolwork, Dustin hated it. Jerad was a peacemaker, never staying mad and always quick to apologize, even if he wasn't in the wrong. If Dustin got mad we all knew it. He was very hard headed and tended to let his mouth get him into trouble. He was confined to quarters more than once. Nathan, at age seven felt he got left out of an awful lot, but lucky for us he was good natured and not one to complain much.

After leaving Puerto Escondido we took our time heading north further up into the Sea of Cortez. We sailed with or criss crossed paths with *Willow* and *Stickwitch,* stopping in the islands to fish and exploring in Bahia Salinas, Isla Carmen, Isla Coronado, and Calida San Juanico along our way to Mulege and Sanispac. Daryl's back was hurting him again and Dustin was running a fever on 103.6 from swollen tonsils so we just took our time. Dustin was fine after a couple of days but Daryl added a hurt finger, a head cold, and numb right foot to his existing ailments.

In Calida San Juanico I took my first solo dingy ride with the outboard motor. The boys had gone to shore for a bonfire and games on the beach with the other boaters. I had stayed behind with Daryl who by now was flat in bed with his bad back. Daryl was sleeping and I was bored so decided to join the others on the beach. Friends had picked the boys up in their dinghy so I had our inflatable Avon with the outboard motor at my disposal. I climbed into the dinghy, let loose of the tether line and started the motor. I was doing just fine and would have made it safely to the beach had it not been for the sandbar between me and the beach that I had known nothing about. The prop hit the sand and bounced a time or two before the shear pin sheared off and the prop got tangled in a mess of kelp. To make matters worse, there were no oars in the dinghy so I was officially stuck. Lucky for me Jerad had witnessed my plight, borrowed a dinghy and came to my rescue!

CHAPTER THIRTY-ONE

NEVER SAY CAN'T

Several memorable events took place while we were anchored in Sanispac. We were anchored close to *Stickwitch* and because their trimaran was the same design as ours and also because they had a teenage daughter, Rachel, on board who was the same age as Jerad, we became good friends. Rachel's mother, Pat, had been a nurse in Santa Cruz, California before sailing south the season before. Her stepdad, Bill, was a funny guy and we enjoyed their company. Pat had decided to get her HAM Radio license and was busy studying for the test. For weeks we had heard sounds of the dits and das coming up out of their open cabin early each morning as Pat practiced her Morse Code letters along with her instructional cassette tape that was a part of her test study material. We didn't know for the longest time what she was doing.

Finally, one morning Jerad decided to go over and investigate the sounds. He wasn't gone long before he returned and said, "Hey, Mom. I'm going to get my HAM Radio license."

"What are you talking about?" I wanted to know.

"All those noises we keep hearing over at *Stickwitch* is Pat learning the Morse Code. You have to know that to take the test. There's a group going up to Escondido in a couple of weeks to take the test and Pat said I could come along if you say it's okay. So is it okay?"

"Jerad. You can't just go take a test. You have to study for it first and know the material. Obviously Pat has been studying for this test for quite some time now. You don't know the Morse Code or anything else about the test. Maybe another time when you have had some time to prepare," I reasoned.

"No, Mom. Pat said I could borrow her book. Besides, how hard can it be?"

Jerad wasn't big in size. Actually, he ended up being the shortest of all my sons. But what Jerad lacked in stature he more than made up for in determination. The word 'can't' was his biggest motivator and without thinking I had used that word. I knew that I would lose any argument with him on this subject so I didn't even try.

Also during this same week on one of Jerad's visits to *Stickwitch* he found Bill doing some sort of mending chore and Jerad started teasing him about sewing. Bill responded by unknowingly using the 'can't' word. "I'll bet you can't sew anything," was Bill's response to Jerad's teasing.

When Jerad returned to *Lunar Glow* his first words were, "Mom, do we have any fabric? I need to make a shirt!"

"Jerad, what are you talking about now? A shirt? I do have some material but we have nothing to sew with. No pattern, no sewing machine. Nothing. And why do you want to make a shirt anyway. You have enough shirts."

"Bill bet me I can't make a shirt, so I've got to make a shirt to show him I can do it," Jerad said.

This was nuts. Now it was Bill that had used that 'can't' word but I was getting stuck with the project. "Okay, Jerad, let's see what we can figure out."

I had a couple of yards of plain tan fabric but no pattern. Jerad had a button down shirt with a collar that we would have to use for a pattern. I had no sewing machine onboard at that time but I did have needle and thread so all the sewing would have to be done by hand. To begin, Jerad had to very carefully pick all of the stitching out of his existing shirt so that we could use all of the pieces as a pattern to cut out a new shirt. This was no easy task but he did it. The next problem was pins. I could only find 10 straight pins on the boat and most of those were rusty and had to be sanded off before they would slide through the fabric. With only 10 pins the pattern pieces had to be pinned and cut out one at a time so that the pins could be removed and reused to pin the next piece in place. Again, a slow process but Jerad did it without help. After all, this was his project. Next, he had to pin the cut pieces together using the same 10 pins and working on one small area at a time. I showed Jerad how to make extremely small running stiches and to keep his seams even. He actually did a remarkable job. The hardest part was the collar. It took him a couple of tries and redoing some of his stitches before he got it to lay right. He even made his own button holes. The finished product looked great. It was rather plain though so Jerad came up with yet another idea. I had some tubes of liquid embroidery on the boat. He took those along with his new shirt around to all of his friends in the anchorage and had each one of them autograph his new shirt. Some of them were quite artistic and others not so much but he had a lasting memory of all of them.

The HAM test was not quite two weeks away from when Jerad first announced that he wanted to take it. Jerad did bring the study guide Pat loaned him home a few days after he had made up his mind to take the test but aside from glancing through it the day he brought it aboard I had never seen him pick it up. The clock was ticking and the test date was getting close. Jerad had also accepted a little side job. Caden from *In Flight* had arrived in Sanispac a few day prior and needed to make a trip up to San Diego to take care of some business there. He asked Jerad if he would look after his boat for him for a few days while he was away so Jerad was sleeping on *In Flight* at night and coming back for schoolwork and chores during the day.

"Jerad. I don't mind paying the money for you to take the HAM Radio test but you will just be wasting our money if you don't even study and try to pass the test." I knew now that Pat was spending even more time studying as the sounds from her instructional cassette were becoming more frequent.

"Don't worry, Mom. I already looked at the book and I know the stuff."

"Where's the book? Let me see it." I thumbed through the manual reading snippets here and there and asking Jerad questions about the material. Every question I could come up with he could answer. Wow, the kid was right. He did know this stuff. I wasn't sure about the code part but he did know the written material. He didn't seem to be concerned about the code so I just let it go.

June 20,1988 was test day. Jerad left early with a group of fellow boaters in *Willow's* van for the ride south to Escondido. Jerad, being the only minor in the group, felt quite elated to be included in this trip. Also on this day Daryl left on a bus out of Mulege to go back to the states. He said his back was hurting so bad that he needed to see a doctor in the states.

It was after dark when Jerad returned back from Escondido. He was exceptionally quiet so I was guessing the test hadn't gone as smoothly as he had thought.

"Hey, Son. The test didn't go so well, huh?" I was trying to be sympathetic and not do the 'I told you so' thing.

"No, Mom. It isn't that. The test was fine. I passed with no problem. The thing is, Pat didn't pass. I felt so bad all the way home that I didn't know what to say." Jerad really did feel bad.

CHAPTER THIRTY-TWO

EARRINGS ANYONE??

The weather in Sanispac was hot. Really hot. We spent as much time in the water as possible. Even cleaning the hulls of the boat didn't seem so bad as we had to be in the water to do that. We noticed that there were a lot of free swimming scallops right around the boat. These are the ones with pretty colored two sided, hinged shells like a clam. They reminded me of a Shell Oil sign. They would propel themselves through the water by opening their two shells at the hinge and then clamping them shut again; sort of like clicking a pair of castanets together. I asked the boys if they would like to collect some scallops and I would fry them up for lunch. Of course they did. I gave them a mesh bag with a drawstring at one end to put the scallops into and over the side of the boat they went, happy with their fun assignment.

It didn't take long for the three of them to fill the bag. Once back on the deck I put a half filled bucket of sea water in the cockpit and the bag of scallops was emptied into it. This would keep the scallops from baking in the hot sun until we could get them cleaned and cooked.

"Hey, Nathan, watch this," Dustin had found a new game. Nathan peered into the bucket of scallops which when left undisturbed would open up their two shell sides exposing the light colored flesh inside. Each time a scallop had its shells open Dustin would poke a little stick inside and then quickly remove it before the two shell sides clamped shut again. As they watched, the same scallops would repeat the process over and over again. Open. Poke. Shut. Open.

"Let me try." Dustin passed the stick off to Nathan who gave several open scallops a quick poke. Sure enough, with each poke the shells snapped shut. This was fun! "What's the matter with that one?" Nathan wondered.

"What's the matter with what one? What are you guys doing?" Jerad was just entering the cockpit from the forward cabin. He looked into the bucket and saw what Nathan was referring to. Each open scallop that was touched immediately clamped shut; all but one, that is. "That one's dead. You probably poked it too hard." Jerad sounded authoritative. After all, he was sixteen. Then Jerad did something stupid and we never could figure out why, except that, well, he was sixteen.

"Ouch! Ouch! My ear! Get this thing off my ear!" For some unknown reason Jerad had picked up the 'dead' scallop which still remained open in his hand and put it up to his ear as if to attach a clip on earring. And with that the 'dead' scallop was suddenly resurrected and clamped down hard on Jerad's earlobe. Jerad kept yelling and dancing around the cockpit as if doing some sort of strange tribal dance. Every attempt at pulling the scallop off his ear just made the darn thing hold on even tighter.

"What in the world is going on out here?" All the noise had brought me up from the aft cabin where I was busy in the galley.

"Jerad got a dead scallop stuck on his ear," Nathan informed me.

"It's not dead, Dummy, Jerad just thought it was," Dustin corrected.

"Dustin. Don't call your brother a dummy."

"Mom, help me! Get this thing off my ear. It hurts!" Jerad continued his tribal moves around the cockpit.

"What's a scallop doing on your ear anyway?" I questioned.

"I don't know. Just help me get it off." Jerad pleaded. I could tell he was in pain. I attempted to get my fingernails between the shell and the flesh of his earlobe. That didn't work. More screaming.

"Son, I just don't know what to do." Daryl had left for the states so I couldn't ask him. On second thought that was no doubt a good thing. He would have just yanked the darn thing off his ear, earlobe and all.

Aha, the single sideband radio. I would just put out a call on our ships radio to the other boats in the anchorage and see if anyone out there had any ideas. "Good Morning. This is the *Lunar Glow.* Say, can anyone tell me how to open up a scallop shell that is clamped shut?" I left out the part about the shell being clamped shut on my teenage son's ear. After all, nobody wants to broadcast the fact that their son is an idiot!

"*Lunar Glow.* Have you tried using a paring knife?" came the first suggestion. The next suggestion was an ice pick. Both of those were out of the question. I didn't want to end up with a Van Gough on my boat.

"*Lunar Glow.* Try dropping the scallops into a pot of boiling water. That usually opens them right up." Boy, that was tempting. Lucky for Jerad I didn't have a pot big enough to submerge his whole head in!

"Roger that. Thanks for the suggestions. This is *Lunar Glow,* over and out." I finally used a butter knife to extract the stubborn scallop form Jerad's earlobe. Even though I hadn't told anyone over the radio the real reason for needing to open a scallop shell I think with all the screaming going on in our open cockpit that several of the boats figured it out anyway. As for the rest of the scallops, they made an excellent meal and all of the empty shells were cleaned and later used to make wind chimes for Christmas gifts.

CHAPTER THIRTY-THREE

WILD RIDE NORTH

Daryl had been gone about a week and a half. We had received a short wave radio message three days after he had left for San Diego letting us know he had arrived safely. He had spent a night at Caden's place in San Diego and then Daryl's nephew, Grant, drove down from Piru and picked him up. As we didn't have any short wave radio equipment on our boat yet the message was sent to another boat in our anchorage who relayed the information on to us.

With Daryl gone the boys and I enjoyed some peaceful days. Along with schoolwork I decided to do a deep cleaning on the boat. We cleaned the boat inside and out making sure all the nooks and crannies were neat and organized. We got a ride into Mulege, picked up mail, and did some shopping. When we returned there was another message from Daryl. He wanted me to call. I had to wait another day before I could catch a ride back into town to use a phone. He didn't give us much information but basically said there was a problem with our house in Nevada and it was important for me to get to San Diego by the weekend. Today was Thursday already and he expected us to get ourselves to San Diego by Saturday. He said he would meet me at the local burger place at the California, Mexico border.

I had one big problem. Jerad was still boat sitting for Caden who hadn't returned from his trip to San Diego yet so he wouldn't be able to leave. I didn't want to leave Jerad alone so we finally decided to leave Jerad and Dustin on *Lunar Glow* and I would take Nathan with me and travel by bus up to San Diego. We were in a safe anchorage, the boat was well stocked, and we had lots of friends on other boats there. They were happy to keep an eye on my boys.

We got a ride into Mulege where we were told the bus would stop. It wasn't much of a bus stop; just a tall pole in the ground at the side of the road with a lot of vegetation growing up around it. Nobody else was at this bus stop so I really hoped it was the right place. If not I wasn't sure how we were going to find our way back to the boat. Finally a bus did come by and stop. I was impressed. It was actually a very large bus. One of the ones that have a couple of steps going up to the seats once you are on board. The bus came to a stop, the door opened, and the driver stepped out. Once I was confident he was going to California he took our one piece of luggage and stowed it in the luggage compartment that he accessed from a door on the lower side of the bus.

The driver stopped us as we attempted to board the bus. He indicated that 'He' needed to get on first and then we could follow him on. That seemed strange, but when in Rome, or something like that. As Nathan and I climbed the steps to the bus I saw what the problem was. The bus was full. Completely full. Not only was every seat taken but the entire isle between the seats was packed all the way to the back. Had Nathan and I gotten on ahead of the driver he wouldn't have been able to get past us to the driver's seat. There was a picnic type ice chest pushed up against the front of the bus right under the big front window and to the right as we climbed the stairs onto the bus. The driver said something in Spanish that I didn't understand. My blank look caused him to point to Nathan and then to the ice chest.

"Nathan. I think he wants you to sit on the ice chest," I said pointing to the blue cooler with a white lid. Because of the configuration of the front of the bus there wasn't enough headroom above the cooler for someone to sit.

"I can't sit on it, Mom. There's no room for my head." The bus hadn't even started moving yet and already we were tired of this ride.

"Then just curl up and lay down on it." It was late afternoon so I figured a siesta wouldn't do him any harm. Nathan timidly curled up on the cooler lid.

"Si, bueno," the driver said, nodding his head and smiling. We were on our way.

I would, of course, be standing for this trip which would last for several hours. With my left hand I held onto a pole that was attached from floor to ceiling just to the right rear of the driver's seat. Maybe two feet in front of my face was the huge front windshield. Wow, what a view. I must have had the most scenic standing spot on the bus!

We drove on for a while then suddenly the bus pulled over and came to a stop. No town here so why were we stopping? The change in motion caused Nathan, who had finally dozed off to sleep, to wake up. The driver tapped my arm and pointed to the door which was just opening with a loud whooshing sound. I grabbed Nathan by the hand and the two of us walked down the two steps and exited the bus. The driver follow right behind. There were two Mexican gentlemen standing there. They had a short conversation with the bus driver which I couldn't understand. I guessed that they, too, needed to get to California but would have to wait for another bus to come by. Wrong. The driver got back on the bus and took his seat then waved Nathan and I back in. Nathan took his place on the cooler and I once again stood to the right of the driver. Then the two Mexican men stepped into the bus. They each stood on one of the two steps just inside the bus door. The door whooshed closed again and we were off. Talk about sardines!

Because we were even tighter then we were before I had to hike up my left hip every time the driver shifted gears. I was sharing my front window floor space with a huge stick shift mounted on the floor to my left. I felt like I was being goosed every time the driver shifted gears. For anyone that has never had the experience of a Mexican road trip, whether it be by taxi or bus, it is similar to a non-stop carnival ride. Sometimes I just had to close my eyes and hang on for dear life. As the time rolled by my legs grew more and more tired as did my eyes. I must have dozed off to sleep at one point but was jolted awake again as the bus swerved and the driver hit his brakes. Apparently I was headed for a face plant into the front windshield when a helping hand from a fellow passenger behind me reached out and grabbed hold of my shirt pulling me back again.

We made another stop just before dark. The driver announced something about 'Bano' so I figured we were stopping to use the bathrooms and stretch our legs. The front door opened with another whooshing sound. The two Mexican men stepped off first followed by Nathan and myself. Next came the bus driver. As he stepped down from the bus, two German ladies stopped him. It appeared that they, too, needed to get to California. As Nathan and I headed for the bathroom I felt bad for those two ladies. There wasn't even standing room left on the bus now so they would be stranded at this remote bus stop until another bus came along.

Once all the passengers had a chance to use the bathroom we all filed back onto the bus in reverse order. First the passengers with seats. Next the ones packed into the isle. Then the driver, followed by Nathan and myself. Lastly, the two Mexican gentlemen climbed aboard taking their steps by the door. We were off again. I don't remember how many hours it took us to reach the border but it was a long night.

I was more than happy to exit the bus at our final destination. By then my legs were like rubber and I was exhausted. Nathan, thank goodness, had slept most of the way but even at that he was glad to be off the ice chest.

The door opened for the last time. Whoosh. The two Mexican men descended. Next came Nathan and myself followed by the bus driver. The driver immediately walked over to the luggage compartment at the side of the bus and slid the long rectangular door up to reveal the compartment along the underbelly of the bus. I will never forget my surprise when the two German ladies rolled out! Only in Mexico!

CHAPTER THIRTY-FOUR

STATESIDE BUSINESS

Daryl met us at the border as had been arranged. He had borrowed Grant's car, the blue Ford Fairmont we had given him the year before. Daryl had seen a doctor in L.A. and didn't seem to be in any great pain. He also didn't appear to be any great hurry so I wasn't sure why we had to rush so fast to get back up north. Grant and Denise put us up at their place.

The people who were renting our house in Stagecoach had suddenly moved out without notice leaving a huge mess behind. We really did need to get back up to Nevada and deal with whatever awaited us there. On Tuesday Grant drove us into Los Angeles where we caught a flight to Reno. We landed safely, rented a car, picked up a few groceries, and made the hour long drive to our now empty house in Stagecoach. The man who was watching over the house in our absence had placed a rental ad in the Carson City newspaper and there were already seventeen responses. Finding new tenants would be the least of our problems.

We made a thorough inspection of the house and yards. The entire inside of the house would need to be repainted. The flooring in the laundry room had been damaged and would need repair. The carpets needed to be shampooed and the yards were a disgrace. We really did have our work cut out for us.

We went back into town early Wednesday morning, bought more groceries, and loaded up with paint. This was a huge house and the painting would take me awhile. I had learned a long time back that doing the painting myself was actually less work then cleaning up the mess from someone else. Daryl was good at many things but painting was not one of them. We also decided that it might be cheaper in the long run to pick up a used car rather than continue to rent one. Besides, we still had to get back down to Mexico and I wasn't looking forward to another bus trip.

I started painting that same day. Daryl worked in the yard and Nathan did whatever he could to stay out of the way. The next day was about the same except for the fact that while I continued to paint Daryl drove the rental car back into town in search of a used car. He came back late in the day announcing that he hadn't found anything he liked yet.

On Friday Daryl went back into town to check out the remaining used car lots. This time he hit the jackpot. He found a 1979 Toyota Celica that he liked for $1,450. Aside from needing new tires the car ran great. He paid for the car then took it directly to a tire shop in Carson City which was located right across the street from the Ormsby House, one of the main casinos there. The time would pass much quicker, he reasoned, playing slot machines in the casino than reading a magazine in the tire shop's waiting area. He settled in at a bank of progressive slot machines and began feeding it quarters. He hadn't been playing very long when suddenly lights began flashing and bells and whistles rang out. He looked at the one armed Barbiet before him and realized that the triple bars were all lined up across the window of his machine. He then looked up an realized he had just won the jackpot for a total of $1,452.68. Almost the exact same price he had paid for the Celica less than an hour before! Once again Heaven had smiled down on us.

Daryl had left the rental car at the used car lot when he bought the Celica. We all drove back into town early on Saturday morning, picked up the rental car and returned it. We didn't linger in town as possible tenants were coming out to look at the house and I wanted to continue on with my painting. We did stop long enough to rent a plumbing snake that Daryl needed to fix a plumbing problem in one of the bathrooms and to buy oil so that Daryl could change the oil in our 'new' car.

On Monday we received a phone patch from friends on a boat named *Michaelanne*. This was one of the boats in the anchorage in Mulege that were keeping an eye on Jerad and Dustin. A phone patch is done between HAM radio operators that have the proper equipment. *Michaelanne* got on their radio and made a request for another HAM radio operator in the USA, preferably someone in Nevada or California, to do a patch. They got a response from a HAM operator in Palo Alto, California. The message was from Jerad. All's well on the *Lunar Glow*. Caden from *In*-Flight had returned from San Diego so Jerad's boat sitting job was complete. Thanks to our neighbor in Stagecoach taking the phone patch, our problem with the Stagecoach property and a possible delay in our return south was explained. The boys assured us that they would be just fine where they were.

We continued working on the Stagecoach house for the next week. Michael drove up on Saturday and stayed for the night. He took Nathan back to the Bay Area with him on Sunday for a visit with Grandma and Grandpa. We signed a rental agreement with the new tenants and by Tuesday we, too, left for the Bay Area. We were enjoying a few days visit with my parents when much to all of our surprise on Saturday Jerad and Dustin arrived at Grandma's front door delivered in a huge motor home.

Inserted here is an account by Jerad Cardoza of what transpired in Mexico and beyond while Daryl, Nathan, and I were in the States.

To a kid, the Sea of Cortez was about as good as it could get. The water was warm, the spear fishing was excellent, and there were lots of boats with other kids anchored nearby waiting out the chubasco season. Best of all, I was making money. When Daryl and Caden took off for the US, Caden hired me to keep an eye out for his boat *Curved Air*. Basically, all I had to do was motor over each night, untangle the anchor lines (if the boat had shifted due to wind direction changes, the lines would twist and chaff on each other), and sleep on the boat to ward off unwanted night visitors. Then the following morning I would check the lines again and leave for the day. We had agreed to the price of one hundred dollars if he returned within a month and two hundred dollars if he was gone longer. It was easy money; our boats were not more than a couple hundred yards from each other and sleeping on his boat was the type of freedom I enjoyed.

When Mom received word that she needed to take off to the states, we decided to make an important change. We lifted anchor on Lunar Glow and moved around the point to another anchorage. Not only would it be a more secure location, but it was also nearer to some of the other cruisers we knew well who would be able to keep an eye on us while we were alone. After all, Dustin was only 11 and I was 15 years old. The new location worked well except for one detail: *Curved Air* was now located around the point and was a fair distance off. With the dinghy and the 2hp Suzuki on the back of it, it took at least 15 minutes to travel back and forth. Still, we secured the anchor and this became our home for the summer.

After Mom and Nathan left for the states, Dustin and I fell into a routine. Each night, I would motor over to *Curved Air*, being careful to avoid the turtle nets set out by the Mexican fishermen, and radio Dustin to let him know I was there and had the VHF on. Even with other cruisers around, he was on his own sleeping on the boat. The following morning, I would motor back and we would throw on a mask and snorkel and hunt down breakfast. It was usually pretty easy to spear a trigger fish or even a small grouper. It was a bit tougher to nail a parrot fish, but when you did, they were one of the best fish to eat. They were also one of the most fun to filet because the meat would continue to quiver, even after it had been cut from the rest of the fish. Once we had caught our food, we would filet it, dip it in breadcrumbs and fry it in a pan.

Needless to say, but, we ate a lot of fish! After breakfast, we would write in our journals, finish just enough schoolwork to avoid feeling guilty, and then the rest of the day was ours to mess around in the water or with friends.

This went on for two weeks.

Our only means of communication to Mom and Daryl was a phone number to a neighbor in Nevada. In the nearby town of Mulege, there was a small store where you could place collect phone calls. We had previously agreed with mom that we would call once a week at a specific time. It was one of the only rules we had been given. By the end of the second week, we were expecting the news that they were en route back to the boat. What we heard instead was the best news ever: we were going to the USA! Now don't get me wrong, Mexico was fantastic, but after having been gone for a year, there was something about McDonalds and 7-11 and Grandma's house that made us wild with excitement. What Mom said was this: "After Caden gets back on his boat, pack up *Lunar Glow* and secure it for the season. Let the other boats know to look after it and then hop a bus for San Diego. Once you are there, you can call us and we will tell you how to get from there to Grandma's house."

I'm going to break away from the story for just a minute to tell you a little about myself in 2019. I am 46 years old and I have three children ages 15, 18 and 20. I consider my wife and me to be fairly normal when it comes to our parenting style. With that being said, when my daughter wants to go to a friend's house, my wife will drive her 5 blocks and then wait outside the house until the door opens and she goes inside—just to be safe. And we would never even consider leaving our kids alone even for one night without an adult to look after them. And yet when I reflect back on the phone call where, after two weeks alone in a foreign country, a 15 and an 11 year old were asked to take a 600 mile bus ride to the US border only to then figure out how to get another 500 miles to the San Francisco Bay area, I have to admit, it felt completely normal. Maybe that was what the cruising lifestyle did to you. We still felt like kids but when we were asked to step up, we just did what had to be done.

A few days later, we attended a big cruiser party on the beach for the Fourth of July. It was a big potluck and there were a bunch of people there. For Dustin and I, it was a chance to brag to the other cruisers about how we were going to be heading back the states as soon as Caden got back to his boat, although we still had no idea when that would be. The party, as it turned out, ended up being the biggest break we could have ever received. While I was talking to some people, Dustin ran up to me and said, "Jerad! I got us a ride to Grandma's house!" It turned out that in the course of his conversations, a man named Al from the boat *Aurora* caught wind of the two kids traveling alone to the states and he approached Dustin with an offer. He told him, "I am actually heading up to Canada in my motorhome to visit my daughter. You guys are welcome to ride along with me up to San Francisco." The only detail that mattered to us was "motorhome." Who he was or what his background was were irrelevant. And there was another catch: he wasn't leaving for another three weeks and his motorhome was parked about 70 miles up the coast. Minor details. We were going to ride in a motorhome!

On the next day set aside to call Mom, we shared the news about what had developed. Having already been alone for three weeks, we told her that we wouldn't be heading north for yet another three weeks. Her reply was simple. She said, "Do whatever you think is best." From this point on, we were calling all the shots.

About 10 days later, Caden came home. It had been just over a month so I gladly collected my 200 dollars, and Dustin and I were finally reunited for the final week or so aboard *Lunar Glow.* To this day I am still amazed at how resilient Dustin was to sleep alone on the boat for an entire month. Our conversations now revolved around how to get to Santa Rosalia where we would meet up with Al and see the motorhome that we had built up in our minds. As luck would have it, there was an old gentleman whose wife had also traveled up to the states, and he was looking to take his boat up to Santa Rosalia by himself. Even though he was set to head there a couple days early, we volunteered to help him crew his boat in exchange for the free ride. Then we would find a motel to stay in until Al was ready to leave. The man agreed and we had yet one more problem solved on our trip north.

On the day we were to leave, we put out a couple more anchors—one more off the bow and another to the aft—in order to secure our location. We knew that if the boat dragged an anchor while we were gone, there would be hell to pay from Daryl and we would be to blame. Then we secured the hatches, padlocked them, and hitched a dinghy ride over to our new crew job. On the ride north, the seas were rough and there was a strong breeze blowing. Dustin and I, having only sailed on a trimaran, were determined to see how fast we could get this monohull to go—it was clearly not built for speed and the two of us sailing it was like trying to make a VW bus drive like a corvette. I have no doubt we broke speed records in that heavy tub. And to add to the drama, the old man—every time he went out on deck, we thought he was going to have a heart attack and fall overboard. But it ended up that we all made it to Santa Rosalia intact and two days before we were to leave with Al.

Upon arriving at the dock, we decided we would find Al and let him know we were there in town. His response to seeing us was something surreal to a teenage: "hey, since you guys arrived early, what do you say we leave tomorrow instead and we can stop at Disneyland along the way?"

Our eyes probably gave away our answer long before our mouths could speak—this was like a dream come true! This wonderful person who my 11 year old brother had met for five minutes on the beach was offering to take us two young boys in his motorhome to Disneyland—I couldn't find any holes in that offer so we gave a resounding YES! And then we went to find a hotel for the night.

Before continuing, let me give a little background on Al that we picked up along the way. As sketchy as the details seem in looking back, Al was a fantastic guy. He was a retired pilot for Canada Airlines and both his boat and his motorhome were top notch. As easy as it could have been for him to be some creep child molester, it turns out that he was simply a really nice person doing an incredibly nice deed. And even given his age, he was still sort of a kid at heart. One of the only stipulations about going to Disneyland was that he wanted to get there early and be the first person in line to go on Star Tours. He got no pushback from us ...

I don't remember a bunch about the ride up the coast other than Dustin and I were now traveling with expired tourist permits; the date had passed a couple weeks earlier so every time we went through a checkpoint, we hid in the closet so as not to put Al in an awkward spot. We were so tanned that we looked Mexican and of course we had no documentation other than our passports. We made it past the border with no issues and stayed the night somewhere between San Diego and Los Angeles. Al treated us to a steak dinner and we talked about what order we would ride the rides the next day.

At Disneyland, Al was true to his word. We were at the front of the ropes on Main Street when they let everyone in and it was everything we could do to stay up with him as he sprinted to Tomorrowland. I remember being yelled at, "WALK!" after which we would take two slow steps and then bolt at full speed once again. We arrived at Star

Tours first and walked straight onto the ride. The rest of the day was a bit of a blur but it was a fantastic welcome back to the United States of America.

The following day was the last day we were ever to see Al. True to his word, he drove us straight to my Grandparent's driveway in San Lorenzo, CA. We had kept many of the details of our travel north a secret from our family so that we could surprise them when we arrived. When we pulled in with this beautiful RV, it was an impressive show to say the least. Nathan wanted to check it out and Dustin was happy to show him around the inside. We introduced Al to Mom and Daryl who, at this point, had made it from Nevada. As payment for the ride, Al had only asked for one thing: we agreed to wash the motorhome before he continued on his way. When we finished, we gave him a hug, thanked him profusely for the incredible trip, and just like that, Al was gone.

People inevitably ask if my parents were crazy or negligent letting two young boys do what we did. To this day, I really don't have an answer to that question. While I would never come close to letting my kids do anything of that nature, I think the circumstances at the time were much different. I will say this: there was nothing that I didn't feel Dustin and I could handle. Was there an incredible amount of luck that went along with us? Absolutely. But I am thankful for the experience and wouldn't change a thing about it.

Daryl and I left the Bay Area on Wednesday. We were nervous about leaving the boat alone for too long. The boys stayed behind so that they could spend more time with Michael and their dad. Grandpa and Grandma were also planning to take them on a trip up the coast to Oregon to visit with their uncle, aunt and cousins there. Now that we had a car we had more flexibility with our travel. We made the two day drive back down to Mexico and were pleased to see that the boys had, indeed, left the boat in A-1 condition.

The car made trips up and down the Baja easier but it also posed another problem. We could tow our dinghy from place to place or haul it up on deck for longer runs, but a car was a different thing. Lucky for us *Stickwitch* and *Willow* both had vehicles on the Baja so we were able to leap frog rides with them to reposition our car. We drove the car on to Escondido and got a ride back to the boat with *Stickwitch*. Daryl and I spent the next three days making day sails from spot to spot as we worked our way back to Escondido. *Stickwitch* sailed along with us so we had someone to visit with and share an evening meal but even so I was missing my young crew.

By now it was the beginning of August and the weather in the Sea of Cortez was extremely hot and humid. We secured the boat once more and arranged for friends in the anchorage to look after her as we headed north again by car. We spent a couple of nights with Grant and Denise in Piru. They were always so hospitable and we enjoyed their company. We headed the Celica north, picked up Dustin and Nathan at Grandma's house, and drove on to Stagecoach where we still had a few yard chores to finish up. The new tenants had moved into the property so we got a motel in Carson City for the night.

I had set up several appointments on our previous trip to Nevada which we now needed to attend to. Daryl's many aches and pains were addressed with our family doctor; we saw our attorney; and lastly Dustin and Nathan had appointments to get some dental checkups and work done. Our doctor arranged for Daryl to have some therapy sessions for the back pains he was having but those wouldn't start for another week yet. So back we went to the Bay Area once again to spend time with the family.

We left Jerad and Dustin with Grandma and Grandpa and took Nathan with us back to Nevada. With the house rented we stayed the night at a Motel 6 in Carson City but realized that even that was going to be over our meager budget for the two weeks Daryl would be getting therapy. We drove back out to Stagecoach the following day, checked with the tenants, and picked up our camping gear from the basement of the house. We would just have to camp out for the next couple of weeks along the Walker River in Markleville where Daryl could drive back and forth for his back therapy. The weather was great and aside from a black bear trying to share our campsite with us it was a relaxing time.

It was now September 5th and we had been away far too long. Our plan at this point was to return our camping gear to the Stagecoach house, drive to the Bay Area and get the other boys and then head back down to the boat within a couple of days time. It had been a fun break for the boys from their boat chores and schoolwork but it was time to get back to "our real world". Then suddenly there was a kink in the plan. When we went to return our camping gear the new tenants informed us that they were having marital problems and decided to get a divorce. They would be moving out in a week's time. Good grief! So now what?

CHAPTER THIRTY-FIVE

A MEXICAN MOTEL

A s per our plan we still gathered up the boys and for the first time we packed all five of us into the Toyota Celica. Needless to say it was really crowded but an interesting trip all the same. We stopped over in Piru for the night then went on to San Diego where we ate some breakfast and renewed our tourist visas for Mexico. Once into Mexico and out onto the open road we gave Jerad his first driving lesson. I'm not sure if Jerad was more excited about learning to drive or just with the thought of getting to trade places with me and not being wedged into the crowded back seat with his brothers any longer. For the subject of driver's ed Daryl would take over as the teacher.

It became obvious that we would not be able to reach *Lunar Glow* before nightfall. Not wanting to run the risk of hitting a cow, horse, or other large animal out on the road and being without any sort of camping gear we decided to find a motel and spend the night then continue on to the boat the next day. We drove on to Gurrero Negro and found a motel just before dusk. Using the five star rating scale for motels this one probably came in at about a half star.

We pulled off the road into the dirt parking area carefully avoiding the fist sized rocks and trash that was strewn about. We got out, stretched, and headed towards the small, whitewashed building up front that we figured must be the office. The room was empty as we entered but a middle aged man soon appeared through a curtain that hung over a door to another room. He gave us a friendly greeting and we used enough of our rather poor Spanish and charades to secure one room for the night for the five of us. It was very cheap but it was easy to see why. We also figured out that he wanted to know if we wanted towels. This would be an extra charge. Yes, we did. "Cinco", five towels. One for each of us. We paid the additional towel charge. He may have asked us if we wanted soap too, but I guess we missed that part because we didn't get any.

The proprietor handed us the stack of towels and a room key attached to a white plastic disk with the number "5" painted on it and pointed us to one of the eight or so doors located on the building at the rear of the parking area. We grabbed an overnight bag out of the car, locked the doors, and headed for Room 5. This place made *Lunar Glow* feel like the Ritz! The room was small. It had one double bed which was actually just a mattress on top of a cement platform. The tile floor was badly chipped but appeared clean. The only other furniture in the room was a small bedside table with a lamp on top. It did have a bathroom although the toilet wouldn't flush without removing the lid and fiddling with the chain inside the tank. There was also a little window in the bathroom above the toilet which was stuck in a half open position. We figured the opening was too small for anyone to fit through it so we didn't worry about that. Besides that it was hot and there was no air conditioning so any added air moving through was a bonus.

I was still examining the room when the boys started to laugh. "What's so funny?" I questioned.

"Look at these towels," Jerad said, holding one of them up. "They're like a puzzle. I've got the feet."

"And I've got a stomach," Nathan piped in.

We unfolded each of the towels. They were thread bare and had at one time been beach towels but had now been cut into thirds. Three of our towels when laid out and arranged properly made a lady laying on the beach.

CHAPTER THIRTY-SIX

BACK TO BASICS

It was nearly 1pm by the time we arrived back at *Lunar Glow*. We parked the car and hailed someone in the anchorage to come and pick us up on shore. We launched our own dinghy and made several trips to and from the boat with all of the "stuff" we had brought back from the states. In addition to our luggage and some food provisions I had some heavy boxes containing the next years school books which had been shipped to my parent's house in the Bay Area.

All was well on the boat, however, our boat papers were missing. These are the papers that must be presented to the Port Captain and Immigration every time you move the boat into a different town. We had given our packet of paperwork to *Stickwitch* before leaving in case there was a problem and the boat had to be moved in our absence. Now we learned that *Stickwitch* had left the day before on a road trip to San Diego. Our boat papers were either with them or on their boat. At any rate we would not be moving the boat anywhere until *Stickwitch* returned.

Our new school year started the next morning. We mainly just went over all of the new books and materials we had received. Schoolwork completed for the day, Daryl and I drove into Loreto for ice and produce. The boys all went into Loreto also to attend a Mexican celebration there, but they motored to town aboard the *Martha Rose* with their friend, Fritz. After having been gone for six weeks the boys had a lot of catching up to do with their friends.

There was still the problem of an empty house back in Stagecoach. Daryl would head back to Nevada try to find new renters while the boys and I stayed in Puerto Escondido. It really did work out well as it was still really hot on the boat, 108 degrees inside the cabin, which made Daryl really cranky. Dustin was behaving terribly and I couldn't figure out why, Jerad had scrapped his knee and was taking antibiotics for an infection, and little Nathan got a salt water boil on his butt making sitting down a pain in the butt! Anyway, given all these problems it really was best that after being back for just two nights Daryl was off again.

Dustin's behavior was a real puzzle. He hadn't been very pleasant on the ride back down the Baja but I figured it was just riding in a very packed car. Then once back on the boat I blamed it on the heat. But as soon as Daryl took off again Dustin got really bad. I suppose he figured that with Daryl gone he could get away with acting up. If I asked him to do something he'd say "No" or just tell me to "Shut up". He refused to mind me and when I'd restrict him to the boat for his bad behavior he would throw terrible tantrums. One night he screamed at the top of his lungs for nearly an hour. He would hit and kick Nathan and when I'd try talking to him to find out what was wrong he'd refuse to talk to me. I was at my wits end. Where had my sweet young son gone? Finally, the pieces of Dustin's behavior puzzle started to fall into place.

CHAPTER THIRTY-SEVEN

PUZZLE SOLVED!

The heat continued to hang on. In trying to keep as cool as possible Nathan asked me to buzz his hair off. I had some old hand clippers which did a pretty decent job. Dustin and Jerad followed suit and soon the boys all had matching buzz jobs. But two days later Dustin was terribly upset about his hair, or rather lack of hair.

"I need to hurry and grow my hair back," Dustin stated, "or else Michael will be mad at me."

"Michael's not even here, and anyway why would your hair make him mad?" I questioned.

"He told me I had to keep it styled the way he showed me and now I can't do that. He's going to be mad."

"I don't care what Michael said," Jerad piped in. "I feel much cooler this way."

Jerad then went on to say that before leaving the Bay Area Michael had told his brothers that they were to stick together in rebelling against

Daryl and myself. Over the next few days many more puzzle pieces began to surface.

My attorney had contacted Joe, the boy's dad, about paying some back child support. He was years behind. This, I learned had made Michael very mad. How dare I ask for back child support. Didn't I realize that Michael's truck payment and auto insurance alone cost Joe over $350 per month. And Joe had other expenses too. He had paid for Michael to take a trip to Europe as a graduation gift. Michael now had his hair styled in a salon while his brothers still had haircuts from Mom, (which would be the case for many more years).

Michael's time living with his dad had been mainly unsupervised and totally undisciplined. He had become vain and materialistic. I loved my son dearly and this broke my heart. At least now I was beginning to understand why Dustin was behaving the way he was. He was very confused about being the sweet boy he was and carrying out Michael's instructions. I felt bad for both of my sons.

As the days passed and I picked up more and more bits and pieces of what had transpired up north I became less and less angry with Dustin. It really wasn't his fault. The boys did their schoolwork each morning followed by lots of chores. Dustin had learned that the worse he behaved the more chores he was assigned. As Dustin started becoming less rebellious he was given more free time off the boat. We heard that Al off of *Spring Moon*, the retired airline pilot from Canada, was back in Escondido. Jerad and Dustin were excited to visit him in his motor home and find out how the rest of his trip up north had gone after he had so graciously delivered them to Grandma's doorstep two months earlier.

By the time Daryl returned from the states Dustin was pretty much back to his old self again. Nathan's boil was better and Jerad's knee was improving daily. Once again, life was good.

CHAPTER THIRTY-EIGHT

A HAM RADIO, A DOG, AND A SURFBOARD

S o what do a ham radio, a dog, and a surfboard have in common? Well actually, nothing, except that they all took place close together. Daryl returned from the states with a big surprise. Ham radio equipment. He said that Jerad's Ham radio license wouldn't be of much use to him if there was no way for him to use it. We were talking more and more about crossing the Pacific Ocean and figured that being able to stay in touch with the rest of the world during our travels wouldn't be such a bad idea. He worked all the next day getting the equipment installed in our little charting area. Jerad was thrilled. Even though his XE2 Ham license hadn't arrived yet we knew that it was "in the mail".

We had had *Lunar Glow* in the water for over a year already and Daryl really thought we should get some new bottom paint put on. He heard that there was a place in La Paz where we could get a haul out. The boys didn't want to make another road trip with the last one still so fresh in their minds. Daryl and I would drive down to La Paz for a quick overnight trip and make arrangements to have the boat hauled out of the water.

Jerad took us to shore in the dinghy then headed back out to the boat. The *Martha Rose* would keep an eye on our boys for us. We picked up the car and drove by the dumps to drop off our garbage. As we did so we spotted a tiny puppy that had been tossed into the garbage heap along with the piles of smelly trash. Not sure if it was dead or alive I nudged it with a stick.

"Daryl, look at this. It moved. It's still alive," I said.

"I believe you're right. I can't imagine anyone just throwing a live puppy in the garbage like that," he replied.

"Well, what shall we do with it. We can't just leave it here to die," I answered.

"There really isn't anything we can do. We can't get it back to the boat. The boys would never hear us calling to them from the shore and they aren't planning to pick us up in the dinghy until late tomorrow afternoon. We can see if it's still here when we get back from La Paz tomorrow. Better yet, just move it out from the trash heap and maybe someone else will rescue it," Daryl reasoned.

"And if they don't it will die. It's nearly dead now. Let's just take it with us."

"In the car. To La Paz. You want to take a half dead puppy on a 215 mile road trip. Are you nuts!" Daryl was losing patience but at the same time coming to realize that he wasn't going to win this round.

I walked over to the car and took a couple of tissues out of my purse then returned and used them to gingerly pick up the puppy. It's eyes were open and it was breathing but not much more than that. It was about the size of a skinny Cornish game hen. There was more movement from the bugs crawling on this thing than from the dog itself. I also retrieved a lid from an empty jar.

"What's the lid for?" Daryl questioned. "We stopped here to drop off trash not pick up more."

"It's for the puppy. It'll need a water dish, right?"

We got into the car and headed off towards La Paz. I laid the puppy on the floor matt at my feet. At this point it was much too smelly and had too many bugs on it to hold it on my lap.

Awhile later I said, "I think it's hungry. We need to feed it."

"Well I'm fresh out of puppy food," Daryl shot back.

"Stop at the next town we come to. We need to find a market and get this little guy something to eat." At this point I hadn't even examined the puppy enough to know if it was boy or a girl.

The market we found was one of those really small ones that doesn't have isles to walk through. There was a counter with a storekeeper behind it. Behind her was a shelved wall containing the total inventory of the "store". I did a visual search of the items on the shelves. The closest I could come up with for something the puppy might be able to eat was a can of sweetened condensed milk. That would have to do.

We returned to the car where I poked a couple of holes in the top of the sweetened condensed milk can with a pocket knife and poured a bit into the jar lid. Using the tissues again to move the puppy I dipped it's nose into the milk.

"Daryl, look. She likes it." By now I had done enough of an inspection to know that "our" new dog was a "she". "Wow, she must have been starving. Look at her go." I poured more milk into the lid. By the time we reached La Paz it was raining really hard and the puppy had consumed a good portion of the milk.

Daryl secured a motel room for the night and I made a mad dash through the rain to the motel room door. It was easy to sneak the puppy in. With the heavy rain nobody was paying much attention to us.

The first order of business was going to be a bath for the puppy. I filled the bathroom sink with nice warm water and lowered the now full puppy into it.

"I think she likes it," I called to Daryl in the other room. Bugs were beginning to release themselves from the dogs light brown hair. I emptied the sink to flush out the bugs and quickly refilled it again with fresh warm water. I repeated this process a few times until I could no longer see any bugs. After a couple of minutes more I called out to Daryl again.

"I think you'd better come here. Something strange is happening with the puppy." It must have been a combination of too much sweetened condensed milk and the warm water because now the puppy's mid section was swelling up like an inflated balloon. Daryl and I just stood there, wide eyed, mouths open, watching the puppy bob around in the water like one of those red and white floats you attach to your fishing line.

Eventually the puppy returned back to normal size but not before throwing up a couple of times. We would have to find something less rich for her to eat. At least now she was clean and as far as we could tell, bug free.

We found the boatyard in La Paz and arranged for *Lunar Glow* to be hauled out in exactly a month's time. We looked all over town for a surfboard for Jerad. His 16th birthday was coming up soon and we knew he would like a new surfboard. Although he still made good use of the big heavy board that had been on the boat when we bought her, we wanted to get him one that was shorter, lighter, and easier to handle. We looked all over town but never did find one so after stocking up on some groceries we headed north again with our now clean puppy in tow.

Jerad met us on shore with the dinghy as we had arranged. The puppy was sleeping peacefully, nestled in a small towel down inside the cloth purse I had slung over my shoulder. Jerad had no idea it was there. We boarded the boat and while Jerad and Daryl brought our bags onboard I called out for the other boys.

"Hey, Guys, we're back. Come on out here. I have a surprise for you." As the boys stepped up into the cockpit I took the sleepy puppy out of my purse and handed it to Dustin. All three boys were so excited. They started shooting questions at us faster than we could answer:

"Where did you get it?"

"Can we keep it?"

"How old is it?"

"What kind of a dog is it?"

"How big will it get?"

"Is it a girl or a boy?"

"Can it sleep on my bunk?"

"No, I want it to sleep with me!"

"Does it have a name?"

The puppy was now being passed from one set of hands to another.

"Slow down a minute and I'll tell you," I said. "We found the puppy in the dumps over past where we park the car. It's a girl and we think she might be two or three weeks old. We have no idea what kind of dog she is or how big she'll get. She won't be sleeping on anyone's bunk and you'll have to come up with a name for her."

After some debate they settled on Dustin's choice, Star. Given that we lived on *Lunar Glow*, Star sounded like an appropriate choice.

Jerad's birthday was now just a week away and we still hadn't found a surfboard. So, you got it! We would make yet another trip up to San Diego. Caden, who now had a girlfriend in San Diego was always looking for a ride north, so we took him along as our excuse for this trip. Nathan came with us while Jerad and Dustin stayed on the boat with Star.

We found a beautiful surfboard for Jerad. It cost us much more than we had planned but we knew Jerad would love it. While at the surf shop we also picked up a bunch of surfboard foam which Daryl later used to build model sailboats with Dustin. Caden remained in San Diego and would return at a later date by bus. This gave us enough room in the car for the surfboard.

Jerad's birthday surprise was a big hit. He loved his new surfboard. Between the boys having pizza on *Endeavor*, free-boarding behind a dinghy with the new surfboaord, and a big party on *Lunar Glow*, the day was a success.

CHAPTER THIRTY-NINE

LIFE IS A BEACH

We had a great time sailing back down to La Paz. We spent some time in the islands outside of Escondido. We played and hiked on shore and even attended a rather interesting horse race in Agua Verde. There were caves to explore and crystals to search for. We had pot lucks on various boats and BBQ's on the shore. There were volleyball games with the other boaters and sand dunes to play in. The fishing was wonderful in these waters. In addition to the many fish we pulled in off of *Lunar Glow*, Jerad was becoming quite proficient with his spear. We were actually starting to get tired of eating so much lobster!

Life was still not all fun and games. We also did schoolwork each day and the never ending boat chores. The water was clear and warm so no one complained much as we swam around the boat and dove down to scrub the bottom paint and waterline. We wanted to make sure it was nice and clean before we had her hauled out of the water.

Once we had anchored in La Paz and had our check in process completed, Daryl headed off to the boatyard to see about the haul out we had arranged to do. Bad news. *Lunar Glow* was too wide to fit into their lift. We were 24 feet on the beam which was wider than most trimarans. We thought we had told them that when we made the haul out appointment a month earlier but apparently our Spanish still needed some work. We would just need to figure something else out.

Our next best option was the dock at the marina there in La Paz and we were in luck. There was an end space available where we would be able to fit and they were happy to have us rent it. That way we could at lease do the work on the inside of the boat as well as paint the decks without the boat swinging to and fro every time the tide changed. Also, there were hot showers at the marina we would be able to use. Caching!

We reconnected with the *Michaelanne* while in La Paz. They had been bird-sitting our little parrot, Sweetie Pie, for several months now and I'm sure they were glad to give her back. We were now a two pet family. We always kept Sweetie Pie in her cage down in the cabin when we were sailing but she was often in the cockpit when we were at anchor. Star, on the other hand, was never allowed down into the cabin areas. She stayed mainly in the cockpit and as she grew larger and was able to hop up onto the cockpit seats and then onto the cabin top she had the run of the outside of the boat. This arrangement worked out well. The floor of the cockpit was fiberglass with removable wooden floorboard slats fitted over the top. Any pee or poop could be easily washed off with a bucket of water sloshed over the top which drained off down the centerboard compartment. The cockpit also had cut out areas under each of the built in fiberglass seats. We usually kept life jackets and miscellaneous items stowed under there. We just emptied out one of those areas and made a bed for Star which she liked just fine.

It was a busy time for us in La Paz. In addition to the everyday routine of school, chores, shopping, laundry, etc., Daryl worked on epoxy repairs, removed a leaky water tank, installed new sink fixtures, and fixed the wet hatches. We had ordered a new desalinater which would turn salt water into fresh water at the rate of about a gallon per hour. Daryl also got this installed. I worked for weeks painting the decks, cockpit, and various interior areas.

After the difficult sewing project Jerad had done months before I had insisted on having a sewing machine onboard. During one of our Stagecoach runs I picked up my portable sewing machine. Daryl made a hand crank for it so that I was able to operate it without electricity. I either had to sew with my left hand and crank with my right hand or when I could talk them into it one of the boys would operate the hand crank leaving me with both hands free to sew. I made new curtains for the stern castle and shorts for the boys. I was also able to patch some worn spots on our sails and made a new Mexican flag.

We motored the boat over to a sand island a short distance from La Paz on December 8th. A big tide was to go out that day so we were able to beach the boat on the sand and then worked like mad to get the new bottom paint on all three hulls before the tide came in again to set us afloat. It wasn't quite like having the boat hauled out at the boatyard to get the work done, but it worked.

This stay in La Paz lasted for six weeks. Before leaving we also got Star to the vet for her distemper and puppy shots and got Mexican car insurance for the Celica. We left the car in the care of Ted from one of the boats who would be staying on the Baja for a while. He was planning on making a trip to the San Diego area and would drive the Celica up there, hand it off to Grant and Denise who would keep it for us until further notice. Ted would then return to La Paz via bus. It was time for us to move along.

We pulled away for the dock at the marina on December 21st and sailed as far as Ballandra and then on to Los Muertos the following day. *Stickwitch* and the *Tao* sailed along with us so we had friends to get together with in the evenings. We were still in Los Muertos on Christmas Day; the weather was warm and calm. We all got together on *Stickwitch* for a big turkey dinner.

The weather turned cool and windy the following day but that didn't stop us from enjoying ourselves while preparing to leave for the mainland Mexico. The winds had continued to increase as we pulled anchor and headed out to sea. The 15 to 20 foot seas made for an exhilarating ride to say the least. It was two days before we spotted land again and entered Bandaras Bay. We were all tired from the sail across the Sea of Cortez but the weather had warmed up again and the anchorage at Punta de Mita was a welcome sight. Jerad was already scoping out some surfing spots.

CHAPTER FORTY

ANOTHER NEW YEAR, A REAL CIRCUS

anada *Goose V* sailed into the anchorage on New Year's Eve day. Jerad saw that there were young girls on board so made it a point to row over and meet them. They were a nice family out of Canada with three daughters ages 12, 14, and 16. We spent the evening with them on their boat sharing stories and plans for the future.

New Year's Day fell on a Sunday and because it was a holiday the boys were given the day off from schoolwork. The boys all headed off to the beach with Star in tow to surf and play on the beach.

It was now 1989 and we started the new year with our usual (or maybe unusual) routine; schoolwork for the boys and I and boat repairs for Daryl in the mornings followed by fun and free time in the afternoons. The *Tao* and *Stickwitch* didn't arrive until Tuesday. Now that the gang was all together again we had a big spaghetti dinner on Wednesday evening and the kids all spent the night on *Stickwitch* for a belated New Year's Eve party. The adults played cards and dice on *Lunar Glow* in the evening.

After a week in Punta de Mita we finally pulled our anchor and made a short sail up the coast of Bandaras Bay to the little town of La Cruz. *Timshell*, who we had originally met in San Diego was already at anchor there. Pam and her husband were a retired couple who had started their sailing trip from Washington state. They were fond of our boys and the boys really liked them as well so of course the boys were delighted when Pam radioed and invited them to check out a circus being setup on shore just a short distance from where we were anchored.

I'm not sure of the name this circus went by. It certainly wasn't Ringling Brothers Barnum and Bailey's Circus although they did have a couple of tents. Pam and her husband picked the boys up in their dinghy and motored it the short distance to the shore. There appeared to be lots of animals in various pens and cages scattered about the area many of which were being fed prior to their "performance" which would take place later that evening.

Dustin was especially intrigued with an alpaca engrossed in eating his meal of dark green alfalfa. He would lean in as far as the alpaca's pen would allow then back away again. The alpaca kept a close eye on Dustin as he continued chewing his meal. Jerad cautioned Dustin to stay back so as not to bother the alpaca but Dustin paid no attention. He was enjoying the stare down with this animal. Then, suddenly, the alpaca had had enough of the game and spit a mouthful of dark green alfalfa in Dustin's direction. Dustin, however, stepped aside just in time for the projectile to hit Jerad square in the face. Jerad stood stunned as the green slime ran down his face and onto his once clean shirt. Dustin rolled on the ground laughing until his shirt was a dirty mess also.

Later that evening (Jerad and Dustin both in clean shirts) the five of us joined our friends on *Timshell* to shore where we bought tickets and attended the circus. There were quite a few of the locals there as well as us boat folks. We all sat on benches made of long planks resting on logs at various intervals. This was a real low budget affair but still lots of fun. Some of the acts included animals such as a huge Bengal tiger that jumped through a ring of fire. Other acts included acrobatics and a knife thrower using a volunteer from the audience as the holder of the target. It may not have been the greatest show on earth but a great show nonetheless.

CHAPTER FORTY-ONE

TO FUEL OR NOT TO FUEL ...

We left La Cruz after our one entertaining night there only staying long enough the following morning to go to town for fresh produce. We headed for Nuevo Vallarta as we needed to fill our water tanks and get fuel and propane and we knew there was a fuel dock there. We arrived in Nuevo Vallarta to find that the fuel dock was closed. It was a Saturday so we supposed they shut down for the weekend or maybe they were still celebrating the New Year. We stayed the night there and when the fuel dock remained closed the next morning we filled our water tanks and moved the boat around into a place called "the pond" for the night. We would need to fill our gas tanks and get more propane before moving on so we did the next best thing we could think of.

"Come on boys, we need to gather up the empty gas jugs and the propane tank and get going," I announced.

"Ah, Mom, can't we just stay here and play with our friends?" Dustin wanted to know.

"Sorry, Son," I replied. "We're going to need all of us to get this done."

We gathered the empty, red, five gallon fuel jugs as well as the empty propane tank, piled into the dinghy and headed for a spot on shore. It was just a short walk to the bus stop where we would catch a bus into town to get our jugs filled. The trip into town was easy. We boarded a bus and each of us took a seat and set an empty jug on our laps. The return trip wasn't quite as easy. With the jugs now full we had the difficult task of getting them back to the boat.

"Mom, how come I have to carry this thing and Nathan doesn't have to," Dustin wanted to know.

"Because he can hardly even lift the jug let alone carry it," I replied.

Daryl was now carrying Nathan's filled jug in one hand and the full propane tank in the other. Jerad, Dustin, and I each lugged our heavy jugs along to the bus stop. When the bus arrived we pulled our jugs up the steps and took seats where we could. Had we been in the U.S.A. we no doubt would have been denied boarding the bus with all that gasoline, but not in Mexico. We actually fit in quite well.

We left the pond early the next morning and sailed on to Ipala where we stayed at anchor for the next three nights. We were able to make phone patches to Mom and Dad and also to our friend, Iris, in Stagecoach, who was taking care of some business for Daryl.

Jerad went diving and caught a large spotted ray which we had for dinner. The rays tasted a lot like scallops but you could only eat the "wings". I would cut the wings in pieces to resemble scallops, batter and bread them, then deep fry them. Really good eating. Jerad went out the next day diving again. This time he speared a large fish that ended up swimming away with his spear gun shaft. He felt bad for a little while but then cheered up when some local kids took he and his brothers out freeboarding. Jerad also sold his wetsuit which he had now outgrown. Having a little cash from the wetsuit also improved Jerad's spirits.

From Ipala we sailed south to Bahia Chamela. The anchorage was good and there was a nice sand beach which was always a plus. There was also a fair sized surf getting to the beach which was usually a minus.

On Saturday we went ashore with Greg and Maria from *Tao* for some fresh, local produce. We got the dinghies through the surf and onto the beach without a problem. Maria and I went shopping while the kids played on the beach. Daryl and Greg tagged along to help carry our purchases back to the boat.

The return dinghy ride out to the boats was a bit more difficult. Maria and I were in one dinghy. We put our groceries on the floor of the dinghy and pushed out through the surf. We swamped the dinghy trying to get in but it stayed upright and we made a safe though wet ride back to the boat. Daryl and Greg also took on some water getting through the surf but then for some reason Daryl stood up about half way back to the boat, lost his balance, and dumped both he and Greg overboard. It was really funny to watch.

A letter I wrote home to Mom and Dad on January 15, 1989 reads in part:

The fresh produce here is wonderful. We went to shore yesterday and found the local market. It's about 12' x 18' but full of nice fruit, vegetables, cheeses, and a few other staples. Prices were good, too. This is a very inexpensive place to be. Nothing to spend money on except food, and we rarely eat ashore so $100 per month is a generous budget ... I think 'Lunar Glow' is ready for her big voyage. I know I am. This waiting to leave is hard. Still not certain of exact departure date but no later than March 15. So many places I want to see.

Jerad is really liking his French course he started a couple of weeks ago. He will have to be our translator in French Polynesia. He does his schoolwork each day without any argument. Dustin and Nathan on the other hand ...

This is such a beautiful place. Quiet and peaceful, too. We have so many friends down here also. We (Daryl and I) play cards - pinochle - most nights with our friends Greg and Maria on 'Tao'. The kids get together and play games or whatever. (The whatever has earned Jerad his new nickname of "hotlips". Heidi and her twin brother, Tyson, from 'Tao', are also 16. Their brother Kalen is 12). For anyone who may think differently, Jerad's social life does not suffer!

Our dog, Star, is growing a little but I think she's about full grown now. She is such a well behaved dog and a very good watch dog. We will dread the day we can no longer have her along with us. She saw her first school of dolphins swimming with 'Lunar Glow' the other day and didn't know quite what to think of them.

Jerad and Nathan are at the beach boogie boarding. Daryl went diving. Dustin is currently grounded to the boat so he is here with me. He cleaned the deck and cockpit and just finished baking cookies so it smells really good in here. I just finished sewing three pairs of shorts …

So aside from the fact that Daryl was depressed and just plain grouchy much of the time, life was good.

CHAPTER FORTY-TWO

A MEXICAN DANCE

After a few enjoyable days in Bahia Chamela we pulled our anchor and headed for Tenecatita. It was quite pretty here and not at all crowded. There were a lot of Americans that lived along the beach here during the winter but we were told they returned to the US during the summer months. These were friendly folks. They volunteered to drive us to town which, we learned, was about two to three miles inland from where we were anchored.

After doing our check in paperwork and picking up some fresh produce we were driven back out to the anchorage. Several of our friends from other boats were also in the anchorage. The *Tao* had sailed down to Tenecatita as well but they chose to go into the inner anchorage so we didn't see them there.

Stickwitch was anchored close to us. After stowing our produce we all went snorkeling with Pat, Bill, and Rachel. They had been in Tenecatita for several days and told us about a dance that was to take place later that evening somewhere on down the beach. It sounded like fun so we agreed to go.

We dressed in our finest clothes, which in reality weren't all that fine. I did have a long skirt to wear and Daryl actually put on long trousers. The boys all wore long pants as well. We dressed, combed our hair, and climbed down into the dinghy for a short ride to shore where we would meet up with *Stickwitch*. We thought we were doing just great when suddenly the dinghy turned sideways as a wave hit us, and, yep, we swamped the dinghy. We climbed out of the dinghy and sloshed the rest of the way through the surf and onto the beach pulling the heavy, water laden dinghy behind us. Our friends, standing on shore, quite enjoyed our 'show'. Well, wet or not, we were off to a dance.

It was actually quite a hike down the beach to the dance. It was being held in a huge cement tank that was about 70 feet across and had cement walls all around it that were about three feet high. We were told that the tank had been built some years before as a government project to protect turtles. The turtles were put into the tank and it was filled with water. That would have been fine except that the hot Mexican sun heated the water to such a high temperature that it cooked the turtles. Now the tank was just used for dances.

Our clothes dried out eventually and we actually had a fun evening. Even Daryl and Jerad danced.

Our stay in Tenecatita lasted only three days but it was a most enjoyable place to be.

CHAPTER FORTY-THREE

PROBLEMS FOR DARYL

The weather was beautiful as we left out of Tenecatita. We let Dustin and Nathan sail on the boat *Surrender* with their friend Josh. We were all headed for Melaque as well as *Stickwitch* and *Tao*. It was okay there except for the fact that there were lots of large noisy hotels along the beach so a very touristy place.

Jerad made a phone patch for Daryl to Iris back in Nevada. He found out that there were problems with his business transaction there so he spent the next several days being extremely stressed out and grumpy. The boys, on the other hand, were having a great time. After schoolwork was done each day they played on the beach, went freeboarding, and even went to watch the Super Bowl at a hotel on shore. They went over to *Stickwitch* in the evenings to watch movies.

After four days of worry Daryl finally decided he needed to fly back to the states to take care of business himself. We went into town where Daryl made plane reservations to fly into Los Angeles the following day.

Pat and Bill accompanied Daryl and I to the airport in Manzanillo late the following afternoon. We went by taxi and I was glad for the company. I had no idea how long Daryl would be gone but we were in a good anchorage and had everything we needed.

Four days after Daryl left, *Stickwitch* headed out for Manzanillo. Jerad sailed off with them to "check things out there". He returned by bus two days later.   Life for the boys and I went on as usual. I sewed, cleaned, and of course prepared school assignments. We took Star into town to get her rabies shot. Dustin baked cookies and caught a pelican while fishing off the boat. Nathan and Dustin spent the night on *Surrender* and went to watch E.T. on *Satori*. They played on the beach and went surfing.

It was ten days before Daryl returned from the states. He came back very sick. We weren't sure what was wrong with him. He was weak, having stomach problems, running a fever and showing signs of internal bleeding. I went into town the day after his return to get some medicine but it really didn't help much. The boys and I went to town for provisions and got the boat ready to go to sea again.

After six days of Daryl laying in the bunk moaning we knew we had to get him down to Manzanillo where we would have a better chance of getting him some medical attention. He rejected the idea of taking him there by taxi. We pulled our anchor and headed south, Jerad taking over as the temporary captain.

By late afternoon we could see that we would not be able to make it into Manzanillo before nightfall. We were very nervous about going into an unfamiliar anchorage in the dark so at 4 pm we dropped our anchor in a place called Bahia Santiago. It was not a very good anchorage and so we weren't surprised to find that there were no other boats there. After making sure that our anchor was secure we stowed our sails and ate some dinner. Daryl remained in bed, unable to eat. We turned in early as we wanted to pull our hook and set sail for Manzanillo at first light in the morning.

Shortly after 10 pm Daryl said he was sick to his stomach. I got him a basin just in time for him to lean over the side of our bunk where he started to vomit. I was horrified when I saw that he had thrown up what appeared to be more than a pint of thick liver-colored blood. He glanced up at me as I was removing the basin, said, "Bye Baby", then slumped down motionless onto the bed. I thought for sure that he was dying and I'm sure he thought so too.

What was I to do? We were totally alone in a strange anchorage. It was a very dark night, the moon having not yet reached its first quarter. At that moment I was thinking of all of the good things Daryl had done and not of the many times that I was exasperated with him. I certainly didn't want him to die. This was awful.

I did the only thing I knew how to do at such a time as this; I prayed. Hard. Then I went up the steps from our aft cabin, crossed over the cockpit, and stuck my head down into the boys forward cabin.

"Jerad. Dustin. Wake up and get up here. I need your help," I whispered down to them.

Within seconds they were both standing in their undershorts in the cockpit with me wondering what in the world I had awakened them for.

"Get some clothes on. I need you to row the dinghy to shore and find a doctor," I instructed. "Daryl has just vomited up lots of blood and I think he may be dying."

"Mom, it's totally dark out there, and besides when we get to shore we don't even know if there's a town there," Jerad reasoned.

"I know that. But you have to try. I don't know what else to do."

My two sons didn't argue with me. They went below, got dressed, and took the money and flashlight I pressed into Jerad's hands. They then unlashed the inflatable dinghy and slid it down into the black water below. They took the oars and started rowing the long distance towards the shore. As I heard their oars slicing through the water I said another silent prayer and went down below to check on Daryl.

I went back down into our cabin. Daryl hadn't moved. I put my ear close to his face and determined that he was still breathing. A good sign. Other than that he appeared to be dead. It was now 10:45 pm.

I don't know how many trips I made up and down our cabin steps that night. I would go below and check on Daryl, then go up into the cockpit and look out over the black water for any sign of my sons returning. What had I done? Had I asked my boys to do the impossible? How would they ever find a doctor, especially during the night hours? And if they did find a doctor, how would they explain to him what we needed? Jerad's Spanish was passable but certainly not proficient enough at that time to explain our situation. Minutes seemed like hours. I continued my silent prayers.

It was just at midnight that I thought I heard something out over the water. I listened then saw the flicker of a flashlight in the distance. My boys were returning! But were they alone? Had they found a doctor? I waited and watched. Then as they pulled the dinghy up alongside the boat I could see that there were, indeed, three people aboard. "Oh, thank you, Heavenly Father," I whispered.

"Help him up, Mom. He's really scared of the water," Jerad called up to me.

I leaned down over the stern and extended my hand to assist this doctor up the steps and onto *Lunar Glow*. He spoke no English and I saw that he was, indeed, very scared of the water. He stepped up onto the deck with his medical bag in tow. As the boys followed him up onto the deck I noticed that they were both soaking wet, yet the doctor was perfectly dry. Later the boys told me that the doctor was so terrified when they got him down to the beach and pointed out across the water to where *Lunar Glow* was anchored that he was refusing to go any further. The boys finally got him to get into the dinghy; then they had to swim it out through the surf until there was no chance of it getting swamped, then they too climbed in.

I took the doctor down into our cabin where Daryl lay, still not moving. I showed him the basin of blood and tried to explain in my very poor Spanish what was taking place. The good doctor examined him and gave him some sort of shot. He actually stayed with us until 1:30 am.

By the time he was ready for the boys to take him back to the beach he had assured me that Daryl was not dying but he must get to a hospital very soon. At first light we would move the boat around to the Las Hadas resort in Manzanillo. The doctor would meet us at the dock there.

CHAPTER FORTY-FOUR

A MEXICAN CLINIC

Jerad, still filling in as Captain, got *Lunar Glow* moved to Las Hadas as planned the next morning. It was now February 12th and boats that were planning to cross the Pacific Ocean and head for the Marquises Islands were already starting to leave. It had been our plan to leave as well, but now, everything was on hold. Our plans would change several times during the coming weeks.

The doctor was on the dock waiting to take us to the clinic as we arrived. Other boats had heard our plight over the radio and as was the norm for the boating community there were many people willing to help. Elan and Letty form *"Lady Star"* accompanied us to the clinic with the doctor. They offered to keep an eye on the boys while we were gone.

I instructed Jerad to watch over his brothers and also to listen to whatever Elan and Letty told them. I stayed at the clinic with Daryl. I'm not sure how Elan and Letty got back to Las Hadas. A taxi maybe. I didn't even know where the clinic we were taken to was located. All I knew for sure was that I stayed in Daryl's room at the clinic sleeping on a thin mat on the floor for five nights.

The room itself was quite small. Aside from the hospital bed there was no other furniture. Not even a chair. No TV, no sink, no bathroom. There was barely enough floor space for the thin mat they brought me to get by without stepping on the mat. And, of course, no blankets came with the mat. At that point I really didn't care.

This was truly a third-world country medical facility. Nothing like I had ever seen before, but, grateful to be there all the same. Daryl was hooked up to an IV and several medications were started. After two days the blood work showed that his blood count was going down. He would need a blood transfusion. The thought of this put Daryl into a near panic. He did NOT want to get blood in Mexico.

Each day someone from the anchorage would come to the clinic to visit. They came not only to see how Daryl was doing but also to give us updates on our boys. They assured us that the boys were doing well. We couldn't have asked for a better group of people to be associated with. And now, once again, they went up and above the call of duty. Learning that Daryl needed blood and seeing his panic at the prospect of receiving blood from who knows where, the call was put out over the radio asking fellow boaters that had A+ type blood for donations. The call was answered and two gentlemen made the trip to the clinic to donate blood for Daryl. The blood was then sent to Colima for testing. If the blood tested okay he would get the transfusion the following day.

One of the first things we noticed at the clinic was that none of the doctors or nurses wore gloves. With no sink in the room we weren't even sure where or how often hands got washed. We tried not to think about this too much until it was time for the transfusion to start.

A nurse brought in the bag of blood and hung it on the IV pole next to Daryl's bed. A flexible tube would need to be inserted into the lower end of the bag and attached to the IV line already running into Daryl's arm. What the nurse should have done was to invert the bag of blood so that the plug at the bottom of the bag would be at the top with no blood pushing against it. Once the plug was removed and the IV tube connected the bag would then be turned tube side down and re-hung on the IV pole.

Instead what actually happened was this. The nurse left the bag hanging on the IV pole and removed the plug at the bottom of the bag. Blood instantly began spraying everywhere; down the wall, on the floor, all over Daryl. The nurse then took her bare, ungloved finger, and used it to plug up the opening in the bottom of the bag of blood while at the same time screaming for someone to come to her aid. Another ungloved nurse arrived and between the two of them they got the bag of now less than sterile blood hooked into the IV line. I was horrified and Daryl was in near heart failure at being a participant in this circus act. Only in Mexico.

Daryl had an allergic reaction of some kind but by the following morning he was feeling a little better so the doctor agreed to release him. We took a taxi back to the port where Jerad met us with the dinghy. We were only on the boat a short time when Daryl started feeling worse again. We were able to get a message to the doctor and he once again came out to *Lunar Glow*. He gave Daryl some shots and said he needed to get back to the clinic. Daryl flatly refused. He said he would only go to a hospital in the states.

We learned that there was a flight leaving Manzanillo for L.A. later that afternoon. We booked two tickets. Once again we would be leaving the boys in the care of friends in the anchorage. I later learned that they had more fun than they dared to let on during our time away. After all, boys will be boys! An open call over the radio went out to any yacht anchored in L.A. The call was returned by someone named Richard on a boat named *Arconseal*. Richard met us at the airport in L.A. and drove us straight to UCLA Medical Center. The world is full of so many good people.

CHAPTER FORTY-FIVE

BACK NORTH ... AGAIN

Daryl stayed the night at UCLA and was given a thorough going over. Although his blood count was still low and he was anemic, there was certainly nothing life threatening at this point. Personally, I think he had worked himself into a panic. All the worry from his business in Nevada coupled with the responsibility of taking the family on a long ocean crossing had gotten his stomach to the point of severely bleeding ulcers. He was given medications for that problem and they were already in the healing process.

Grant and Denise picked us up from UCLA on Saturday, February 18th and took us to their place in Piru for the next two nights. We picked up our Celica which was still there in Piru and headed out for Santa Monica. The doctor at UCLA had told us of a walk in clinic in that area where we could go each day to get Daryl's blood work checked. In the meantime, back in Manzanillo, Jerad had done the check in process for *Lunar Glow*.

We visited the clinic each of the next four days. Daryl was to begin taking iron for his anemia and also started blood pressure pills to try to keep his blood pressure under control. With nothing more to be accomplished by daily visits to the clinic we drove on down to San Diego.

Our friend, Caden, was now back in San Diego living with his girlfriend. He helped us get a phone patch through to Jerad. All was well on the *Lunar Glow*. We also made phone calls to Michael and Mom and Dad and Daryl was able to call Reno and conclude his business transaction. Best of all, Caden wanted to buy our Celica. That would work well for us as we were ready to fly back to Manzanillo and no longer had any use for a car. Caden took us to pick up our plane tickets and then drove us to the airport. It was now March 2nd.

CHAPTER FORTY-SIX

NEW PLANS, AND
MORE NEW PLANS

O ur flight back down to Manzanillo was uneventful and we found everything in order there. Las Hadas is a huge, luxury resort and the boys had had a wonderful time in our absence.

Here's Dustin Cardoza's story of when my mom left her kids in Mexico ... ... again.

If you look at a satellite image of Manzanillo, Mexico, you will see it sits along the Pacific ocean on a very large bay. In the center of the bay is a very pronounced peninsula that pushes out westward into the Pacific ocean and basically splits the bay in two. On the south side of that peninsula is an area called Las Hadas. Today, it's home to a fancy marina, a yacht club, and a large resort with a wonderful beach and tons of restaurants oh and don't forget the enormous swimming pool with islands and live iguanas swimming around. And in early 1989, it was exactly the same. As kids, we spent an awful lot of time away from civilization. Or maybe not civilization, but 1st world type of civilization. Places like Las Hadas weren't usually on the list as a "port of call" for Lunar Glow. Granted the circumstances in which we end up at Las Hadas weren't ideal (sick step-dad, about to die) what I can say is this: If you are going to get left in Mexico, get left in Las Hadas.

In early 1989 I was 11 going on 12. Like any normal 11 year-old I'd already successfully survived an extended stay in Mexico without any parents to keep tabs on me. So one might say I was already a veteran when my mom and stepdad needed to make an emergency trip to the states. Last year Jerad and I had spent an amazing 5-6 weeks totally carefree inside Sea of Cortez. But this go round found Jerad (16), Nathan (8) and myself were all together for an unknown length of time until mom and Daryl suddenly re-surfaced again south of the border.

Now we weren't completely unsupervised, after all we had Jerad there and as far as 16 year-olds go, he was really quite responsible. There was only one small detail. For the few weeks that mom was gone, I only recall seeing Jerad a handful of times. Typically we'd see Jerad in the mornings when we'd all wake up and crawl out of our bunks. But for the most part, how Jerad got back into his bunk at night is still a mystery to me. To his credit, he did show up every night and I'm sure checked on Nate and I before he passed out in his own bunk.

The mornings were a special time back then because we got our fix of daily gossip on "The Net". Of course this wasn't the internet. Instead, this was a group of boats that all had VHF radios. Every morning, at about 8am or so, all the boats in that vicinity would tune into a specific channel and we'd basically have a town hall type of meeting. As I remember, it was Elan from "Lady Star" that ran The Net every morning as the moderator. We'd start with role call, and each boat would, in turn, check in. I didn't think about it much back then, but I'm sure most of the other boats tuning in each morning were anxiously waiting to hear a young boy's voice speak the words "Lunar Glow, here". (Jerad was always cool about letting Nate or I be the radio operator) Fact is, most of the boats at anchor there knew our situation and the fact that we were kinda fending for ourselves while our mom and stepdad were up north trying to get some first-world medical treatment. For us, The Net provided us the one thing kids need, entertainment. We could find out things like, who was new in the anchorage, was anyone planning to leave, did anyone have something for sale (or free), did anyone have access to a car and need a ride somewhere, etc, etc. My favorite morning of The Net started with a song and while nobody officially claimed ownership, I'm convinced it was Elan because he was just that kind of guy. But that morning, at 8am sharp, rather than starting The Net like normal, we sat through the entire song of "Don't Worry, Be Happy" by Bobby McFerrin. At 11, I thought it was the coolest thing ever and it was the first time I'd ever heard that song.

I mentioned we didn't see a whole lot of Jerad during this time. It's no mystery that as a strapping 16 year-old with a libedo, that Jerad was pre-occupied with chasing tail and hanging with his buddies. (and as I came to learn much later in life, getting drunk) Remember Las Hadas wasn't like most places we visited and honestly it was the only place like this we visited during our entire trip on Lunar Glow. Las Hadas had it all! With beaches, hotels, pools, and restaurants, there was no shortage of places for us to explore or things to do. I'm not sure who was responsible for pumping Jerad full of Cuba Libres (rum, Coke, and lime juice) but those were apparently pretty easy to come by. Nate and I spent most of our days hanging out together and doing pretty much whatever we wanted. Getting school work done was definitely not on the list of things to do (well, not on my list anyway). We had enough food on the boat to get us by without having to go shopping. I'm sure mom left us some money, but I don't ever recall needing it. The funny part about being in this situation was how well you can play the sympathy card. Boaters tend to be genuinely nice people and really do look out for one another. Everyone in that anchorage felt so bad for these poor boys that had been left all alone. They all wanted to help however they could. And pretty much every evening that "help" came in the form of free dinner! It was usually just Nate and I, but we were either eating on someone else's boat or on shore at one of the many restaurants. Eating at a restaurant!!! Are you kidding? Mom and Daryl would NEVER take us to a restaurant. That was way too expensive. The closest we got to eating at a restaurant with Mom and Daryl was a ceviche tostada stand! Some nights Nate and I had multiple invites for dinner. We could actually be choosy about what and where we ate. THIS was living. I'm sure these wonderful people had no idea how much we were actually enjoying the freedom of not having our angry stepfather hanging around barking orders at us all the time.

We did a great job of staying out of trouble for the most part. There was one incident that landed us in a little hot water and Jerad was actually with us that night. The incident we refer to as "Yum Yum Tower". With zero adult supervision, we had no actual curfew. So we tended to stay out as late as we felt like staying out. I've no idea if we stayed up until 9pm or midnight. Time wasn't really a factor for us. One night we were out looking for mischief. It was myself, Nate, Jerad, and another teenager about Jerad's age. We had somehow scored this bag of candy. Think of them as a Mexican version of Skittles. I have no idea what they were really called because we just called them Yum Yums. Yum Yums will be key in just a minute. Las Hadas has a tower that sits high up above the hotel. It's almost like a lighthouse type of tower with a winding concrete staircase that wrapped around the outside. If you google "Las Hadas Costalegre" you are sure to find a picture of this exact tower. At the top of the staircase is a wonderful view of the bay and it's a popular romantic spot for vacationing couples to visit as part of a nice post-dinner stroll. Also at the top of that staircase is a door which leads inside the tower. Inside the tower there is another spiral staircase made of metal, which gives access to the roof. This section isn't intended to be accessed by the public and in early 1989 it was definitely gated off with a tall metal gate at the bottom of that spiral staircase. But in early 1989, that metal gate had a hole in the top of it. And that hole was JUST large enough for us to climb though. So here we all were, sitting on the TOP of that tower with some rather impressive views. But when you are a kid, you don't give a crap about impressive views. Instead, one of us (and I don't recall who) produced a bag of Yum Yums, which we started eating. Then we started dropping the candies off the side of the tower to watch them bounce off the stairs and roofs way below. The natural progression from here was to start dropping them on tourists. Because how funny is it when they get hit by a falling piece of candy? I can tell you it's pretty funny when you are 11 and sitting on top of that tower WAY past your normal bedtime. In fact, it's really funny until one of those tourist ladies looks up and you drop a piece of candy and it hits her in the eye and her husband is with her and he's SUPER pissed off! Then all of a sudden it's not funny. (in all honesty, if some kids did that to MY wife today, I'd be super pissed off too) But our plan to bombard unsuspecting tourists with these small candies had one serious flaw. We had no escape route. And remember that hole in the top of the gate? The one that we could barely squeeze through? Well that super angry husband managed to squeeze through as well. So up the stairs and onto the roof he came. We were totally screwed. I thought this guy was gonna toss US off the roof! Lucky for us he didn't throw us off the roof, but instead decided to march us all back down to find our parents. Good luck with that one dude! I hope you don't mind marching all the way to Los Angeles or wherever the heck our parents actually were during this time. Turned out his wife's eye was just fine albeit she had a nice big welt right next to it. In the end, he felt that just giving us a good verbal lashing was enough. I'm sure that couple has an awesome vacation story about the time they went to Mexico in 1989 and these punk kids dropped candy on them and the dude had to crawl through a gate in order to teach those kids a lesson!

Like most amazing adventures, this one had to come to an end. Eventually, Mom made it back down to Manzanillo and of course found her sons all healthy and quite happy. We were happy to see her too, despite her having brought Daryl back as well. Jerad and I tell this story to people often and sometimes perhaps it gets slightly embellished. I think maybe there are parts of the story that Jerad leaves out and that's ok. That's his story. Nate was just young enough that he only remembers bits and pieces, which is a bummer. I had a lot of fun with him at Las Hadas. It's another one of the many experiences I got to share with my brothers that I'll get to carry with me my whole life. One might say my mom is kinda nuts. And on some accounts I'd agree. One thing is for certain, however. No matter the situation we were put in, we always figured out a way to push though. Somehow she knew this about us and had complete faith in our ability to take care of ourselves and each other. Some people find that crazy, but others find it to be awesome!

Because of all that had taken place over the past month we decided that we should postpone our trip to French Polynesia. Instead we would sail the boat back to the Baja and head north up the coast maybe going as far north as Washington state. Several of our friends had sailed down from there and told us how nice it was.

We rested up on the boat for a couple of days. Jerad and Dustin cleaned and greased all of our winches. They were learning a lot about boat maintenance. We had some mail and other items that we were to deliver to some of the boats that had already left for the Marquasis Islands. Now that we had decided not to cross the Pacific this season we took everything over to *Northern Lights* so that they could deliver the items. They would be leaving any day.

Two days after deciding to sail back up to the Northwest we changed our minds again. We would just go up into the Sea of Cortez and spend another season there. We really did like that area and besides it would save some wear and tear on the boat.

We checked out of Manzanillo and set sail for Malaque and then on to Tenacatita the following day. We got busy on schoolwork once again. We scrubbed our boat and cleaned all of the rigging. The weather was beautiful and the fishing was great. The boys enjoyed taking Star to shore and playing in the surf during the afternoons.

We celebrated Dustin's 12th birthday on March 14th. Life was pretty much back to normal. We continued jumping from one anchorage to another until we finally sailed back into Nuevo Vallarta on March 18th. Daryl was feeling pretty good overall but would feel much better if he could be given a clean bill of health. We were told of a big, modern hospital in Guadalajara that had English speaking doctors. Daryl had been told of a Dr. Angelo Lopez, a gastroenterologist, that worked out of that hospital. Daryl really wanted to go see him.

It was Saturday when we arrived in Nuevo Vallarta. We wouldn't be able to do our check in paperwork over the weekend so we decided to take a bus into Guadalajara first thing on Sunday morning. Daryl and I walked into town and found the bus station. We took the seven hour bus trip to Guadalajara and found a motel for the night. First thing Monday morning we made our way to the hospital and were able to meet with Dr. Lopez. The hospital was, indeed, clean and modern, and the doctor was extremely nice. He did an endoscopy and said everything looked good. No evidence of any ulcer or scar tissue. We told the doctor of our original plan to cross the Pacific Ocean in our sailboat. The doctor said he saw absolutely no reason why we shouldn't go, so … yep, you got it. Our plan changed yet again.

We rented a car and drove the seven hours back to Nuevo Vallarta where we told the boys our good news. We were going to the Marquesis Islands after all. We used the rental car the next day to check not only in and out of Nuevo Vallarta but out of Mexico as well. Daryl had gotten the necessary visas and paperwork needed for French Polynesia when he was in the states before all of this medical fiasco started. We also took advantage of the car to do some heavy duty, last minute provisioning. We returned the rental car and after a good night's sleep we were ready to go.

CHAPTER FORTY-SEVEN

AUDIOS MEXICO

The day was beautiful and it was with mixed emotions that we sailed out of Nuevo Vallarta. We had spent many wonderful months in Mexican waters and had a treasure chest of special memories to carry with us in our hearts. We loved the Mexican people; had learned and experienced so much here. We would miss this chapter of our adventure.

But it was time to move on. It was March 22, 1989. We were actually just one week past our original departure date of March 15th. The wind started out brisk but died off after about four hours. We set up a schedule for standing watches. Daryl, Jerad, and I would rotate through four hour watches around the clock. Dustin could do some relief watches during the daylight hours of an hour or two at a time.

The person on watch was in charge of keeping the boat on coarse as well as watching out for anything going on around us. Sometimes that meant altering our coarse slightly to stay out of the way of freighters, especially if we were going through shipping lanes. Boats, like aircraft, cars, etc., have certain routes that they tend to follow even if you can't see them. We always gave way to the big guys. There were also the occasional floating objects to watch out for, like a shipping container that had fallen off of a freighter ship. Although large containers would float only the top portion could be seen above the water. Sort of like an ice burg. It would be almost certain destruction to run into one.

Then there were changes in the wind and weather. The increase or decrease of the wind speed as well as the direction of the wind could require an adjustment of the sails or in the case of an approaching storm, a complete sail change. These things were all very important, not only to keep our vessel on course, but for our safety as well.

The person on watch stood at the wheel and "steered" the boat. A large compass was mounted just in front of the wheel and whoever was on watch had to keep the boat on a specific compass course. The compass course was determined by charting our position on a large chart of the area we were sailing in. I did most of the navigating, which I really enjoyed. We had an electronic device at that time called a Sat Nav. It took readings from satellites out in space and about every four hours it told us of our exact position at that moment. That position was marked on the chart and by drawing a line from where we were to where we wanted to end up would give us the compass direction to follow. To stray off course by even a degree or two would cause us to miss our intended destination by hundreds of miles. Not a good thing when you are in the middle of a huge ocean.

The Sat Nav, as well as our running lights and radio equipment were keep powered by our solar panels and wind generator. Although we had installed a desalinater we used it for only a total of three hours crossing the ocean as it used too much power which we needed to be very careful with.

We also had a sexton on the boat; a navigational instrument that was first developed in the early 1700's. This is a handheld device used to find your position. It measures the angle between two objects; mainly the horizon and the sun or stars. It was fairly easy to determine latitude and I got to where I could do accurate noon sights on a clear day, but beyond that I did a pretty poor job. I had the calculation tables and all that but it was still a difficult process for me. I just prayed our Sat Nav kept working, and it did.

CHAPTER FORTY-EIGHT

WIND, FISH, AND SHELLBACKS

Crossing the Pacific Ocean between Nuevo Vallarta, Mexico and the island of Hiva Oa, which was one of a small cluster of the Marquesis Islands and a part of French Polynesia, took us 22 days. The wind during those days was anything but consistent. We started out with good wind but it died out about 4:30 in the afternoon of our first day out and continued to be light for the next couple of days.

Although we had our 25 H.P. outboard motor we carried very little gas. Using the motor in the middle of a 2000 plus mile journey would have been pointless. The motor was strictly for emergencies and for getting us in and out of ports easier. So, when the wind was light, or as happened after a couple of weeks, there was no wind at all, we just went very slow or drifted. I didn't like when that happened because if we weren't sailing through the water then the ocean currents would pull us off course. When that happened we would have to refigure our position when the wind started up again and get back on course.

What we liked best was when the wind was coming from behind us.

We would pull our big mainsail which was attached to the boom out to one side of the boat and hold it in place there with a pole designed for that purpose. Then we would attach our big genoa sail to the mainstay at the front of the boat and pull it out in the opposite direction from the mainsail. We called this flying wing and wing, and with all the wind these two sail held we truly did feel like we were flying through the water.

Sometimes the winds were fluky and required us to do a lot of sail adjustments. If it was just to let a sail out or pull it in to a better angle to the wind that was easy. When we had to actually do a sail change it was much more work. Jerad and I worked together to do the sail changes. Although Dustin had just turned 12 and could do a lot of things on the boat, sail changes out at sea was not one of them. We would put on our harnesses and attach our tethers to the front railing of the boat. We had a strict rule when we out to sea. Nobody went out of the cockpit without wearing a harness and fastening our tether to the boat.

Once we had ourselves secured we would begin to lower the sail we had been using. Daryl, at the wheel, would keep the boat on course while Dustin loosened the halyard on the mast which had kept the sail in place. Jerad and I would then begin pulling the sail down the mainstay, unfastening the hanks that held the sail in place, and stuffing the sail into a large nylon sail bag as Dustin continued to keep control of the halyard. We would then reverse the process with a larger or smaller sail depending upon the wind and sea conditions.

Sail changes when the seas were fairly smooth weren't too bad, however, rough seas was a whole other story. Remember that we were standing on the very bow of the boat. If the seas were rough the bow of the boat tended to plow down into the waves. This meant that we had to stop for the moment, hold tight to the front railing of the boat, and close our eyes while getting drenched in a very salty shower. The large fancy boats didn't have to go through this drill. They had something called 'roller reefing'. By pushing a button in the cockpit their sails would automatically wind in or out on the forestay so that they could adjust the sail to any size they needed. They never had to remove the sail at all. But we were hard-core sailors all the way.

For the most part our weather was good on this crossing. We did encounter a few rain squalls, however. During the daylight hours you could see them coming and get things buttoned down before they hit. It would look like a big dark wall coming at you. Not knowing what kind of weather the nights would bring we would reduce our sail before nightfall in order to eliminate any sail changes during the night. We felt safer doing this even if it meant losing some of our speed during that time. Even so we averaged about 100 miles a days. Not bad for no motoring.

All in all the fishing was good crossing the Pacific. We caught several dorado in the waters closer to Mexico but the further west we sailed we tended to catch mainly blue fin tuna. These were really good eating fish. It was my job to gut and fillet the fish we caught then cook them. This had to be done right away because with no refrigeration the fish wouldn't keep. It wouldn't have been so bad except for the fact that for some reason we almost always caught a fish just as I was going off my watch in the early evening and was anxious to get into my bunk for a few hours sleep before it was time for my next watch. Anyway, I'd cook the fish, we would eat our fill, give some to Star, then had to throw the rest overboard.
We caught fish almost every day but once in awhile we even got fish we didn't try for. Those were the flying fish. Sometimes they would fly up onto our deck and once we even got two inside the cockpit. We never did attempt to eat these fish. We just returned them to the sea.

About a week out of Mexico the boys landed a 3 1/2 foot thresher shark. Boy was that exciting. There was no way I was going to clean and cook that thing. I was all for just cutting the line and sending it on its way, but Dustin was adamant about getting his lure back. He made almost all of our lures and I must say they were quite impressive. Retrieving a lure from a shark's mouth isn't quite the same as getting one out of the mouth of a tuna. Even though this was a fairly small shark it still had a mouthful of razor sharp teeth. Daryl and the boys pulled the shark up alongside *Lunar Glow* and then with the aid of our big fish net hauled it on up onto the boat. It was thrashing around and nobody wanted to get too close to it. Jerad finally used a portion of his life line to wrap around the shark's tail in order to bring him a bit more under control. With the rest of us trying to do our part in subduing the beast, Daryl used a large pair of pliers to extract Dustin's lure. That done we released the shark to his ocean home.

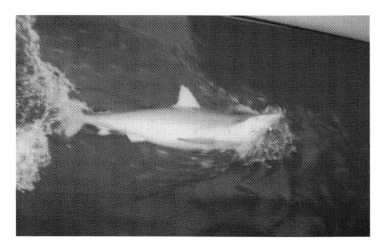

Lunar Glow finally crossed the Equator on April 7th. The day was beautiful with good wind and calm seas. A perfect day for in initiation celebration. I didn't know much about maritime traditions but apparently crossing the Equator by sea for the first time has long been a big deal.

Before embarking on our adventure I had seen some "Shellback Certificates" in the Downwind Marine store in San Diego. I had inquired as to what they were and not knowing if or when we might ever have need of these I had purchased a certificate for each of the boys and had them tucked away on the boat.

We were watching our position and at the moment we determined that we were crossing the Equator Daryl announced that it was time for the "crossing the line" ceremony to begin. Daryl sort of made the whole thing up as he went along. First he explained to the boys that up until that time we had all been "slimy pollywogs", but at the moment we sailed across the Equator we had become "nobel shellbacks", and a member of Neptune's Royal Court.

I guess the old time Naval initiation was quite brutal but I had no idea what took place. Apparently it has been tamed down a bit in more recent years but either way I had no idea what it entailed.

First, Daryl to told the boys that they had to drink their own pee. This, of course, brought lots of "yuck", "gross", and "no way" comments. Daryl said he was sorry but he couldn't change the rules. This was just part of the initiation and it had to be followed; if not the boys would have to remain slimy pollywogs. Nobody wanted that. The boys each took their cup and went off to collect their urine. They returned their cups to Daryl who was sitting at the settee in the galley. He taped their name to each cup then sent the boys up into the cockpit to wait. He then dumped the urine down the sink, rinsed the cups, and poured a mixture of lemonade with a dash of soy sauce into each of their cups and delivered the new "urine" for them to drink. I don't think the boys were fooled but they went along with the ruse anyway.

Next we had the boys remove their shirts and sit on one of the nets set into the wing deck just outside the cockpit. They hooked their tethers to the boat and waited in anticipation of the next part of their initiation. I had a gallon of root beer syrup onboard. I had bought it in error thinking that it was actually a gallon of root beer that we could drink on a special occasion. I had pulled it out on Dustin's birthday and realized that it was syrup that had to be mixed with carbonated water in order to drink it. Now the thick, dark, syrup was just taking up valuable space and weight on the boat. It would become part of the initiation ceremony. Daryl took the syrup and dumped the entire thing over the heads of the three boys while saying some sort of "I now dup thee … " whatever words. It ran down their faces, chests, and backs. Their white harnesses, as well as their shorts and the net they were sitting on were all a sticky brown color. Star, hearing all the screams and laughs from the boys, jumped out onto the wing deck and began licking the boys off as fast as her tongue would allow. The boys then had to remain on the net while buckets of sea water were hauled up and dumped over them until at long last all of the root beer syrup had been washed through the nets and into the ocean waters below.

Lastly, after the boys were dry and changed I presented them with their official Shellback certificates which had been signed by the captain. All in all, it was a fun day and one I'm sure they remember to this day.

CHAPTER FORTY-NINE

LAND HO!

We had really good communications with folks on the mainland while we were crossing the Pacific. Jerad had set up a regular schedule on the HAM radio so that those following our progress would know when we were on the radio. We always used GMT (Greenwich Mean Time) when at sea so that we didn't ever have to worry about what time zone we were in and neither did those folks on the radio. It was really fun to hear from HAM operators from all over the place that were tracking our trip. We never had a problem getting one of them to make a phone patch to my parents back in California.

Dad had hung a huge world map from National Geographic on the wall of their spare bedroom. Every time we talked to them we would give them our longitude and latitude and Dad would mark it on the map with a stick pin. It put their minds at ease to hear our voices and know that we were safe and it also gave us a feeling of security knowing that so many people knew where we were as well.

Life was fairly routine for us during that three week crossing. Some of my journal entries during that time say: *nice day with good wind, nice day but not much wind, Daryl repaired cockpit floorboards, worked some sun shots, saw 3 freighters, hooked and lost 2 fish, caught 2 dorado, Kay not feeling well, caught 2 blue fin tuna, Nathan barfed up his dinner, shut down Sat Nav for awhile to save battery power, fluky winds, hit the NE trade winds, light showers in a.m., found 2 cracks in boat at port ama joint, no fish today, baked banana bread and coconut pie, tired today, Daryl set up third solar panel, Jerad completed English course, looks like squalls coming, more wind out of E and SE, lumpy, lost a BIG fish, Daryl not feeling too good, confused seas, rough ride, Nathan is seasick, rain squall hit us about 2:30 a.m., Dustin caught 25+ pound tuna, cloudy and rainy all day, stove acting up, steep seas,* and finally, *land in sight!!*

As we got closer to where we thought the island of Hiva Oa should be, Jerad would climb up the mast every so often with the binoculars in order to look out further onto the horizon in the hopes of spotting land. The islands of the Marquasis were very tiny in respect to the size of the ocean. Any miscalculation in our navigation would send us right past our destination without us ever knowing it. Each time Jerad descended the mast without spotting land the knot in my stomach got bigger. But finally, his shouts came. "It's there. Land. I can see land," and we all climbed up onto the cabin top to see what it was that Jerad was seeing. It would be a while longer for the top of the island to come into view from lower down on the boat.

The boys were so excited that Dustin too, climbed up the mast where he joined Jerad. The two of them sat on the first spreader and started singing a song that they seemed to make up on the spot. It was simply: *Land Ho! Ho, Ho, Ho.* They sang it over and over and over again with Nathan joining in from below. Finally, their voices beginning to go hoarse, we made them get down. We had to get busy getting things ready for our first landing in French Polynesia.

Although it wasn't the time for our regular HAM radio patches, we did get a fellow operator to get a message to Mom and Dad that we had land in sight. That done, the boys and I began cleaning up the boat and putting everything in order. Daryl, meanwhile, attended to our outboard motor. The motor hadn't been lowered on the track at the stern of the boat since our departure from Nuevo Vallarta. Daryl changed the spark plugs then lowered the motor into the water. He pushed the starter and the motor came to life. Hurray. Daryl shut the motor off again and pulled it back up the track and secured it into place. We were all set for our entry into Hiva Oa though it would still be several more hours until we arrived.

We could see the island much more clearly as we sailed closer. It was like a huge volcano with the top being so high that it was actually obscured by a large cloud that seemed to hover right above the peak. The sun was going down and we knew that we would never make landfall before dark. We weren't worried though. After all, we had a chart of the island which showed the passageway into the harbor, and Daryl had started our motor. All we needed to do was sail in a safe distance from the island, ease the motor back down the track, drop our sails and motor on into the anchorage. No problem. Right.

Wrong! It was 1:30 a.m. when we reached the island. Jerad lowered the motor and Daryl hit the starter button. Nothing. He tried again and again without luck to get the darn motor started, but it just wouldn't go. So we did the only thing we could do at that point. We stayed off shore for the remainder of the night and we would just have to sail into the anchorage once it was light again.

At first light we sailed towards the island once again. Unfortunately, as we got close to land the island blocked the wind. Without wind we didn't go. So we went back off shore once again where Daryl tried again to get our motor to start. Still no luck. Well we had no motor and no wind. We were so close and we couldn't just hang around out in the ocean forever hoping something would change. We launched our dinghy and tied a line from the back of the dinghy to the bow of *Lunar Glow* and with Dustin and Jerad each rowing with all their might they towed our boat right into the inner anchorage at Atuana, on the island of Hiva Oa. The date was April 13, 1989.

CHAPTER FIFTY

AHH ... PARADISE

This was an extremely beautiful island. Friends on *Jo Hanna III* were already at anchor here and they came over for a visit. It was fun to see familiar faces once again. We waited until the next day before we went into town to do our check in and change some money at the local bank. This was a French speaking island group and their currency was the French franc. We were quite used to using pesos in Mexico but now we were going to have to figure out this currency thing again.

It had rained hard during the morning, but once the rain stopped and we made our trip into town we took the boys to have a look around and found the local swimming hole. It was great fun and the boys met some local kids who gave them lots of bananas and mangos. We found that this was the norm all through the Polynesian islands. I don't think we were ever without fresh fruit of some sort.

This was also our first introduction to French baguettes; long thin loaves of French bread which we usually picked up straight from the bakery and still warm from the oven. We usually bought an extra loaf that we pulled apart and ate on the way back to the boat. I cut way back on my bread making throughout French Polynesia as the baguettes were so good. And they were one of the few food items that wasn't outrageously expensive. Butter, rice, and powdered milk were also affordable. Friends from other boats told us we would need to "order" our vegetables and they would be delivered within a couple of days. This was different.

I spent a couple of days getting caught up on the laundry that we chose not to do during our crossing. What laundry we did do had been washed in salt water so it needed to be rewashed again to get the tacky salt water feel out of the clothes. It took Jerad and Dustin two days but between the two of them they got all three hulls scrubbed clean. After school and chores the boys would head off to the swimming hole or they would go surfing.

After five days Daryl gave up on trying to fix the outboard motor himself and was able to locate a mechanic in town that agreed to work on it. Daryl would get it to the shore the following day where the mechanic would pick it up. With the motor being taken care of Daryl started to work repairing the cracks that had developed in the wing deck during our crossing. This also turned out to be a several day project.

Three days later our outboard motor was returned to us. The good news was that it worked great. The bad news was that it cost us $335 US dollars. Ouch! The mechanic, however, was a really nice man gave us 13 pomplemoose and a breadfruit. The pomplemoose were like huge, thick-skinned grapefruits and the breadfruit tasted a lot like a potato. Both were very good and over the next years we ate as much of them as we could.

We had been in Hiva Oa for eleven days already and except for the prices and the miniscule, knat-type bugs they called no-see-ums that were eating us alive, we loved this place. But the South Pacific is covered with islands and we knew there was more to see so after topping off our water tank and jugs and doing our check out in town we pulled our anchor and headed out of the harbor.

From Hiva Oa we went the short distance to Tahuata. Except for the bugs, this, too, was a beautiful place. There were only two other boats here with us. The water was clear and warm and wild horses and goats roamed on shore. We stayed for two nights while Daryl finished his repairs on the wing deck. It was a great place to swim; at least until Dustin encountered a shark while snorkeling. Jerad made a phone patch to Mom and Dad so we were able to give them a General Delivery mailing address in Tahiti to send mail to. We weren't sure how long it would take us to get to Tahiti but it would be nice to have mail waiting for us when we did arrive.

At 10:15 p.m. of our third day in the anchorage at Tahuata, we pulled our anchor and set sail for the island of Ua Pou. The wind was good and we decided to make this a night sail in order to arrive during the daylight hours. We anchored about 11 a.m. and after stowing our sails, went to shore to check in. The Gendarme was closed so we took a walk around town instead. We were in yet another very beautiful, quiet, and calm anchorage. Aside from a French Navy ship and a Swiss boat, we were the only ones here.

The following day, being a Friday, Daryl decided to do the check in and out process at the same time in case we wanted to leave Ua Pou over the weekend. We strolled around town once again and admired the lush, green foliage and flowers everywhere. Jerad and Dustin did some surfing and then Dustin and Nathan hiked to the top of a hill with some new friends and accepted an invitation for a visit to their house. None of the boys ever had trouble making new friends, even when there was a language barrier.

The waves were getting bigger so the boys took advantage of them and went out surfing once again. The seas were building to 6-8 meters and the Gendarme put out a message over the radio that no boats were to leave the harbor. Jerad made a phone patch back to Nevada in response to a message we had received the day before. Our house in Stagecoach needed a new septic system. Well, I guess it was life as usual outside of Paradise. The boys finished off the day by attending a local dance on shore.

We had purchased a movie camera during one of our trips up the Baja to San Diego but we really hadn't used it much. The surfing had been so good the day before that, after school, the boys asked us to take some movies of them surfing. We all went to shore for the filming, however, as luck would have it, the seas and waves had calmed down from the day before so their surfing was no more than average. One of Dustin's new friends saw us on shore and brought us a bag of oranges. By evening the French Navy ship had left but there were now a total of seven sailboats in the anchorage.

Monday was another nice day although quite windy. I decided to do some laundry on the deck which I hung along the lifelines to dry. Then, of course, it rained and the nearly dry laundry was wet once again. Daryl was beginning to get bored so we figured we would head out the following morning. The boys went into town to see their friends for one last time and returned to the boat with a huge gunnysack full of fruit; bananas, mandarin oranges, limes, mangos, and pomplamose. Yum.

CHAPTER FIFTY-ONE

GROW AN ORANGE TREE??

We left Hakahua, Ua Pou about 7a.m. for the short sail over to the island of Nuka Hiva. Although the distance wasn't far it was a rough sail with rain squalls most of the way and wind on our nose. By the time we dropped our anchor Daryl and I were both beat.

"Hey, Guys. Daryl and I are going to take a little nap. Just straighten up out here and do something quiet for a while. As soon as we get up we'll put the dinghy in the water and go to shore to explore."

We left the boys in the cockpit and went down the stairs into our aft cabin and climbed up onto our bunk. I scooted over to the inside part of the bunk and Daryl immediately fell asleep on the outside of the bunk near the stairs. Before long, I, too, was sound asleep.

"Pssst, Mom." I opened my eyes to see Jerad at the top of the steps looking down the open hatch into our bunk. I put my finger to my lips indicating that I wanted him to be quiet. I then waved my hand for him to go away. I laid my head back down and closed my eyes. It was quiet again for maybe three or four minutes.

"Pssst, Mom," and Jerad's head appeared once again.

"What do you want?" I mouthed silently.

"Dustin got a mandarin seed stuck in his ear."

"He what?!"

"Dustin stuck a mandarin seed in his ear and we can't get it out," Jerad whispered back to me. I pointed down at Daryl sound asleep on the outside of the bunk and put my finger to my lips once again. I knew that if Daryl got woken up from his nap he would be a real bear. I raised myself up onto my knees and as quietly as I could I made my way across Daryl and onto the cabin steps without waking him.

"Dustin," I questioned as I entered the cockpit, "what in the world is going on here?"

"Well, we were eating some of the mandarins and spitting the seeds over the side and Jerad said there was so much dirt in my ears that I could probably plant one of the seeds in there and grow a tree. So I did," he said.

"Did what?"

"Put a mandarin seed in my ear to grow a tree but now it hurts and I can't get it out. Jerad tried to get it out only he couldn't get it out and now it hurts worse."

"Oh, brother," I said, rolling my eyes. "Let me see." I turned Dustin's right ear into the sunlight and looked inside. "I can't see anything." I pulled down on his earlobe trying to get a better look inside. "I still can't see anything. Nathan, will you get me the flashlight from the chart table? Be quiet so you don't wake Daryl."

Nathan returned a minute later with the flashlight in hand. I shined it into Dustin's ear and peered inside. Yeah, now I could see it way down inside his ear canal. Now, how was I going to get it out?

"Maybe we could suck it out with the vacuum," Jerad suggested. We had a little 12 volt canister vacuum on the boat which had proved useful in sucking dirt and sand out of small crevices around the boat. Well, it was worth a try.

"Okay, Jerad, go get the vacuum and we'll give it a try." Jerad descended the forward stairs to retrieve the vacuum which we stored in the head. He returned less than a minute later with the little vacuum in tow. I took the end of the cord which had a 12 volt plug like the kind you would plug into a cigarette lighter. Our only 12 volt outlet was in the aft cabin bulkhead; right next to our bunk where Daryl was still sound asleep. I tiptoed down the steps, plugged in the cord, and tiptoed back up the steps and stretched the cord as far away from the sleeping Daryl as I could. It reached almost to the center of the cockpit.

"Dustin, sit down here on the floor and hold still. Jerad, you need to shine the flashlight down into his ear. Good. Ready? I hope this works." I attached the little funnel shaped attachment to the end of the vacuum hose, inserted it into Dustin's ear canal and pushed the toggle switch to the 'on' position. The vacuum roared to life as I pushed the funnel attachment as far into Dustin's ear as it would go. I tried for about 30 seconds to suck the seed out but it was no use. It wouldn't budge. The only thing we accomplished was to wake Daryl from his nap.

"What's going on out here?" Daryl growled as he came up the aft cabin steps into the cockpit. "I said I wanted it quiet while I got some sleep."

"Sorry," I apologized. "We're trying to get a mandarin seed out of Dustin's ear."

"What in the hell is a mandarin seed doing in Dustin's ear?" Daryl was in a really foul mood. This was not a good sign.

I made a quick explanation of how the seed got into Dustin's ear and how we were attempting to get it out.

"Here. Let me try." Daryl grabbed the vacuum from my hand and roughly inserted the tip into Dustin's ear once again. Jerad flipped the switch to the on position and again the vacuum came to life. Dustin howled in pain but the seed still did not budge. "This little vacuum just doesn't have enough suction to do any good," Daryl stated the obvious.

We all stepped back trying think of another way we could get that dang seed out. "Mom," Nathan said after looking around at the other boats in the anchorage. "Look, *Jo Hanna III* is anchored over there. Maybe they have a bigger vacuum on their boat."

"Well, they might," I replied.

"Jerad, put the inflatable into the water and row on over to *Jo Hanna III* and see if they have a vacuum," Daryl ordered.

Jerad launched the dinghy and within a short time he had rowed over to the other boat and had gone aboard. Not wanting to tell them that his stupid little brother had put a mandarin seed in his ear he just asked if they had a vacuum we could borrow. A couple of minutes later we got a call over the single sideband radio. It was Jerad's voice: *"Lunar Glow, come in. This is the Jo Hanna III."*

"Go ahead Jo Hanna III, this is Lunar Glow."

"Mom, they said they don't have a vacuum but they have a whisk broom and dust pan we can borrow."

Oh great! *"Son, just tell them thank you anyway and come on back home."*

Jerad returned and we all sat around for several minutes trying to figure out a way to extract the seed. Daryl made sure that Dustin knew what an idiotic thing it was to try to plant a seed in his ear. I think Dustin had already figured that out on his own.

"I've got it," I exclaimed. "Crazy glue. We can put some crazy glue on the end of a toothpick, stick it into Dustin's ear, and glue that to the seed and then pull the seed out of his ear."

"And then what are you going to do when the crazy glue hits the inside of Dustin's ear canal. Now he'll now only have a seed stuck inside his ear but a toothpick glued to the ear canal as well. How are you going to explain all that when we have to take him to a doctor that only speaks French?" Daryl did have a good point there.

"Okay, well what about this", I said. "We cut off a cocktail straw about an inch long. We then cut the end off of a toothpick so that it's flat on the end. We slide the toothpick inside the straw until only the flat end sticks out. We then put the crazy glue on the flat end of the toothpick and pull it back inside the straw, then very quickly insert the whole thing into Dustin's ear canal before the glue has a chance to set, then push the toothpick back out of the straw and onto the seed and hold it tight until the glue dries on the seed. Then we pull the whole thing out."

We all looked from one to another thinking this was a really goofy plan, but we had to try something. I went down into the galley to find a toothpick and cocktail straw. Daryl got the crazy glue and we all gathered around the settee to perform the seed extraction.

"Dustin," Daryl instructed, "come over here and lay your head on the table. Jerad, Nathan, you two need to help hold him still so that he doesn't move."

Dustin knelt down on the settee seat and laid his head on the table so that we could work on his ear. I prepared the toothpick and straw. Daryl applied the crazy glue and I quickly pulled the toothpick back into the straw and inserted the whole thing into Dustin's ear. I had to push down fairly hard so that the glue would stick to the seed. Dustin screamed that we were hurting him and I had no doubt but what he was right. We held him, screaming the entire time, for a good two or three minutes until we felt sure that the glue had dried. I then pulled the whole works back out of his ear and we all cheered when we saw that mandarin seed glued tight to the end of the toothpick. That seed with the toothpick glued to it remained on our boat for the rest of our sailing days as a sort of reminder to never stick anything into any orifice where it doesn't belong.

CHAPTER FIFTY-TWO

BUGS IN PARADISE

Nuka Hiva was a gorgeous, lush island with high mountains carpeted in every shade of green imaginable. It also had a beautiful bay. We were anxious to get to shore to have a look around, however, by the time we finished Dustin's "ear surgery" and got the boat cleaned up and ourselves ready to go it was too late in the day to do our check-in. That could wait.

We rowed to shore and spent some time exploring the little town there. We located the Inn and picked up a packet of mail that we had had sent there. Getting mail was always a highlight for us. We passed a bakery and stopped long enough to buy a few baguettes. The long, slender, French bread always smelled so good and was just too hard to resist. We pulled of chunks and ate as we walked along. The fresh bread helped to distract us from the ever present "no-see-ums" that had continued to plague us ever since arriving in the Marquasis Islands. Although they were too small to see with the naked eye their bite was mighty. They itched like all get out.

They seemed to be worse on shore than out on the boat, however, some of them still managed to find us out there.

The following morning Daryl and I went back to shore to find the Gendarme. We did our check-in and check-out process at the same time so that if we decided to leave over the weekend we would be ready to go. The boys weren't up to swatting off the no-see-ums on shore again and chose instead to visit friends on some of the other boats at anchor.

We bought a chicken for dinner and also ran across a stone carver and spent some time just watching him perform his craft. The carvings were quite large and we marveled at the man's skill. It had started to rain and there didn't appear to be an end in sight so we headed back to the boat.

By evening time I was beginning to worry about Nathan. He was never one to complain but it was obvious he didn't feel well. He seemed to be having a bad reaction to his many bug bites. For the rest of us our bites very much resembled an ordinary mosquito bite, but not for Nathan. His bites were becoming much larger and raised and were circled in a bright red ring about the size of a quarter. And he had a lot of them. Because of the warm humid weather the boys seldom wore a shirt so Nathan's back and chest as well as his arms and legs were covered in bites. The Calamine lotion and ointments I had onboard didn't seem to help at all.

By the next morning Nathan was even worse. From information we got in our sailing guide plus input from other yachts over the single sideband radio it looked like there was a hospital of some sort on shore. We decided to try to find it so with Nathan in tow we headed for shore in the dinghy. Our propane tank was almost empty so we took that along with us as well. The town was nearly deserted; all of the shops were closed. We walked the streets and finally located the hospital but that, too, was closed. So was the propane filling station. This was strange. It was midmorning on a Thursday. What was going on? Eventually we ran into someone who informed us that it was a holiday though I never did figure out which one.

We headed back towards the anchorage, still carrying the empty propane tank. It was here that we first met, Alberto, one of the most interesting characters we would ever encounter. He had just made landfall after several weeks of sailing singlehandedly in a dug out log that he had made in Panama.

Alberto was rather tall and had a very weathered look to him. He was as impressive looking as his log vessel was. The log was about 12 feet long overall. The back half was hollowed out with the top portion removed. This was where Alberto spent his time at sea. He had made a sail of sorts attached to a tall pole which he could stand up and secure in a spot he had designed for that purpose. He also had a bench type seat carved into this stern area.

The front half of the boat was used for storage. That portion had been hollowed out but the top part of the log was still in tack making it look like a cave. Here he had his water jugs, food stores, tools, and a few personal items lashed down to the inside. He explained that occasionally he would be hit by a wave that would roll his log so if he and his belongings weren't lashed down to the boat they would be lost at sea. Alberto wore a wet suit and said he never really slept while at sea although he did rest his eyes from time to time. He navigated totally by the stars. I don't remember where Alberto was from originally but he could speak English although heavily accented. We would cross paths with him several more times while in French Polynesia.

During the afternoon *Jo Hanna III* came over for a game of Pictionary. Although Nathan's infected bites continued to worsen the game was a good distraction for him.

We headed back to shore right after breakfast the following morning. We already knew where the hospital was located so we headed directly there. As we had suspected, the hospital staff spoke only French and of course we did not. By pointing to Nathan's sores and performing some of our charades they understood why we were there though the propane tank which we once again had brought along to fill no doubt confused them. They gave us some packets of medicine free of charge and tried to explain how to use it. We smiled, nodded our heads and said some *mercy boques* and headed on our way. We filled our propane tank, stopped for baguettes, and returned to the boat to start the new treatments for Nathan's infected bites.

The doctor at the hospital had given us a bunch of packets of a purple, powdery substance which we understood him to say needed to be dissolved in bath water and in which Nathan was to soak. This was fine accept for the soaking in a bath part. We had no bathtub. We did, however, have a large dishpan so that would have to do. As the dishpan was too small for Nathan to actually sit in it we did the next best thing.

We stripped Nathan down naked and had him stand in the dishpan which we had filled with warm water and had set on the floorboards of the cockpit. I had dissolved several of the purple packets into the warm water. I then took a cup, filled it with the warm, purple solution and ladled it over Nathan's body starting at his shoulders and allowing the warm water to pour over his entire body from the neck down so that it covered all of the infected areas which by this time were looking quite bad. I'm not too sure time wise how long I kept up this ladling routine but when Nathan pointed out that his feet were beginning to look like prunes we decided it was time to stop the treatment. We placed a towel on the floor for him to step out onto and wrapped his wet body in another one. It was about this time that we looked down and noticed Nathan's feet. Standing in the purple solution for so long had dyed the skin of Nathan's feet to a couple of inches above his ankles. They were now the color of really dark tea. It sort of looked like he was wearing a pair of socks but, of course, he wasn't.

Boy was Nathan upset. We tried washing his feet with soap and water but nothing we did helped. To make matters worse, the boys had been invited over to one of the other boats to watch the movie, "Willow". Nathan had really wanted to go along with his brothers but now he said he wasn't leaving our boat again with his feet that color. We finally convinced him to wear a pair of socks to cover his feet. He actually looked even sillier wearing white socks with flip flops but, of course, we told him that nobody would even notice, so off he went.

CHAPTER FIFTY-THREE

OFF TO THE TUAMOTOS

We left the Marquasis Island group on Saturday May 6th with light winds but smooth seas. Except for the bugs, we had enjoyed our stay in the Marquasis and would always remember the beauty of the islands and the friendly people there. It would be four days of sailing to reach our next anchorage on the atoll of Kauehi which was part of the Tuamotos Island group. This group of islands were called atolls as they were flat spots of land rising just above sea level. Their highest points were the tops of the many palm trees that covered the islands. It was quite a contrast from the mountainous Marquasis.

Our sail to Kauehi was smooth and uneventful. We took turns, it seemed, at not feeling so well but nothing major. Nathan's infections continued to heal but by the time we reached land Dustin's bites were actually worse so we had begun the purple treatment on him as well. The good news was that there were no no-see-ums in the Tuamotos; only mosquitoes when we went to shore. We could deal with those.

We dropped our hook in a beautiful lagoon which had lots of fish.

We caught two tuna coming in so we would be set for dinner. Jerad went to shore soon after landing and, of course, met some new friends which he was very good at doing. The population here was extremely small. You could actually walk around the perimeter of the atoll and not even be tired out at the end. There didn't seem to be anyone to check us in or out so we didn't worry about that.

The local people lived very simply and were extremely hospitable. They used every part of the numerous coconut palms that grew everywhere from the milk and fruit inside the coconut to the husks and large palm leaves. They used these for the roofs of their houses and to weave mats, fans, hats, and many other things. Most of their food stuffs and other necessities came from supply boats that came into the lagoon every few weeks. The supply boat would anchor in the lagoon and the locals would row out in their small boats to pick up the goods.

We worked on schoolwork and projects around the boat. I was trying to make a sail for our hard dinghy while Daryl made a rudder for it as well as working on our 2 H.P. dinghy motor which had begun to act up. We made trips to shore and visited with friends on the other boats at anchor there. On our third night there, we, along with several others from the anchorage accepted an invitation for dinner and a dance at the home of Edward, a local resident in the village.

Edward was an extremely large Polynesian man but actually reminded me a big Teddy bear. His home wasn't large by any stretch of the imagination but somehow we all managed to fit inside where a large spread of food had been prepared and we all ate buffet style. This was our first true experience with authentic Polynesian food and we found it to be quite good.

After we had all eaten our fill, the food and tables were cleared away and the music and dancing began. A local gentleman came over and asked me to dance. I had no clue as to how to do this kind of dancing so I just mirrored everything the man did. All the Polynesians began to roar with laughter. The more they laughed the harder I tried to imitate my partner. It wasn't until sometime later when we were in Tahiti watching all of the dancing there that I realized why Edward and his friends had been laughing at my dancing. The ladies part of the traditional Tamari dance is totally different from the man's part, and of course, I had been dancing the man's part. I suppose I was rather comical.

The following morning, *Lunar Glow,* along with two other boats from the anchorage, *Cannibal* and *Mistral,* loaded up 35 of the local villagers and took them on an outing to one of the small atolls in their island group which they called Tuka Tuka. Our boat transported 14 of them there and 18 on the return trip. It was a fun time and we finished up the day back at Kauehi where we all got together again for a big BBQ on the beach.

The following day being a Sunday I accepted an invitation from one of the locals and attended church. Of course I understood none of what was being said but it was a good experience all the same. The boys played volleyball in the village and we finished off the day with dinner at Edwards house once again.

We had enjoyed our outing on Tuka Tuka so much we decided to go back out there to explore for a couple of days. We had met a young 19 year old local boy by the name of Calvez. He had learned a few words of English and wanted to go along with us. *Mistral* would sail along with us as well.

The five of us, along with Calvez, got the boat ready for our trip out to Tuka Tuka. Calvez was quite tall and wanted to help with everything. As far as we could figure this would be his first overnight trip away from home. The 25 H.P. outboard was lowered into the water so that we could motor out of the lagoon and into the open sea. We raised our sails and as they filled with air Daryl cut the outboard and we headed towards Tuka Tuka.

Daryl, standing at the wheel, called out that the motor needed to be pulled up the track so that it wouldn't be dragging through the water and slowing us down as we sailed.

Jerad took his cue and headed towards the back of the boat with Calvez at his heals, but what happened next turned into one of the worst hours we ever experienced aboard *Lunar Glow*.

As Jerad leaned over the stern rail of the boat to pull the motor up the track, Calvez reached past him and in a very well meaning attempt to help, grabbed hold of the pulley rope and pulled on it. Hard. Calvez was not only older than Jerad but taller and much stronger as well. What would have been a much slower hand over hand pull for Jerad to raise the motor was a quick, hard pull for Calvez and the motor shot up the track. The problem was that he pulled it so far up the track that it actually pulled off the track on one side and was left hanging sideways and precariously close to falling off altogether and toppling into the ocean below. Jerad was shouting for Calvez to stop and trying with all his might to hang onto the dangling outboard motor.

Daryl, hearing the commotion at the stern of the boat but not yet knowing what had happened, turned the wheel over to Dustin and made his way aft. As soon as he saw the outboard hanging by a thread he started yelling at Jerad.

"What's going on here?" Daryl growled, pushing past Calvez and getting in Jerad's face. "You know you can't pull the motor that far up the track. What were you doing, showing off because you have a friend here?"

"It wasn't me," Jerad shot back. "Calvez pulled the motor up."

"So now you're passing your job off to someone else," Daryl accused.

"No. He just reached over and yanked on the rope. I couldn't stop him. He was just trying to help." Jerad was now raising his voice to match Daryl's.

"Don't you raise your voice to me," Daryl snapped. "Go get me a rope to tie this motor off with."

Jerad backed away and headed towards the cockpit with Calvez following. I had heard all the yelling and came up from the galley to investigate. Daryl was still raging like a madman hanging onto the motor with both hands and my attempts to calm him down did no good at all, and in fact, just made him all the madder. "You're always defending Jerad no matter what he does," Daryl yelled.

Jerad returned a minute later with the requested rope and assisted Daryl in getting the motor secured to the back of the boat then made a speedy retreat with Calvez to a spot on the boat as far away from Daryl as possible. But Daryl wouldn't stop. He continued yelling at Jerad and actually started pushing him around. Jerad cut loose with some language that I had never heard come out of his mouth before. As Daryl lunged at Jerad I jumped onto Daryl's back in an attempt to stop him. It was a very ugly scene and I'm sure Calvez was wishing he had never come along.

Although none of us spoke the words out loud I was sure the boys and I were all thinking the same thing. "It would sure be nice if we could just push this Captain Bly overboard and be done with his madness once and for all," but, of course, we didn't do that. Instead we just continued on to our destination of Tuka Tuka.

The rest of the sail to Tuka Tuka was uneventful and it was actually a beautiful day for sailing. We dropped our anchor and stowed the sails and the boys were ready for some fun. They jumped into the water and before long had speared us some fish for dinner. *Mistral,* who had anchored nearby joined us that evening for a fish fry on the beach. Nathan spent the night with his friend on *Mistral* which gave us some extra bunk space.

The following morning after collecting Nathan, we decided to move the boat to a more protected spot. We found a beautiful place and set our anchor. We turned the boys loose to go to shore with Calvez while Daryl scrubbed the bottom of the boat and I cleaned the water line. I never minded doing this job when we had beautiful clear water to work in.

Once our chores were completed we join the boys on shore. Calvez was showing the boys how to hunt for coconut crabs. Coconut crabs are extremely large land crabs with pinchers as powerful as bolt cutters. The crabs would climb the coconut palms and get the coconuts. We had seen lots of palm trees with sheet metal bands nailed to the tree about a foot in height circling the trunk about a third of the way up the tree. Calvez explained that this was how they kept the crabs from climbing up and stealing all of their coconuts. The crabs would climb up as far as the slippery sheet metal and finding nothing to grab onto they could climb no further.

The crabs were very good at hiding. We never did find any ourselves but somehow Calvez knew exactly where they would be. He would point to a pile of large rocks, find an opening, push in a big stick and pull out a coconut crab clamped onto the end of the stick. He made it look so easy! Calvez used palm fronds to make a harness and tether for the crab. He ripped the large leaf into strips which he somehow weaved into a harness which he put around the crab. Other strips were used to tie the pinches closed. He then made a leash or tether with still more strips of leaf which he tied to the harness at one end and secured the other end to a tree trunk. This way he was able to leave the crab while he went in search of another one.

Back on *Lunar Glow* Calvez cooked and prepared the two crabs he had caught for our lunch. Although they were wonderful I knew that coconut crab would not become a part of our menu. Even with their powerful pinchers tied closed I was still intimidated by them.

We went back to shore in the afternoon where Calvez gave the boys lessons on climbing palm trees. The boys remained on shore while Daryl and I returned to the boat. Daryl was complaining of pain in the right side of his chest. He said it had pulled something during his tirade the day before I couldn't feel sorry for him. In fact, I thought it served him right.

The boys spent the following morning sailing our little sabot while Daryl and I got *Lunar Glow* ready for our sail back to Kauehi. The sail back was uneventful and Calvez seemed to have had a great time. Dustin's infected bug bites were getting worse, however, and Jerad's hand was becoming infected where he had cut it some days before. We started both boys on antibiotics.

The next day, May 18th, was our fifth wedding anniversary. Only five years … it seemed like forever. We said good bye to our new friends on shore and also to our friends on the other boats in the anchorage and set sail for Tahiti.

CHAPTER FIFTY-FOUR

TAHITI

I t was a two day sail to Tahiti. We went through some squalls and
had a very fast ride. We caught a tuna each day so had plenty of fresh
fish. We talked to Mom and Dad and also Michael on the radio to
let them know we were fine and gave them an update on our plans. We
arrived in Papeete, Tahiti on May 20th. It was Michael's 19th birthday. I
wished he were with us to experience the beautiful islands and celebrate
his birthday with us.

Several of our boating friends were already in Tahiti when we arrived.
We backed our boat up into an empty slot along the dock at the edge of
town and after stowing our gear went to visit our friends. The boys were
happy to reconnect with their friends on *Tao* and *Dreamweaver* and Daryl
and I were anxious to get the lowdown on Tahiti. As we had arrived on
a Saturday we were unable to do our check-in with the authorities until
Monday.

Our first few days in Tahiti were filled with the routines of daily living.
We went to town and collected our mail; I bought material and began

sewing shorts for the boys; Daryl bought parts for the 2 H.P. outboard and started working on that; we exchanged dollars at the bank for francs; we did laundry, scrubbed the decks, and did more laundry; I gave the boys haircuts and Daryl actually shaved off his beard. Nathan managed to get a fishhook imbedded into his knee while fishing off the dock. Removing that was not a fun experience for any of us.

There is an annual celebration in Papeete every year called Fet. It goes on for weeks. It started the week after we arrived in Tahiti so we had plenty of entertainment while we were there. The festival has competitions from all of the different island groups in the South Pacific. There are wonderful dancers performing all sorts of their native dances. (It was here that I realized I had been dancing a man's part of the tamari that night in Edward's house). There was native music, coconut husking contests, tapa cloth making, weaving with palm leaves, long boat and dugout canoe races, palm tree climbing, and many other contests taking place.

We got together almost every evening with the *Tao* to play cards or dice, sometimes on our boat and other nights on theirs. Our mornings were still filled with schoolwork and chores but then the boys were off to explore and spend time with their friends. Our friends on *Dreamweaver* had already located the Mormon church before we arrived. The boys and I attended church on Sundays and during the week they went over to the church to play basketball or volleyball. We attended several church activities and were even surprised with a farewell party when we left the island complete with leis for the whole family.

Alberto arrived in Papeete a couple of days before we left. He was the Argentina man who sailed to the South Pacific from Panama in his dug out log. We invited him over for dinner and caught up on his adventures since we had seen him last. He was having some trouble with his rudder so Daryl helped him work on it for the next couple of days.

Although we loved Papeete and would have liked to have stayed longer, it was very expensive for our meager budget. After three weeks we knew it was time to move on.

CHAPTER FIFTY-FIVE

MOOREA

I t was a cloudy day as we sailed out of Papeete but the sail to Moorea was a short one. We pulled into Cook's Bay, Moorea and anchored close to shore. By the next day it had begun to rain which made it an excellent day for schoolwork and sewing. Once the rain cleared the boys went out freeboarding behind one of the fast dinghies from one of the other boats. Daryl kept himself busy by installing a new pump in the toilet. We spent a couple of days exploring the village and surrounding areas then on Monday we pulled our anchor and motored from Cook's Bay over to Baie de Opunohu.

While sailing throughout the South Pacific we referred often to a large soft covered book titled <u>Charlie's Charts</u>. On the front cover of this book was a picture of Baie de Opunohu, Moorea. As we motored into the anchorage we compared the picture of the cover of the book to the breathtaking sight before our eyes. The two sites were identical. The water in the bay was a pristine azure blue. Straight ahead and set back from the water was a high mountain; I think they called it "Sharks Tooth

Mountain". To our left as we entered the bay was a tall palm tree growing close to the water's edge with its top bending way out over the water. Because our boat had such a shallow draft we were able to anchor very close to the shore. We chose a spot near the bent over palm tree and dropped the hook. There were only a couple of other boats in the bay; both anchored further out from the shore.

Once the boat chores and schoolwork were completed the boys grabbed some rope and headed for that bent coconut palm. Dustin, who was extremely good at knot tying, was given the job of climbing the tree and securing the rope to the trunk. I guess his palm tree climbing lessons with Calvez had paid off. He then pulled the other end of the rope up to where he was, held on tight and swung out over the water. As soon as he was sure he was clear of the shore he let go and plunged down into the bay. All three boys had a great time climbing that tree with the free end of the rope and swinging out over the water.

Friends on a little boat, *Spindrift,* arrived the next day and tied up next to *Lunar Glow.* Their only daughter, Laura, was Nathan's age and she was happy to join the boys playing on the rope swing. The following day Daryl and I decided to join Laura and her folks on a hike. We headed inland through lush green vegetation where we stumbled upon some very ancient looking remains of what appeared to be old burial grounds. We understood that such places were very sacred to the native people so were especially mindful to not disturb anything or act in any way which might be disrespectful. Further on we came across a vanilla plantation where workers were trimming row upon row of vanilla plants. It smelled wonderful here. We were allowed to gather some of the dark brown vanilla beans laying on the ground and take with us back to the boat. (We would later use these to make our own vanilla extract).

More than seven hours had passed before we got back to the boat. I was tired and wanted nothing more than to sit back and enjoy a peaceful, quiet afternoon. This, apparently was not to be. As we emerged from a grove of coconut palms and crossed the dirt road which bordered the shore where our boat was anchored we were met by an unbelievable sight. We had been invaded by what I thought at the time to be every native kid on the island.

"Jerad," I shouted, looking to locate my son among all the chaos. "What in the world is going on here?"

"Well," Jerad started, "when we finished our schoolwork we went out to swing on the rope some more. A couple of local boys came by and saw us and wanted to have a try, so we let them. They seemed to be having fun but then they left so we went right on swinging. Then awhile later they came back only this time they brought their friends. And then they just kept coming."

I looked at the long line of kids waiting for their turn at the rope swing. Then I looked over at our boat. The decks of *Lunar Glow* were covered with local kids. I was waiting for Daryl to erupt but thankfully he held his tongue, probably because Ed and Marilyn from *Spindrift* were with us.

"And the kids on our boat? What are they doing there?" I questioned.

"Well, some of them seemed real interested in the boat so Dustin has been taking them aboard in groups to have a look around. He's been serving them those cookies you baked yesterday," Jerad explained. "I think they really like them."

We had learned that the island people are not only friendly but generous and hospitable as well so to shoo everyone away just didn't seem right. For the rest of the day we felt like we were living in the middle of a Disneyland attraction.

Our dog, Star, was enjoying all of the attention she was getting from so many new friends. We had begun to worry about what we were going to do with our little pet as we had read in Charlie's Charts that we would not be able to take a dog into Samoa. The time was coming for us to begin looking for a new home for our dog.

One young boy seemed to really like our Star. Dustin asked him if he would like to have her. We said he would have to ask his mother and father first. He left for a while then returned with a smile plastered across his face. Permission had been granted.

We all felt sad. Star had turned out to be an excellent boat dog and we all enjoyed our time with her. We got a piece of rope and tied it to her collar and handed the other end to her new master, said our goodbyes, and watched with long faces as the two of them walked down the road and out of sight. We turned in early that night. Not only had we had a long busy day but we were all feeling down and already missing our dog.

Just at daybreak the following morning we were woken up by a strange sound. We could hear the sound of something slapping the water outside then hitting the side of our boat. We laid still for a couple of minutes trying to figure out what was going on. We decided it had to be one of two things. Either it was some of the kids from the day before coming back for more fun aboard *Lunar Glow*, or it was a good sized fish jumping out of the water and hitting the side of the boat now and then. I was hoping for the latter. Daryl and I finally got up to investigate. To our great surprise it was neither kids or a fish, but our little dog, Star.

Apparently Star had been tied up with the rope we sent her off with. Sometime during the night she decided she wanted to come home and chewed the rope in half and returned to the boat. She had swam out to the boat and was paddling around and around the boat. Every now and then she would try to jump up onto the boat which, of course, was quite impossible. We scooped her up out of the water, dried her off, and took her down into the boys cabin for an early morning surprise. Star would remain with us a little while longer.

The next three days passed in much the same way. We tried hard to get schoolwork done before the local kids arrived, but this was a challenge because they came early and stayed late. I was beginning to wonder what they did before we arrived. Nathan had done something to his hand and it was becoming infected. A red line was running up his arm to just above his elbow. I started him on some Penicillin and once again was thankful for a well stocked medical supply.

We really loved this anchorage. It was unbelievably beautiful, but after six days Daryl was becoming very nervous. I never would have thought anything like this but Daryl was worried that if one of the local kids got hurt on the rope swing or on our boat that we might get sued. He finally insisted that the rope be removed from the tree and we had to move the boat further out into the anchorage away from the shoreline. In looking back I think it was just an excuse to keep all the kids away and thus restore some peace and quiet.

We stayed in the bay for another week. It was pretty much business as usual; school, chores, shopping, and so on. The boys went to shore each day to spend time with friends they had met there. There was one family in particular that we became friendly with. We had gone to their house and they had all come out to the boat for a visit. It was Saturday, June 24th when we decided it was time to leave and head out towards Bora Bora. Six members of the Rupea family came down to wish us a fond farewell. Each of them wore five handmade shell leis around their necks and we were each presented with a beautiful lei from each of them for a total of 30 shell leis. No two were alike. It was such a touching jester of friendship. They also brought us two huge stalks of bananas. Oh my.

It had rained hard the day before but the skies had cleared and it was looking a little better. We left our new friends on shore and rode the dinghy back out to the boat. We pulled the hook and waved good-bye but as we started to motor out of the bay the sky started to darken and the wind was kicking up. Nathan slipped in the cockpit and put his teeth through the underside of his tongue. We were getting ready to hoist the sails as we reached the mouth of the bay but immediately changed our minds. The wind was hitting us hard and one look out at the horizon told us that a huge storm was coming in fast. There was no way we wanted to head out into that. What we wanted to do was to turn around and get ourselves tucked back into the bay for protection but after the wonderful farewell we had just been given it just didn't seem right. Instead we headed out to the reef where we anchored and spent the following two days bouncing around out there until the storm had passed.

CHAPTER FIFTY-SIX

AND ... PARADISE CONTINUES

We left the reef on Monday at 4:45pm for a night sail to the island of Huahine. It was fast sailing once again and we were anchored by 9am. Jerad, Daryl, and I were tired from our night of sailing so spent much of the afternoon napping. Dustin and Nathan rowed the dinghy over to watch a movie with their friend, Kim, from *Balleaux*, a big fancy sailboat out of England.

After a couple of days we moved the boat into a very pretty little bay where we could get closer to shore. The bay wasn't very deep so the single hull boats with the deep keels couldn't get in there. We had the bay to ourselves. Jerad was able to get a HAM radio patch through to Mom and Dad in the states to give them an update on our travels and let them know where they could send mail. Bora Bora would be our next place to pick up mail.

Huahine was another very lush green island. The boys and I rowed to shore to do some exploring. Daryl was still puttering around with our 2 H.P. dinghy motor so stayed behind. We found a dirt path a short ways off the water and started to follow it. We had no idea where we were headed but the island wasn't very big so we figured we couldn't get too lost.

One of the first things we did when arriving at a new island was to look for the church. We knew that more than likely if we could find a basketball court then we would have also found the church. Usually the only basketball court on the island was at the Mormon church. We hadn't walked very far when, to our surprise, here came two young men riding bicycles towards us. They were wearing white shirts and ties and were unmistakably Mormon missionaries. They stopped and we chatted for awhile. They told us where to find the church and invited us to attend on Sunday. We assured them that we would be there. We walked on awhile more before returning to the boat.

Before returning to the boat we came across some young kids. I'm not sure why but they ended up giving us a huge stalk of bananas. We were still eating bananas off of the two stalks we had been given when we left the anchorage at Opunohu. The bananas were the little finger bananas. They were really good but with three stalks now tied to our rigging we now had hundreds of bananas. Even the dog had started eating bananas. Star would climb up onto the cabin top where she could reach the bananas. She would pull one off the stalk, hold it down with a paw, then peel it with her teeth. She loved the bananas but she left the peels scattered all over the decks.

The boys friend, Kim, was having a birthday party on *Balleaux* the following day. They were still anchored out in the deep anchorage but we had keep in contact with them via the single sideband radio. Kim's folks came into our little bay and picked up the boys in their high powered dinghy and then delivered them back after the party. Whoever said that my boys would miss out on a social life if I moved them onto a boat was just plain wrong.

The boys and I found our way to the church on Sunday. The service was in French, the main language in French Polynesia, but the missionaries we had met a couple of day earlier, sat behind us and translated for us. It was really a fun experience. We were introduced to lots of friendly people. One family wanted to come out to our boat for a visit. Actually, because of my not understanding the French language I didn't realize that until after we had returned to *Lunar Glow* and heard someone calling out from the shore. Jerad rowed over to the shore and ferried this nice family back to the boat. They came baring gifts; yep, two stalks of bananas. We were now up to five stalks and having to become very creative in finding places to tie them up to. Conversation was difficult but we all smiled and laughed and ate cookies so it was all good.

The missionaries had also arranged for us to have dinner that evening at the home of a local family. They actually came and picked us up in a pickup truck. We tied our dinghy to a tree near the water's edge and off we went. The missionaries were also at the dinner so we had some translators making conversation a bit easier. After an enjoyable evening we were once again loaded into the back of the pickup truck and returned to our dinghy. We were loaded down with armloads of fresh fruit, and yes, more bananas!

We left Huahine the following day and sailed on to Tahaa for the night. My journal simply reads: *Windy. Eating lots of bananas!*

CHAPTER FIFTY-SEVEN

BORA BORA

I t was a short sail from Tahaa to Bora Bora. We picked up a free mooring near the Oa Oa Hotel. Soon after, the boys went in search of the church basketball court while Daryl and I went to check on mail. Nothing yet. Jerad ended up having dinner on shore with a family he had met at the church while Dustin and Nathan accepted an invitation to a 4th of July party on *Flying Dolphin.*

The weather in Bora Bora remained beautiful. The boys spent their days after schoolwork riding bikes, playing basketball and visiting with friends on other boats. We took long walks and went to church on Sunday. After a week we moved the boat over to an anchorage near the Bora Bora Hotel and finally got around to checking in with the Gendarme.

One day the boys were out sailing the sabot and Daryl decided to go to shore. I'm not sure how he did it but as he went to climb into the inflatable dinghy he managed to flip it over. I thought it was quite funny except for the fact that the 2 H.P. motor he had finally got running well went under water and was dead once again.

The following day Jerad hiked into town to see his new friends. He ended up taking a ride in a motorboat around Bora Bora with them and then spent the night in town at their house. While Jerad was off with his friends Daryl decided to take *Lunar Glow* up to the dock while we went into town to stock up on groceries, do some banking and get some information from the Gendarme's office.

"You two stay here with the boat while your mom and I go into town," Daryl instructed Dustin and Nathan.

"Can we get off the boat if we stay on the dock?" Dustin questioned.

"And Star, too?" Nathan added.

"Yeah, fine. Just make sure you keep an eye on the boat. We shouldn't be too long," Daryl said.

Daryl and I headed off in the direction of the bank to get our errands started. We were gone for about an hour then returned to the boat dock. *Lunar Glow* was still tied up to the end of the dock and Nathan and our dog, Star, were standing guard next to the boat. We assumed that Dustin had gone down into the cabin as he wasn't visible on the outside.

"Okay, ready to go?" I asked Nathan. "Dustin, come on up. We're ready to untie the boat now," I called out toward the boat.

"Mom," Nathan said. "Dustin's not here."

"What do you mean he's not here. Where did he go?" I questioned.

"I told you guys to stay right here and watch the boat," Daryl snapped.

"I'm watching the boat," Nathan responded.

"Okay, so where's Dustin?" I asked again.

"Out there," Nathan said, pointing out toward the water.

"Nathan, knock it off. There's nothing out there but the *Windsong*," Daryl said looking out at the beautiful five masted cruise ship sitting at anchor way out beyond the harbor. "Now, where is he?"

"On that boat out there, honest," Nathan said. It was then that I realized that Nathan was telling the truth.

"Why is he out there instead of here with you where he should be?" I questioned.

The story as told by Dustin went something like this. The boys were sitting in the cockpit when they noticed a man in a white uniform of some sort walk to the end of the dock where *Lunar Glow* was tied up. He wasn't looking at our boat but off into the distance at the beautiful cruise ship sitting at anchor. Dustin realized that this man must be one of the officers from the cruise ship and was stranded on the dock.

"Excuse me, Sir," Dustin called over to him. "Would you like to use our radio to call your boat?"

"Oh, thanks for the offer but a tender should be coming out soon," the man replied.

"Oh, okay," Dustin replied but then began asking the officer all sorts of questions about the cruise ship. Then two American ladies walked to the end of the dock also looking out towards the *Windsong*. They, too, were obviously waiting to be tendered back out to the ship. About ten minutes later a tender could be seen motoring in towards the harbor. It was then that the officer asked Dustin if he would like to come out and have a tour of the *Windsong*.

"Yeah, sure," Dustin replied. "I'm supposed to be watching our boat but my younger brother is here so I guess he can watch the boat. And with that he jumped off *Lunar Glow* and climbed aboard the tender along with the officer and the two American tourists.

Once aboard the *Windsong* the officer took Dustin and the two ladies up to the bridge where they got a firsthand look at the wheel and all of the navigational instruments. The officer then asked the two ladies if they would take Dustin on a tour of the ship. They took him on an extensive tour from top to bottom, forward and aft. Finally, he was taken back to the tender which would return him to the Bora Bora dock. He was all smiles as he disembarked the tender with a large sack of fresh fruit that he had been given as a gift from the *Windsong*.

We remained in Bora Bora for another week after Dustin's tour of the cruise ship. Jerad spent several nights with his new church friends on shore and Dustin and Nathan spent a couple of nights sleeping on the beach with some of the local kids. They met a young boy that got permission from his mother to take our dog, Star, when we got ready to leave Bora Bora. We decided to keep Star on the boat until we were ready to set sail as we didn't want a repeat of the last time we thought we had a new home for her. On our last night on the island Dustin and Nathan were invited to spend the night at the home where Star would soon reside. They returned to *Lunar Glow* the following morning.

"Hey guys," I greeted as the boys returned the next morning. "How was your sleep over with Marco?"

"Oh. It was good. We all slept in his mom's big bed," Dustin replied.

"And where did his mother sleep?" I questioned.

"She took a matt outside to sleep with Marco's dad," Nathan said.

"His dad? I thought you said Marco's dad had died."

"Yeah, he did die," Dustin answered back. "He's buried out in front of their house. Marco says his mom sleeps out there with him a lot."

Wow. We were all getting an education of the cultures of other countries.

CHAPTER FIFTY-EIGHT

GOOD-BYE BORA BORA

We had enjoyed Bora Bora but once again it was time to move on. We checked out, bought groceries, and bid farewell to the local families we had met there. Our last job was to drop Star off with her new family. We would miss her a lot but at least she had a beautiful island to live on.

It was only a short distance to our next stop. It was the island of Maupiti. It was late when we arrived so we anchored near a moto just inside the pass for the night. In the morning we moved *Lunar Glow* to an anchorage in front of the village of Maupiti. We all took the dinghy to shore and walked around the entire island. The boys spent the remainder of the afternoon sailing the dinghy.

By our second day Jerad was beginning to feel sick. We worked on schoolwork and did chores on the boat. The day was cloudy and there was a persistent light rain. There wasn't much to do on the island so on day three we moved the boat back out to the moto. *Balleaux* was now sitting at anchor there so Dustin and Nathan were able to spend a good part of the day having dinghy races with Kim. By now Jerad had a fever, headache, and aches and pains all over. I knew he must really be sick when he took a pass at the dinghy racing.

Our goal was to reach Pago Pago, American Samoa before the beginning of hurricane season. We had read that Pago Pago was the safest hurricane hole in the entire South Pacific so we would be spending several months there to stay safe.

We left Maupiti on Sunday July 23rd. Jerad was still feeling sick the following day and Daryl's back was giving him trouble. We had no wind for most of the day and then a storm front came in. Thank goodness Dustin was now taking more watches which gave me a bit of a break. By the following day Jerad was feeling a little better but now Dustin and Daryl were sick. We had high, rough seas and lots of wind. I was getting really tired but at least Jerad was feeling well enough to take some watches.

The seas started to moderate on our third day out and there was still lots of wind. By now Dustin was feeling better but not Daryl. He remained sick the remainder of this leg of our journey which left the sailing of the boat to Jerad, Dustin, and myself. The seas were just too rough to turn the wheel over to Nathan. He did fine in calm conditions but not in this stuff.

After five nights at sea we finally reached the Cook Islands. We dropped our hook in an anchorage just off the shore of Suvarrov. Besides *Lunar Glow* there were five other boats in the anchorage. One Italian, one French, one German, one Canadian, and two from the United States. We bagged our sails and tidied up the boat a bit then went to shore where we were met by Frances, the immigration lady. Frances and her extended family were pretty much the only permanent residents of the island. The island was small and flat and covered with coconut palms. It was pretty and we liked it there. Everyone from the anchorage had dinner with Frances and her family that evening and the boys all ended up spending the night on shore with them.

The following day was a Sunday. Dustin and Nathan remained on shore playing with their new friends for most of the day while Jerad got ahead on some of his schoolwork. Daryl and I decided to take a walk and explore. We did a circumnavigation of the island which really didn't take very long as it is such a small island. There is a lot of reef around the island and in one spot a jetty that went quite a ways out from the island and across the reef. It was a narrow strip of land probably not more than three feet wide so we had to walk single file along it to keep from falling off into the water. As we made our way along the jetty we started to notice fins cutting through the top of the water not more than a couple of feet from where we were walking. We stopped walking and focused on the water to either side of us. There were reef sharks swimming all over the place. They weren't very big but there were a lot of them and we for sure did not want to fall into the water and go swimming with them. We later learned that this was where the kitchen garbage was dumped so the sharks had an easy feasting ground there.

We had a baking contest that evening on shore. Each of the boats made a baked dessert and brought up to pot luck dinner we put together. Frances and her husband, Ti, were the judges. I don't remember who the "winner" was or even if there was a winner, but it was a lot of fun trying the special desserts from different countries.

It rained the following day so it was a good day to catch up on some schoolwork. I gave Daryl a much needed haircut and he spent yet another day working on the 2 H.P. outboard motor. The folks on the island had built a good water catchment system to capture and store the fresh rainwater. Without a desalinator on the island these people depended upon the rainwater and were very careful not to waste it.

They also had no electricity. They did have an old generator but apparently it wasn't working. Because of this the people went to bed when the sun went down. But this night things were different. One of the boats had a portable generator onboard. They brought it to shore along with some videos and set it up in Frances's

house. The local kids as well as those from the various boats spent the evening watching videos. This was as much of a treat to our boys as it was to the kids living on the island.

There were lots of shells on this island. Many of the small ones were used to make shell leis. Daryl and I had canvas sailing hats made for us by a friend in La Paz, Mexico. We wore them to shore one day and when one of the local ladies saw them she sat down on a palm frond matt and started working with her shells. In no time at all she had made each of us a beautiful shell hat band which she pulled down over the crown of our hats. She explained that the weight of the shells would keep our hats from blowing off in the wind. And she was right.

We ended up staying on Suvarov for nine days. Again it was hard to leave our new friends. Their lives were hard with no frills but never a complaint and always a smile and a friendly word. I left feeling nothing but respect for these kind people.

CHAPTER FIFTY-NINE

PAGO PAGO HERE WE COME

I hadn't felt very well our last couple of days in the Cook Islands and was still a bit off as we set to sea again but the sailing was nice and we were having an enjoyable ride. By day two I was feeling better but the wind had really calmed down and by day three there was no wind at all and the temperature was getting hot. There we sat; becalmed.

As was the norm, Jerad used this time to do as much school work as possible while Dustin and Nathan did as little as they could to get by. For some reason the two younger boys were in the mood to bake. Dustin made bread two days in a row while Nathan baked cookies.

Day four is a day I will forever remember. We finally picked up the trade winds and were moving along at a good clip. Once we started moving again we let out the fishing lines we trolled off the back of the boat. We were ready for some nice fresh fish. We had a very nice deep sea pole and reel on board but we rarely used it, but today Jerad wanted to fish with that in addition to our troll lines.

"Daryl," Jerad said. "Can I try using the big fishing pole?"

"Yeah, I suppose you can. It's all set up and ready to go," Daryl answered. "Just drop the line over the front end of the boat so you don't get tangled in the troll lines. And remember to hold on tight to that pole."

"Okay." Jerad attached one of our big flashy lures to the line and dropped it over the bow. He stood there patiently for a few minutes without any action, then suddenly he came to life.

"I think I got a hit," Jerad shouted. "Yeah, I feel something."

"Let me see that," Daryl said, grabbing the pole out of Jerad's hands. "Yeah, I think you're right. I feel it too," he said passing the pole back over to Jerad."

"Give the pole a yank to set the hook in the fishes mouth," Daryl instructed.

Jerad complied, but a minute later he began yelling excitedly. "I can't reel him in. My line keeps going out."

"That's okay, Jerad. Let him have a little line, then reel in a little at a time. Dustin, you go back and pull in the troll lines. We don't want them to get in the way of this fish," Daryl called out.

"He's pulling really hard. I can't reel him in at all."

"Just hold on tight to that pole. Give him a little more line. Kay, help me get some of this sail down. We've got to slow the boat down."

We pulled the sails down so that we were pretty much still in the water. Jerad continued to play with the fish. We had no idea at that point what it was but from the way it fought we knew it was big. Jerad had moved towards the stern of the boat as the fish swam in that direction. Every now and then we could hear the zinging sound of the fishing line pulling fast off the reel.

"Don't let him take all the line, Jerad," Daryl told him. "When he slows down or turns this way reel in as much as you can."

"I think he's coming back towards the boat. See, the angle of the line has changed." Jerad was excited to have hooked such a big fish but we could tell he was getting tired.

"Let me reel him in Jerad. I want a turn," Dustin begged.

"No. You're too small, and besides, this is my fish. It was my idea to use the pole and I hooked him."

"Man." Dustin was clearly disappointed. He was actually our most avid fisherman and made almost all of our nice big lures.

"Hey, I think I'm gaining on him," Jerad called out. "I'm actually getting some of the line reeled in."

Jerad had been playing this fish for well over half an hour and we could see that he was getting tired out.

"Do you want me to work him for a while?" Daryl asked.

"No thanks. I've got it." It was about this time that Jerad announced that he thought he had lost the fish. "I can't feel it tugging any more. He must have broke loose or something."

Jerad, thinking he had lost the fish, relaxed and loosened his grip on the pole as he continued reeling in the line. A couple of seconds later we all had the surprise of our lives. The fish hadn't broke loose at all. He had swam back towards the boat giving the line plenty of slack which was why Jerad had been able to reel in so much of the line. The fish then shot up several feet out of the water not far from the boat and we were able to see the beautiful big marlin that Jerad had been fighting. But as it did so the line tightened again and as Jerad had loosened his grip on the pole we all just stood there with our mouths open as the marlin completed his arc through the air and reentered the water taking our only deep sea fishing pole, reel, line, and lure sailing through the air along with the marlin.

Jerad, of course, felt terrible, and in fact, we all felt bad. The fish and the fishing rig were gone. I felt bad for the marlin, too. He was left swimming through the ocean with a big lure stuck inside his mouth and a fishing pole trailing behind him. Daryl just couldn't contain himself and spent some time yelling at Jerad about not holding the pole tight and not letting Daryl reel in the fish. He had a real knack for making a bad situation worse.

During his tirade Daryl announced that he was going to return to the States when we got to Samoa. This was sort of a pattern with Daryl. When he would get really mad he would threaten to return to the States and leave us stranded without a captain for our boat. I think he was hoping we would beg him not to go. What he didn't know was that we were all silently cheering him on because life was usually much more pleasant when he was gone.

We got the boat sailing again and headed west towards Pago Pago, the harbor in American Samoa where we arrived the following morning.

CHAPTER SIXTY

MEN IN SKIRTS

I t was a beautiful, sunny morning when we entered the harbor of Pago Pago. (Pronounced Pongo Pongo). I was cleaning up the galley as we pulled up alongside the Custom's Dock. As Daryl motored us in and cut the engine Jerad and Dustin tied the boat fenders to our starboard ama and jumped off the boat onto the dock to tie us off to the cleats there. The Immigration officer was standing on the dock along with another gentleman. Nathan, who had remained in the cockpit took one look at the two men on the dock and called down to me in a very loud voice, "Mom, there are two men out here wearing skirts!" Oh great. Nathan insults the authorities before we even have a chance to introduce ourselves.

The other gentleman on the dock that day turned out to be Captain Patane, the assistant harbormaster. We learned that about one third of the male population wore lava lavas; a rectangular piece of cloth, usually colorful, which they tied around their waist and did, indeed, resemble a skirt.

We went through our check in procedures for the tune of $50.00 and then found an empty spot in the crowded harbor to anchor the boat. There would be lots of boats waiting out the hurricane season here in Pago Pago.

Our first order of business after getting everything on the boat tidied up was to take care of the laundry. We hadn't wanted to use any of the precious fresh water in the Cook Islands for laundry and washing clothes in salt water left them feeling damp and sticky. We loaded our laundry in tote bags and rowed to shore. Because American Samoa is a US territory many of the people spoke English. Some spoke it well and others not so good or not at all. We asked directions to a launder mat then walked to our destination where we were pleasantly surprised to find brand new Maytag washers and dryers. Wow. This place was like heaven.

There was a phone booth on the customs dock. I called and talked to Mom and Dad to let them know that we had arrived safely. I also tried to call Michael. He was planning to come to Samoa for a visit and it had been quite a while since we had talked. We would not talk this day either as apparently he wasn't at home.

The following day we finished the laundry and set off to do some exploring. We learned one thing that made us sad though. According to the information we had read in our travel guides nobody was allowed to bring a dog into American Samoa. We saw now that was not the case. There were lots of dogs running around and several of the boats had come in with their dogs without any problems. We had left Star on Bora Bora to save her from being put down and now found out that that would not have happened. We still had our little parrot, Sweetie Pie, with us.

We found the post office and, as always, we were happy to find mail waiting for us in General Delivery. We inquired about getting our own post office box as we knew we would be here for several months but were told that there were no boxes available at that time. We got put on a waiting list.

Our rolls of films were piling up. We found a place in town to get them developed and dropped them off. We discovered the market with the best prices and replenished our depleted food stores.

Jerad wasted no time in finding a way to earn money. Within two days of arriving in Pago Pago he had found work on one of the other boats in the harbor,

Northern Lights. He spent many hours over the next two weeks sanding and varnishing the wood on that boat.

We had located a Mormon church building as we wandered around Pago Pago so the boys and I attended church that first Sunday. The service was all in Samoan so, of course, we recognized the order of things but not the words. It was to our surprise when the Assistant Harbor Master, Brother Patane, came up and greeted us. He was surprised to see us. We had no idea that he was LDS. He spoke very good English. He told us to come and see him the next day and he would find an excellent spot for *Lunar Glow* in the harbor.

We took Brother Patane up on his offer to get us a prime spot in the harbor. On Monday morning we went to the Harbor Master's Office. We were told to raft *Lunar Glow* up to a large barge that was anchored in the harbor close to the shore. This was great. Being tied up to the barge meant that we didn't have to have an anchor out so would not have to worry about swinging back and forth on the anchor or having the anchor drag.

We stayed busy all week. Besides school work Jerad continued his work on *Northern Lights.* We found the local medical clinic and spent an afternoon there catching up on our medical needs. The charge, thanks to the US taxpayers, was just $2.00 each regardless of what you needed to have done. Nathan got his tetanus booster and started on the first of three Hepatitis B shots. Daryl got a blood pressure check and had some blood work done. I had a pap smear and tetanus shot.

Jerad and Dustin spent most of Wednesday and Thursday attending a youth conference at the church that Brother Patane had told them about. Daryl went into a travel agency in town and bought an airline ticket for himself. True to his word he would fly back to the states by the weekend. The purchase of the ticket made a big dent in our very meager budget. I went into the Manpower Resources office to find some sort of job and bring in a few dollars.

With Daryl gone I got busy doing some deep cleaning on the boat and started sanding the walls of the galley to get it ready for a new coat of paint. The boys were becoming more familiar with the lay of the land. They had found the library and Jerad and Dustin would go there to work on their schoolwork. Our friends on *Dream Weaver* arrived in Pago Pago and rafted up next to us on the barge so they once again had plenty of friends around.

When I wasn't sanding, cleaning, or doing schoolwork, I spent my time working on sewing projects and filling out job applications. The sailboat, *Tiva,* arrived with Leslie on board. She was a dental hygienist and cleaned my teeth as well as each of the boys teeth for a total of $20.00. What a bargain!

Jerad continued working on *Northern Lights* and started sanding down our hard dinghy. He had completed his schoolwork for the eleventh grade and was ready to start his senior year. Because we planned to stay in Samoa for the hurricane season Jerad said he really wanted to go to a "real school" for his last year. He kept reminding me how much money we would save by not having to buy another years worth of text books and manuals.

On August 31st I took Jerad to the high school to get him registered. During the registration process some of the school rules and traditions were explained to us. One was that every Friday the students were to wear the school colors; blue and white. This was fine with Jerad except for one thing. The blue part was a lava lava. Jerad emphatically stated, "I am NOT wearing a skirt to school!"

I looked around at the several, very large, Samoan males walking around the campus, most of which were wearing lava lavas, and said to Jerad, "Which one of these guys do you want to tell that you are not going to wear a skirt to school?"

Jerad took one look and said, "I'll wear a skirt to school."

By the time we left Samoa all any of my boys wanted to wear every day of the week was a lava lava.

CHAPTER SIXTY-ONE

TIME FOR WORK

The day after we got Jerad registered for school I received word that I had been offered a part time job. I was to become the new librarian of the South Pacific Elementary, a private English speaking school located outside of Pago Pago. Daryl was still in the states so had no idea about any of these recent happenings. School was to start the following week so I did the best I could to finish up the sanding and painting I was doing on the boat.

Lucky for us American Samoa had a very good bus system which became our main mode of transportation during our first months on the island. All of the buses were privately owned and generally had seats for about 20 to 30 people, depending on the size of the passengers. Each bus was painted on the outside and decorated on the inside according to what the owner wanted. Some had fringe or tassels or whatever hanging on the inside and the outside was always brightly painted in a rainbow of colors. There were no actual bus stops. If you wanted a bus you just stuck out your arm and waved as a bus approached heading in the direction you wanted to go. If it had room it would stop and pick you up. If it was full it would keep going. The fare was always a quarter which you would toss onto the front dashboard. When you got to the place where you wanted to get off you just flipped your fingers on the roof of the bus and the driver would stop and let you off. It was not unusual to find someone with a chicken or other animal riding along with them on the bus. Nathan would shoot me daggers with his eyes every time we boarded a crowded bus and one of the many very large Samoan women would scoop him up and sit him on their lap. This happened several times.

Jerad had finished the work he was doing on *Northern Lights* and had already located another job. He was now going to work at the local bowling alley after school and some Saturdays. Jerad would also be taking a Seminary class at the church each weekday before school so he would be extremely busy.

Daryl returned from the states the day before Labor Day and my first day at the school library was the day after Labor Day. Dustin and Nathan decided that they, too, needed to find some sort of job. Not far from where the boat was docked was a covered, outdoor area where the local bingo games were held. The players sat on the ground with their bingo cards spread out all around them. They played bingo several times each week and my young boys decided that they would provide a snack service for the players. They got busy baking. First it was pieces of cake then cupcakes that they would bake and sell. The bingo players loved it and the boys were really excited to have their first money making business. Unfortunately, after a couple of weeks the authorities caught up with them and informed them that they would need a permit from the Health Department in order to continue their cupcake business.

My new job as librarian of the private school was a part time position so most days I just worked in the mornings. I rode one of the local buses to school and back. I learned on my first day that the school had never had a library, thus my first task was to arrange the mountain of books I found piled on the floor of my library room into an organized library. Nobody had thought to mention this to me when I was applying for the job. At least the room was lined with book shelves. By the end of my first week I was beginning to see the light at the end of the tunnel and felt that by the following week students would actually be able to visit and find a book.

With Daryl back home again he was able to keep an eye on Dustin and Nathan while I was working. I went to work and the boys did their chores in the mornings and we did schoolwork in the afternoons. Jerad continued to work at the bowling alley after school and did homework in the evenings. This was pretty much our routine throughout the month of September and into October.

CHAPTER SIXTY-TWO

ANOTHER VISIT FROM MICHAEL

Wanting Michael to see as much of Samoa as possible we took an all day tour of the island with our friend, Fili. We had met Fili at the outdoor bingo hall some weeks before. He was a taxi driver and like with the buses, he owned his own taxi. His offer of a tour was greatly appreciated.

Michael had graduated from high school and was now working and living on his own in the Bay Area in California. He seemed happy to be spending some time with his family and we were glad to have him there. He spent time with his brothers playing basketball or just goofing off. He attended church with us on Sundays although he had pretty much stopped attending church when he had left home some years before.

Nathan was baptized while Michael was there. In our church children don't get baptized until they reach the age of eight years old. Even though Nathan had turned eight some 10 months before we had never had the opportunity to have him baptized. Now that we were in one place for a prolonged period of time and going to church every week it seemed like the time was right. Nathan was baptized in Pago Pago by Brother Patane, the Assistant Port Master we had met on the day we arrived in American Samoa.

The following Saturday we took an unusual excursion into the jungle. Jerad, Dustin, and Nathan took a bus over to the village of Leone to watch a school football game. Michael came with Daryl and I on a 'bat count'. There are great big fruit bats on the island of Samoa and every so often the Department of Marine Resources tries to figure out what the bat population is looking like.

There were maybe 15 of us folks who had volunteered for this project and I don't think any of us had a clue as to what we were doing before we set off. We were transported to somewhere that was covered in very dense foliage. From there we set out on foot with instructions to keep our eyes peeled for any fruit bats we might see. They are quite large and easy to see when in flight.

There was no beaten path for us to follow. Our guides, of which there were two, simply cut their way through the jungle foliage with large machetes. It was quite hot and humid so not the most comfortable of outings, however, for me it was okay because it was like a mini adventure. We took a water break at one point but having no water one of the guides scaled one of the many coconut palms and threw down several green coconuts. The two guides then took their machetes and whacked the tops of the nuts a few times until a hole opened up on the end. They passed a coconut to each of us and we enjoyed the refreshing coconut juice.

Continuing on our way, we "bat counters" started to remark to each other that it was strange that aside from our guides there were no other Samoans with us. We also thought it was odd that between all of us we had only spotted a total of two fruit bats, and at the end of the day that remained our final count. We concluded that perhaps we "non-natives" had just participated in the Samoan version of a good ole American snipe hunt. Oh well. It was a fun day all the same.

Michael flew out on October 17th; a day he will long remember. As he was flying home a huge 6.9 earthquake was taking place in the Bay Area. A freeway collapsed and there were many deaths. His plane had to be diverted making his long trip even longer.

CHAPTER SIXTY-THREE

SCHOOL DAZE

ichael left on Tuesday and on Thursday, Daryl, yep you guessed it, flew back to the states again. I suppose he figured that now that I was bringing in a few extra dollars he might as well take a trip and spend them. For someone who had said if he could do anything in the world that he wanted to do it would be to "get a boat and go sailing", he sure spent a lot of time and money flying back home. Oh well, we would manage without him. We had done it plenty of times before.

There was a PTA meeting that evening at the high school. Trying to be a supportive parent and keep up on what was happening with my son's new school, I took a bus to the school and attended the meeting. Unfortunately, the meeting was all in Samoan so I had no clue what was being said. At least Jerad's classes were given in English.

Without Daryl to keep an eye on the two younger boys while I was at work I had to figure something else out. Dustin would be fine on his own for a few hours each morning. He had plenty of chores and homework to keep him busy. Nathan would just have to come to work with me. This actually worked out quite well. Never having attended a real school before it was a fun, new experience for him. I had made friends with, Marina, the third grade teacher at the school. She was kind enough to invite Nathan into her class whenever I was working so he had something besides my little library to look forward to.

Jerad had already been a student at the high school for over two months and I got notice of his parent teacher conference. Jerad assured me that the teacher I was to meet with spoke excellent English so I was happy to go and meet with her. She gave Jerad a glowing report. She said whenever she asked the class a question, Jerad's hand always went up first. She said he could not only answer the questions correctly but he could also tell you the page number and paragraph of the book he had learned the answer from.

Island wide testing was to be done in Samoa the following week. There was some sort of military test given at the high school of which Jerad got the top grade for the entire school. I guess his home schooling hadn't hurt him too much!

The South Pacific Elementary where I worked was giving IOWA tests. They would go on for three days. I got permission from the school to have both Dustin and Nathan given the tests as well. I really wanted to see if they were keeping up academically with the schools expectations on a nationwide basis. So for three days running I took both Dustin and Nathan with me to work. Both boys had excellent test results.

It was about this time that I was given more opportunities at the South Pacific Elementary. I was asked to be a substitute teacher. They didn't seem to care that I had no teaching degree or even a college degree for that matter. I had been home schooling my own children for quite some time now and that was good enough for them. Now that my little library was put together I had more time to spend elsewhere. Most of my substituting was in the 7th grade but I also spent time in the 6th and 8th grades. I worked in the kindergarten a couple of times but I much preferred the higher grades.

Usually I would just work in the classroom if a teacher called in sick but during the holidays some of the teachers wanted to take a trip to the states to spend the holiday with family there. During those times I would teach in a classroom for a week or more at a time. I liked this because I got to know the students better.

Daryl finally returned to Samoa the week after Thanksgiving. He had been gone for six weeks this time. The boys and I had spent our Thanksgiving together on the boat. It wasn't much of a celebration but it was Nathan's ninth birthday. We actually had his party the following day so that our friends who were celebrating Thanksgiving the day before could join us.

Even though Daryl had returned I continued to take Nathan to work with me. Marina didn't seem to mind having him in her classroom and Nathan was having fun there. This way I wouldn't worry that the two younger boys would argue giving Daryl something to complain about.

CHAPTER SIXTY-FOUR

HO HO HO OR BOO HOO HOO

Our first Christmas in Samoa would be different for us in a number of ways. The boy's father, Joe, had offered to pay for plane tickets to fly the three boys back to California for Christmas. They would be leaving in mid December as soon as Jerad's school let out for the Christmas break. We were kept busy getting them ready for their upcoming trip. Jerad took his SAT test as he was now thinking about going off to college. He also had a Marine Symposium report to complete. I gave all of the boys haircuts and bought them new shoes. Then, of course, there was Christmas shopping and getting them packed. With everything completed, we got the boys to the airport for a 2:30 am flight back to the states.

Daryl and I wouldn't spend the Christmas holiday on *Lunar Glow* either. One of the American teachers at the South Pacific Elementary, Jean, and her husband, Van, were going to visit their family and asked me to housesit for them during the school break. Their house was in the village of Leone. Fili, our taxi driver friend, picked us up and delivered us to the house in Leone. It would be nice to have a change of scenery and more room to move around but there would be no Christmas tree or decorations. Beside that we were now too far away to walk into town or visit with our boat friends. It was probably for the best though because I was so sad with the boys gone I wouldn't have been very good company anyway.

There were no presents under our non-existent Christmas tree. I figured that Daryl had given himself enough presents with his many trips back to the states. He did have something for me, however. When he returned from the states a couple of weeks prior he brought with him a large, heavy-duty, used Phaff sewing machine. I asked him why he bought that big thing when my little hand cranked machine worked just fine for the things I sewed on the boat. He said that this machine was able to sew through sails and canvas so "I" would be able to make extra money doing sail repairs and making dodger tops and settee cushions for the other boats. It was touching how he was always thinking of "me". Anyway, he brought the sewing machine, still in the box it had traveled in, out to Jean's house in Leone and set it up there so that I would have something to keep me busy.

Daryl took a bus out to the boat each day to work on boat projects. He said it was much easier to get things done there without the boys and I getting in his way. I'm not sure how much he worked and how much he napped but he was gone a lot during that time. Just before Christmas Daryl informed me that he had talked to Fili about finding a rental house on the island. We had sustained some structural damage to one of the wing decks on the boat during our crossing and although it didn't seem to be urgent we would need to get it repaired before doing another ocean crossing. He said that if we could move onto land for a while then we could have the boat lifted out of the water making the repair work easier.

Fili drove us to several places around the island where he knew of houses for rent. Unfortunately they were all either way too far from the boat or they were way too expensive for our budget. We would have to keep looking. And now Daryl came up with yet another idea. A car. He said he thought we would also need to find a used car to get around with while we were in Samoa. Apparently he was planning on my getting lots of sewing jobs to pay for all of these new ideas of his.

CHAPTER SIXTY-FIVE

A NEW YEAR AND
AN OLD HOUSE

Christmas passed as did New Years. Fili showed us a couple more houses but still nothing that would work for us. I talked to the boys every few days. They were staying mainly with my parents and having a great time so I was glad for that. We returned to the boat just before New Year's minus the sewing machine which Jean said could remain at her house in Leone for the time being. I returned to teaching the 8th grade class the day after New Years. It was now 1990.

The first week of the new year passed by rather routinely. I worked at the school and Daryl puttered on the boat. The boys finally returned home on Sunday, January 7th, their 7:10 pm flight finally arriving at 11:45 pm. I didn't care. At least they were back.

Fili showed up again on Wednesday afternoon. He had found another house for us to look at, and this one was actually in Pago Pago. He warned us that it wasn't much and needed a lot of repairs but he wanted us to see it and meet the owner, Mrs. Tiai, anyway. We agreed.

Well Fili was right. This house wasn't much. For starters it didn't have electricity. It also had no kitchen appliances, i.e. a stove or refrigerator. There were three bedrooms, a kitchen (minus appliances), and a large living room. There was a bathroom of sorts. It consisted of a toilet and a shower, each of which had a separate door and was located about ten yards down a little path from the back door. Oh yeah. And if you looked down through the slats of the floor boards you could see the earth under the house. The outside had been painted white with blue trim at some point in time. It was now chipped and peeling so badly that the house had a curly look to it where there was still any paint left and a bleached wood look otherwise. But the good news was it had running water, cold only, and it could be ours 100% rent free as long as we agreed to "fix it up" at our expense. We agreed.

The boys hadn't been with us when we found this house so the following day between school getting out and Jerad going to his job at the bowling alley, Fili took us all back up the hill to the Tiai compound. We called it a compound because it actually consisted of three houses (if you could even call ours a house). The boys looked around and finally gave us the "Oh my word, you've got to be kidding" look but knowing that this wasn't really all that bazaar for this family.

The largest house in the Tiai compound was occupied by Mrs. Tiai. She was a widow in her early sixties at the time although she appeared to be much older. Her husband had died a few years before and was buried in the front yard. She was a large woman and defiantly the one in charge of the family. She ran a tight ship. Living in the big house with her was her oldest son, Tiai Tiai, (yep the first and last names were the same), his wife, Lupe, and their two children, Sine and Mafutaga. The daughter, Sine, was about ten at that time and, Mafutaga, about eight. Tiai had suffered a severe accident a few years before and was left quite handicapped in both body and speech. Also living in the big house were Junior and Bennie, two sons that seemed to come and go, and Tina and Uli, Mrs. Tiai's two youngest adopted daughters whom we didn't interact with very much. And then there was Liai, who was fourteen at the time and would become like a part of our family. Liai was actually Mrs. Tiai's granddaughter by her oldest daughter, Tua. Tua, had given birth to Liai out of wedlock while stationed in Colorado when she was in the military. After four months it became obvious that Tua couldn't care for this baby so sent her back to

Samoa to be raised by her parents. The problem was that the baby's father was black which was quite apparent. Because of this many of the Samoan people never really accepted Liai.

There was another house in the compound. This one was occupied by Frank, another of Mrs. Tiai's sons, along with his wife and young son, Rambo. Frank was in the US Army Reserves so would come and go.

The following week was a busy one. Between work and school we bought a used car, a 1986 Toyota wagon and gave Mrs. Tiai $75.00 so that she could have a power pole installed at our house. We would need electricity in order to repair this house. We started buying materials for the house and moving some of our tools from the boat.

We started a couple of days later working on the floors. I didn't mind the cute little geckos that wandered in and walked along the walls but I really didn't like the thought of other "things" getting in and so we nailed thin sheets of plywood over the existing floorboards to cover up all the gaps between the boards. Daryl ran wiring for the house and we had a refrigerator and a propane stove delivered. We brought one of our two propane tanks from the boat to connect to the stove.

By the end of January things were looking up. The plywood floor work was done and we had ordered some carpeting. The wiring had been run and the power hooked up. We had a stove that worked and Daryl was building some kitchen counters. I was putting vinyl tiles on the kitchen floor and had washed down all the walls and ceilings. Our furniture consisted of the sewing machine Daryl had picked up from Jean and Van's house in Leone and the foam mats from our bunks on the boat. There were also a couple of crates to sit on. Real homey! And then everything went crazy.

CHAPTER SIXTY-SIX

HURRICANE OFA

On February 1ˢᵗ Nathan and I went to work at the South Pacific Elementary as usual. We had had a lot of wind and rain for the past several days but today it was official; Hurricane Ofa was heading directly towards Samoa. This couldn't be happening. Samoa hadn't had a hurricane for 24 years which was why we decided to sit out the hurricane season here. The radio kept repeating the hurricane warnings and telling people to get away from the shore lines and up to higher ground. They closed the school early and sent everyone home.

Nathan and I went back to the house in Pago Pago. I left Nathan there with Dustin and picked up Daryl. We headed down the hill to the harbor where there was a hive of activity going on. Despite the wind and rain the yacht owners were scrambling around their boats tying down everything they could and putting out extra anchors. We took as many of our belongings off the boat as we could stuff into our car, moved the boat away from the barge, and set out extra anchors. *Lunar Glow* ended up looking like a bug in the center of a giant spider web.

We returned to the boat the following morning to make sure the anchors were holding. We picked up a few more of our belongings and were about to leave the harbor when a couple of our boat friends approached us. Don and Kathy and their son Sean didn't feel safe staying on their boat *Gallatea* and our friends from *Spindrift* were worried about their daughter, Laura. Could we possibly put them up at our "house" until the storm was over. Well, sure. But they had never seen our "house". We all piled into our car and drove back up the hill in Pago Pago. Don brought his VHS and some movies which would keep the kids entertained.

The winds increased throughout the day and our power would flicker on and off. Don helped Daryl board up the windows on the north and east sides of the house. I started laying vinyl tiles on the 2nd bedroom floor.

The next morning the adults took a ride to pick up a few groceries and to check on the boats again. *Lunar Glow* was fine but *Galletea* and *Spindrift* had to be moved and reanchored. That done, we returned to our house in Pago Pago. I finished the floor tiles on the second bedroom. It was extremely windy. Ofa was hitting us hard. The winds were over 100K when the weather station blew out so we were no longer getting weather reports. Towards evening I put a couple of frozen pizzas, which we had picked up at the store earlier in the day, into our oven. This would be the first meal I had cooked in our new oven. It was just 6 o'clock when I was pulling the pizzas out of the oven. Suddenly there was a horrible noise which sounded like a freight train racing through the house. I was alone in the kitchen and holding the hot pizza pan in my hands as the roof and ceiling of the kitchen peeled back and blew off. Wood and debris toppled down all around me but not one thing hit me. I suppose I was in shock as I wasn't thinking clearly. I remember thinking, "should I put the pizza back in the oven or go serve it to our guests?" The power flickered again then went out completely. It appeared as though the whole house might blow apart at any minute. It was total confusion. We looked outside only to find broken off tree branches and power wires flying through the air. We all grabbed pillows to cover our heads with and ran down the path to the main house as it still appeared to be intact. The house was dark, of course, with the power out, but the family welcomed us in. Daryl left at this point in the car. He said he wanted to try to make it back to the boat before any more trees went down to block the roads.

The Tiai family welcomed us into their home. Mrs. Tiai wasn't there. She was in Apia over on the island of Western Samoa visiting family members there. By now it was dark so all of the younger kids found a spot on the floor and were soon sleeping soundly. The adults and older kids listened to the howling wind and rain and speculated on the amount of damage being done across the island. After a couple of hours we started to witness more of the hurricane damage firsthand as the roof of the Tiai house began to tear loose. As more and more of the roof was ripping away it became clear that we would have to relocate once again. I had no idea where to go but the Tiai's did. Their Aunt Pago Pago lived just down the hill. She had a block house that might hold together better. We would all relocate to her house.

We woke the sleeping kids and made sure that everyone had a pillow. Outside there was corrugated sheet metal which had ripped off of roofs of houses flying through the air as well as all sorts of other debris ready to slice into anyone who ventured out into it. As the storm raged on we noticed that every now and then there was a short lull as if the storm was stopping for a minute to catch it's breathe. We waited for one of these lulls then with a pillow protecting our head we all ran as a large group down to Aunt Pago Pago's house. I didn't know many of the people there but that didn't seem to matter. There was a disaster happening and we were all welcome to the safety of their home.

The worst of the storm had hit us on Saturday. Daryl made his way back up the hill on Monday. The boat had weathered the storm fairly will. Only one of the anchor lines broke loose and the outboard motor was pulled off its track but that could be fixed. It was still real windy but we went back over to the house to assess the damage there. We moved the new stove and refrigerator out of the kitchen and into the living room. The back part of the house was a total loss. There was still a floor but that was about all. Then we looked out back where our toilet/ shower rooms had been. All that remained was a cement slab with a toilet bowl sitting on it. No walls, no toilet lid. Nothing.

By Monday night Don and Kathy from *Gallatea* returned to their boat and I went back to *Lunar Glow* with Daryl. All of the kids remained at Pago's house. The wind and rain continued but not at hurricane force. Mrs. Tiai returned from Apia on Wednesday and moved everyone back up to her house. The damage there was minimal compared to our house. The heavy rains continued through Thursday but many of the roads had been cleared and were passable. We loaded the car with as many members of the Tiai family as we could fit in and took a tour of the island to see what the storm had done. It was terrible. Damage everywhere. So many people had lost their homes. We went by the South Pacific Elementary to see how the school had faired. There was roof damage over much of the school but my new library was gone. The roof had been ripped off and all of the books were a total loss. Well that would be the end of my library job.

Friday was the first day that the sun came out and the wind stayed away. We ordered some wood at the lumberyard to build new trusses with. There was plenty of clean up to do until the wood came in.

The boys and I went to church on Sunday as was our habit. We were given a much appreciated gift from the Bishop as we were leaving; two big tarps, a huge bag of sugar, and a case of canned fish. I gave the sugar and fish to Mrs. Tiai and the tarps were a big help to us.

CHAPTER SIXTY-SEVEN

FEMA

It was still raining on Monday. We put the tarps over the roof which helped some and started to work building new trusses for the back part of the house. We took a break to take Dustin out to the medical clinic. He had been coughing for quite some time and we wanted to get him checked out.

Dustin was given a thorough going over and tested for TB. We were instructed to return in two days to see the results of the TB test. When we returned two days later we were told that Dustin tested positive for TB but they wanted to do some additional testing. They did more blood work and did a chest x-ray. The conclusion was that although Dustin tested positive for TB he didn't actually have TB. What he had was something they called atypical bacterial disease. He was put on the same medication that was used to treat TB and would have to take it for a full year.

We continued with the clean up and repair work on the house. Nathan, Daryl and I were sleeping on the boat at night while Jerad and Dustin stayed at the house. The power had still not been fixed but we were assured the power company was working on it. Daryl ran new wiring through the house so that it would be ready when the power was restored.

It had now been a full two weeks since the hurricane. The overall damage to the island was enormous and as with any disaster, some homes weathered the storm better than others. Because American Samoa is a US possession the people who had sustained damages would be given help from the United States government through the Federal Emergency Management Agency, otherwise known as FEMA. The FEMA representatives would be giving out applications for relief funds at the Lee Auditorium in Pago Pago. Daryl, Nathan, and I, along with Mrs. Tiai drove down to the Lee Auditorium where we found what appeared to be the entire population of the island. After a five hour wait we were able to sit down at one of the many small tables which had been set up around the room and talk with one of the government workers who helped us fill out our application and set a time for an inspector to come out and see the house. Mrs. Tiai's application would need to be separate from ours even though the property all belonged to her.

The FEMA inspector actually showed up on Monday, just two days after having filled out the application. We were pleasantly surprised and impressed with the speed at which this government agency responded. The inspector looked through the house, inside and out, making notes in his notebook. He did the same for Mrs. Tiai's big house. When the inspector left he instructed us to go back to the Lee Auditorium where the Red Cross was giving out food vouchers.

We gathered up Mrs. Tiai and a couple of the smaller children and headed back to the Lee Auditorium. This time the crowds of people filtered through much faster as no applications needed to be filled out. We picked up the food vouchers and returned home to continue working on the house.

The relief check from FEMA arrived exactly one month from the day Hurricane OFA hit. Our check was in the amount of $7,248. Holy Cow! This was more than a year's income for our family but we knew it would take at least that much and maybe more to rebuild the house. Mrs. Tiai wanted us to give the money to her but we knew that if we did she would spend the money on whatever and the house would never be rebuilt. She had tried to talk the FEMA representatives into having the check sent to her in the first place as she owned the property but they refused saying that because we were living in the house they couldn't do that. She also got a check for the damages to her big house; more than $22,000, but very little of it was actually spent on repairs. Most of it was just spent on whatever.

CHAPTER SIXTY-EIGHT

REBUILDING

With so many people rebuilding their homes building materials were in short supply. As soon as new shipments arrived at the lumberyard there were lines of people waiting to purchase them. Sometimes we were able to get what we needed and other times we just had to wait. In the meantime life went on as always.

Jerad continued to do well in his senior year at the high school and the other two boys did their home schooling assignments with and without grumbling. Dustin turned 13 on March 14th and we had a big party for everyone with pizza, ice cream and cake. I was getting enough sewing jobs to bring in a few extra much needed dollars. The boys and I continued to attend church each Sunday and participate in other church activities throughout the week.

In early April Jerad took the written test for his driver's license permit. The process is a little bit different there. Even though he passed the written test he was not able to pick up the permit until the following week.

We were able to get some nice ceramic tiles at the lumber yard so Daryl tiled the floor of the new outhouse type bathroom and shower that he rebuilt down behind our house. I put a coat of paint on it and it actually looked quite nice. Much better than the original one that had been blown away.

I took the kids to an Easter party at the church on the Friday before Easter. Someone there told us about some art classes which were to begin the following day. I liked taking the boys to these kinds of things in order to round out their home schooling curriculum. Dustin and Nathan attended the entire series of art classes and had a great time. At one class they made life-sized drawings of themselves and another time they actually made their own paper and painted a picture on it. I was so impressed with Nathan's painting that I pressed it between two pieces of cardboard and toted it around with us throughout the remainder of our travels. Today it has been professionally framed and matted and hangs on my living room wall but I must confess I have no idea what the picture is supposed to be.

Daryl got the exterior of the house completed so that we were protected from the elements. The interior would be done as we were able to get building materials. I was the main painter. I had painted our bath/shower outhouse and by mid April I had the exterior of the main house painted as well. From the outside it looked pretty good; inside, not so much.

Lunar Glow had sustained some minor damage during the storm so between waiting for materials to work on the house Daryl would go down to the harbor and work on the boat.

One day while Daryl was at the lumber yard he noticed a new radial arm saw that had just come in. The price on it was unbelievably low; they were almost giving it away.

"Hey," Daryl questioned the salesman. "Is this price right. What's the catch?"

"No catch. It just arrived with the last shipment of lumber but it won't turn on. We don't have room to store it and just need to get it out of here. Do you want it?"

"Sure. If that price is for real I'll take it."

"Okay, Sir. For $25.00 it's yours."

"Oh, just one other thing," Daryl added. "I think it's too big to fit in my car. Do you think it could be delivered?"

"Sure. We can do that for you". And they did.

Daryl was exceptionally good at analyzing and repairing things. Once the saw was delivered to the house he started looking it over. What he discovered was a safety cap that had been put over the on/off switch to protect it during shipping. Once that was removed the saw started right up and worked perfectly. It was truly a God send in helping us rebuild the rest of the house.

Jerad was having a busy month. In addition to school he continued to attend a Seminary class at the church each morning before school. He was a great student and was inducted into the National Honor Society. Jerad got his court and police clearance papers for his driver's license and on April 30 he went in to take his driving test. Unfortunately, he failed. He retook it the following day and this time, because he now knew that he had to actually turn his head to look and see if traffic was coming before changing lanes, etc., and not just look in his mirror, he passed.

Although I was no longer working as a librarian at the South Pacific Elementary I had been asked to do some substitute teaching. I usually worked a day or two each week bouncing around between the 1st and 8th grades. It was sort of fun and I enjoyed it.

Nathan and Dustin completed their art classes towards the middle of May and I took them, along with Nathan's little buddy, Mafutaga, to register for Little League baseball. We seemed to spend a lot of time going to baseball practice but now that Jerad was driving he was able to help out driving sometimes.

CHAPTER SIXTY-NINE

MORE TRIPS

Mother's Day was extra special for me that year. My boys knew that it had been a long time since I had seen my parents in California. Much to my surprise, Jerad had been working with the family to collect enough money to buy me a round trip plane ticket to see my family in the states. He had saved up money from his jobs on the island and got contributions from Michael and my parents. It was almost as great to see the pleasure it gave my sons to give me this gift as it was to get it. I wouldn't actually make the trip until after the school year ended and Jerad had graduated from high school.

It was only a few days after the boys had given me my Mother's Day surprise that Daryl decided that he needed another trip back to the states himself. After all it had been about six months since Daryl had made that trip. Some things never changed.

Jerad's high school graduation was on June 13th. He looked so nice in his white shirt and blue lava lava wrapped around his waist. He also wore a beautiful fresh flower lei around his neck. He was an excellent student and had become a fine young man. I was so very proud of him. The Tiai family had a graduation party for him at their house after the ceremony at the school.

Jerad had earned an academic scholarship to BYU in Hawaii and was excited at the prospect of another new adventure. He would make a trip back to California to spend some time with his dad, Michael, and my parents before heading off to Hawaii at the end of the summer. We were busy trying to get everything ready for his trip. I made him a padded travel bag for his surfboard and sewed him a very impressive briefcase out of heavy canvas. We would shop for new school clothes in California.

Daryl flew to LA two days after Jerad's graduation and would stay with Grant and Denise. Jerad left three days after that. I missed Jerad so much it hurt. There was still a lot of work to do on the interior of the house and I was getting lots of sail repair jobs as well. I drove down to the harbor early each morning to check on the boat and pick up sewing jobs. Between working on the house, sewing, doing school work with the younger boys, baseball practice and games, I stayed busy.

For some reason there didn't seem to be much sheetrock to be found for the interior walls. We could, however, get sheets of masonite so that is what we covered most of the interior walls with. I ordered more masonite after Daryl left for the mainland and between Dustin, Nathan, and myself we were able to get the interior walls nearly finished. By the time Daryl returned to Pago Pago on July 10th we not only had the walls up but I had them painted as well.

I was scheduled to leave for my trip six days after Daryl returned. This would be the first time I had left Daryl in charge of the boys. They were old enough to take care of themselves and with the Tiai family next door I knew they would be okay but I was still a little bit nervous.

Flights out of Samoa are always in the wee hours of the morning. I had to leave for the airport at 2:30am in order to catch my flight. Daryl was sick and said he had to stay in bed.

"Dustin, Nathan, wake up. I need you to come with me." I was shaking my sons awake out of a sound sleep.

"What's wrong? Why do we need to get up?" Dustin questioned.

"Do we get to go to Grandma's house too?" Nathan wanted to know.

"No. But Daryl says he's sick and can't drive me to the airport. If I don't leave soon I'm going to miss my flight."

"Do I get to drive you?" Dustin was wide awake now.

"No. I'm going to drive. What I need for you guys to do is to go with me and when we get to the airport I'll find you a taxi and you will bring the car keys back home. Then when Daryl is feeling better he can take a taxi back out to the airport and pick up the car. Hurry up now and get some clothes on."

We got to the airport on time and I was able to find a taxi for the boys. I paid the driver and gave him directions back to our house. I went to check my luggage only to find out that my flight would be delayed by three and a half hours. As if this wasn't bad enough, the delayed flight would make me miss my connection in Hawaii so I had to sit in Honolulu and wait an additional seven and a half hours more. It was 5:30 am the following day when I finally arrived in San Francisco. Mom, Dad and Jerad were all there to meet me. I was really tired but so happy to see them all.

I spent a little over five weeks in California. Michael was excited to show me his apartment and introduce me to his new girlfriend. I visited with aunts and uncles and cousins and friends. We went to ball games and plays and out to play miniature golf. We went out to eat and to the movies and worked in the yard. We took a road trip to Nevada so that I could check on things at our house in Stagecoach. We shopped a lot trying to get Jerad ready for college, but mostly we just spent quality family time together which was great.

The plan was for me to stay with my folks until Jerad was ready to leave for Hawaii. I would accompany him that far and get him checked into the college then return to Samoa.

CHAPTER SEVENTY

COLLEGE

My time in the Bay Area seemed to fly by and before I knew it, it was time for Jerad and I to leave for Hawaii. We said our goodbyes at the San Francisco International Airport and boarded our plane. Our old friends from *Stickwitch* were now living on their boat in Honolulu. Pat, Bill, and Rachelle picked us up at the airport and delivered us to the BYU campus on Oahu's north shore. They would pick us up later and take us to Bill's father's condo at the Turtle Bay Hilton. It was currently empty and we would be able to stay there for the next three nights.

Jerad and I lugged all of his belongings, including the surfboard, to the main office where we checked in and were assigned a guide to show us around the campus. Our guide was a clean cut, polite young man. Our first stop would be to Jerad's new dorm room where we could deposit his stuff.

"Now I want to warn you before we go in that the dorm rooms are really small," our guide said in the way of an apology before he opened the door. "Jerad, you have a roommate. His name is Edward and he has already checked in so his things are already in the room." We nodded our heads as he swung the door open. The room was long and very narrow. It reminded me of one of those tandem garages where you park one car directly behind another one rather than side by side. Along the left wall were two single size beds nearly touching one another head to toe. On the right side of the room was a built in desk/dresser unit built along the wall. Each occupant had a desk area with some drawers for storage and a tall closet space of maybe two feet where clothes could be hung up. There was just enough room between the beds and desk space for a person to pass through providing they weren't too large. At the end of the room was a small bathroom.

"WOW! This is great!" Jerad exclaimed as he surveyed the room.

Our guide's mouth dropped open and he looked at Jerad as if in unbelief. "Nobody has ever said these rooms are great."

"Oh, you don't understand", I explained. "Jerad has been living on a sailboat where all of his belongings had to fit into a cubbyhole about two feet wide and three feet deep. His bed has been a two inch piece of foam on a hard surface. In comparison this is a mansion." We completed our tour and I felt peace of mind at knowing that this would be a good environment for my son while we were so many miles away.

The following two days passed quickly. Jerad completed his paperwork and took some placement tests. We explored more of the campus and spent time at the Polynesian Cultural Center which was quite near the school. Most of the employees of the Polynesian Cultural Center were actually BYU students, most of which came from the many islands of the South Pacific.

My flight back to Samoa was late on Sunday afternoon. Pat, Bill, and Rachelle went out to lunch with Jerad and I then took me on to the airport. I can't even start to explain how hard it was for me to get on that plane and leave Jerad behind. I cried all the way to Samoa. Not just quiet tears. I sobbed and sobbed. By the time we landed my eyes were red and swollen. I knew I looked a sight but I didn't care. At least I would be with my two youngest sons again. Life would go on.

CHAPTER SEVENTY-ONE

BACK TO THE GRIND

All was well when I returned to Samoa. In some ways things had even improved. Daryl and the boys had seemed to form some sort of bond and were getting along well together. Daryl had even been able to handle the one incident requiring a visit to the emergency room while I was gone. While Dustin lay sleeping on the foam mat in his room that served as his bed an unwelcomed centipede crawled in and bit him on the ear. The centipede was captured in a jar and taken with them to the emergency room at the Clinic. All turned out well.

They had started rotating the cooking duties and each one had their specialty dish. It became apparent that on Nathan's night we knew the menu would be cooked pasta covered with Prego, cooked frozen vegetables, frozen French fries, and canned fruit for dessert. It worked, and after all Nathan was only nine. Dustin almost always something he called chili cheese potatoes. It was really quite good.

The house itself was looking good. Most of the work on the house had been completed and Daryl no longer needed the radial arm saw. He sold it for $400.00.

Lunar Glow had sustained some damage during Hurricane Ofa plus the wear and tear of crossing the Pacific Ocean had taken its toll on the boat. With the work on the house about finished we turned our attention to the boat. There were many things that could be done while the boat sat in the water, however, it really needed to be hauled out in order to do some of the necessary work. Samoa didn't have a boatyard that could haul us out. We knew there was one in Fiji but we were really nervous about sailing that far for repairs plus it was really too late in the season for us to take off there. Someone told us that they were pretty sure there was a place in Tonga where we could haul out and gave Daryl the contact information. Daryl was able to talk with someone at the boatyard in Tonga. He explained to the man the size of our boat (primarily that we were 24 feet wide) and was told "yes", they could accommodate our boat. He reserved a date for us in late October.

Our plan was to do as much work on the boat as we could here in Samoa for the next five or six weeks then sail to Tonga, haul the boat out of the water and spend a week or two doing dry dock repairs, then return to Samoa where we would stay until the following April. At that point we would pack up and head out for good.

Mrs. Tiai was very pleased with the way we had rebuilt our little house; now she wanted Daryl to build her a new house as well. He was having nothing to do with that. It was already September and Mrs. Tiai had already blown through a good portion of the $22,000 she had received from FEMA and nothing had been done on her house. Finally some family members from Western Samoa arrived to do the work. Daryl helped some at first but when he saw the kind of work they were doing he threw up his hands and walked away. Even Nathan could see that the work they did might keep some rain out but if the wind blew very hard the whole thing would blow apart. They said, "Oh well. If it blows apart FEMA will give us more money!" The US Government is great at handing out money but not at following up on how it is spent.

I gave the boat a thorough cleaning during this time and made new curtains for the seatee and head. We went to the clinic for dental appointments and check ups with the doctor. Nathan had several planters warts on his feet that had to be cut out and stitched. Then he fell on his bicycle and split the back of his head open; more stitches. I took several of the Tiai family members on errands to the lumberyard, feed store for pig feed, to the clinic, pick up and drop offs at the airport, and just shopping in general. I had become their personal taxi driver.

By now Liai had become very close to our family and when she learned that we were getting ready to leave for Tonga she wanted to go with us. We loved her and would have been delighted to take her with us. With Jerad gone we would have an empty bunk on the boat. She had just learned a short time before this that her real mother was actually Mrs. Tiai's oldest daughter. Liai and I both wrote letters to her mother, Tua, in Texas asking for permission for us to take Liai with us. We got a response back from Tua. She said that would be fine with her as long as Mrs. Tiai didn't care. We went to talk to Mrs. Tiai. She said no, Liai could not leave because she did too much work around the house and they needed her there. We were heartbroken.

As we were working on the boat Daryl found a spot where termites had entered. It wasn't bad but we weren't taking any chances. We had the exterminators out to fumigate the boat. We went to see Captain Patane, the Port Captain to let him know we were taking a trip to Tonga. He assured us that he would keep our spot in the harbor open for us when we returned. Things were just about ready for us to go. We had been on land for too many months so I think we were all just a little bit nervous about taking out to sea again. I celebrated my 41st birthday on October 15th and the next day we loaded up the boat. We did our check out the following day and left the dock in the late afternoon.

CHAPTER SEVENTY-TWO

OFF TO TONGA

We left Samoa under a sunny blue sky and calm seas but by the following night the seas were rough and stormy. Daryl and Nathan were sick which left most of the sailing work to Dustin and myself. There was a lot of wind. We reefed the mainsail down but there was still way too much wind and it tore one of the reef points right out of the sail. This meant that we had to reduce the sail down even further. We sailed through the night and the storm continued. By the next morning Nathan was feeling better but Daryl was still sick.

As the sun rose on day three we could see Tonga in the distance. The weather had turned nice once again and Daryl was now feeling better. We reached the anchorage and had our hook in the water by noon. Some local kids swan out to the boat to greet us and Dustin and Nathan were happy to have some new friends to play with.

The water in Tonga is beautiful, clean and clear. Perfect for swimming and snorkeling, and to Dustin's delight, spear fishing. There are many small islands and dozens of anchorages. We anchored in many of them.

Sometimes we would have our own private island with beautiful white sand beaches. Was this heaven? Often the local people would row out to our boat to sell or trade fruit or hand crafts. Many of them spoke some English which was certainly a plus for us. The fruit and vegetables there were excellent and cheap. For example, you could buy three nice pineapples or three large papayas for one Tongan dollar which was equivalent to about 75 cents US.

At one island we met the local policeman. He invited us to a Tongan feast at his house. He was having roasted baby pig in addition to the many other dishes his wife prepared. The pig had been skewered with a sharp stick which ran right through the pig from its mouth to its rear. It was then hand turned over an open fire in the yard for a full two hours. Several men took turns turning the pig. It was so tender and yummy! Dustin and Nathan ended up spending the night there with the policeman's kids and we all accepted an invitation the following morning to attend church with his family. They attended the Free Church of Tonga which we found quite interesting.

There was no electricity on many of the small outlying islands including this one. In the evening, however, they would fire up small gas generators so that they could have lights. I don't know how many islands there are total in Tonga but I do know that a person could easily spend a year here and never see all there is to see. There are three main island groups in

Tonga. We had sailed into the Vavau group which is the northern most group and located about 330 miles SW of Samoa. The boatyard where we had a appointment to haul *Lunar Glow* out of the water was actually in Neiafu. We had given ourselves plenty of time to explore this new territory before our haul out date and we took advantage of it. We sailed from one island to another where we would go to shore and hike the island and swim in their pristine waters. We continued doing schoolwork and boat chores each morning so it wasn't all fun and games. I also got the torn out reef point in our mainsail repaired and also fixed a tear we had gotten in our Yankee.

We finally sailed into Neiafu on the appointed day of our haul out appointment. There was actually a hotel here with a dock so we pulled up there. We filled our water tanks and did our laundry and while the boys went swimming in the hotel swimming pool, Daryl and I went in search of the boatyard.

We found the boatyard and it was really quite nice. Only one problem. It could not haul out a boat as wide as ours. I wanted to scream! I love the Polynesian people but sometimes they are so agreeable that they give out misinformation in an attempt to be friendly. This was the case with the gentleman saying yes they could haul our boat out when in reality they could not. Another example of this had occurred a few months before. I had gone into the local hardware store in Pago Pago in search of some rust remover. After looking through the shelves of various types of cleaners and chemicals and not finding what I was looking for I went in search of a salesperson. I found a sales lady and asked her if they had any rust remover and explained what I needed it for. "Oh, yes we do," replied the lady.

"Good," I said. "Could you tell me where it's at? I didn't see it on the shelf where I thought it would be."

"Just go down this isle to the very end and then turn to your left," she said pointing me in the right direction. "It's in the back corner."

I thanked her and headed off in the direction she had pointed out. Once in the back corner of the store I looked around and couldn't find anything. There was literally nothing there except a door to the bathroom. Strange. Well maybe they kept the rust remover in the bathroom for some reason. After all, this was Samoa and some things were just beyond reason. I entered the bathroom. Nothing there but a toilet and vanity with a sink.

Okay so maybe they kept it under the sink. I opened the vanity doors and looked through its contents. Paper towels, toilet paper, a can of cleanser, but no rust remover. Dang. It was then that it hit me. The sales lady had heard the word 'rust remover' and decided it was 'restroom'. From then on she stopped listening to what I was saying and just wanted to help me by pointing out where the restroom was. And, no, I found out later, they did not carry rust remover.

We stayed on for another week in Tonga. As long as we were here we might as well enjoy ourselves. We sailed back out to one of the pretty bays and dropped our anchor. The weather was beautiful for several days but by the time we returned to Neiafu to go to the market and do our check out procedure it was becoming overcast and gloomy. We decided to sit out at anchor until the weather cleared and we could return to Samoa. We were now into the first week of November.

After three days Daryl stated that we had waited long enough. Bad weather or not, we were heading back to Samoa. This turned out to be our very worse sail ever and one I will never forget. We pulled our anchor at 7:30am and headed out. The seas were rough and we had strong winds on our nose. We hadn't been out long when Daryl informed me that he was sick … again, and had to lay down. Nathan wasn't feeling too good either. Dustin and I took turns at the wheel throughout the day and we tried to get some sleep in between. We had our two dinghies lashed down to the boat on either side of the cabin top. We had also tied down everything else we thought might blow off the boat. By nightfall Nathan was feeling better but Daryl was still in bed sick. In nice weather we would let Nathan take a turn at the wheel during the day and Dustin could even do some short night watches. This, however, was nowhere near nice weather. It was, in fact, the worst I had ever seen.

Before dark the boys and I were able to reduce our sails down as much as possible. We reefed down the main and had our storm jib up. After that I wouldn't even allow the boys to be up on deck at all. The wind was blowing something fierce and even standing upright was becoming a challenge. There should have been some moonlight but the skies were so cloudy the moon couldn't shine through. I had donned my foul weather gear not only because of the rain but for the waves which would crash over the boat every few minutes. Our wheel was in the center of the boat in our cockpit. It had a compass mounted just behind the wheel which had a light on it. I knew the course we needed to stay on to reach Samoa and also knew that I couldn't let the boat get sideways to the waves. If this happened, one of the big waves coming at us could flip our whole vessel over. I spent approximately eight hours with my feet planted in the exact same spot in front of that wheel. I had to squint through salty eyelashes to see the compass as the waves broke over *Lunar Glow* and rained salt water over my head. My yellow rain hat helped to keep my hair out of my face and that was a plus. I was scared. My knees knocked together so hard that I feared by morning they would be bruised, if indeed, we saw morning. And I can tell you I have never prayed so hard in all my life. I know the Lord helped me through that awful night because I never could have done it on my own.

The following day was much the same; Daryl was still sick, I was still tired, and the storm raged on, but somehow things don't seem quite as bad in the light of day. What we did discover on this morning was that we somehow lost our Avon inflatable dinghy during the night. We thought it had been tied down good enough but apparently not and with the noise of the wind, rain, and crashing waves I never heard it go.

We got through day two much the same as the first. Dustin was taking a turn at the wheel when suddenly there was a big crash. Our strobe light which had been attached to the top of our 45 foot mast blew off and crashed onto the deck not two feet from Dustin's head before bouncing off into the sea. Again I knew we were being watched over.

By the third morning the seas were still rough and the wind remained strong and on our nose but the rain had stopped and Daryl was feeling better and able to take over the wheel for a while. We pulled up at the Customs Dock at 7:30pm. It had taken us a total of 60 hours to make our return trip; it felt like much more. We remained at the Customs Dock all of that night and most of the next day waiting for clearance from customs and immigration. We were back on Samoan time!

CHAPTER SEVENTY-THREE

ANOTHER CHRISTMAS

O ur boat was in desperate need of repair. After the terrible pounding it took returning from Tonga it was even worse than before. We knew we couldn't make any long passages with her this way. In mid November we went to talk to the Harbor Master, our friend, Captain Patane. We explained our dilemma to him and asked if he had any suggestions. He told us that there was a government crane that should be big enough to lift us out of the water. He would arrange for the crane to set our boat right there on the Customs Dock so that we could work on it. The bad news was that the crane was down for repairs. The good news was that it should be fixed in a couple of weeks time. This would be a wonderful Christmas present! But we should have realized that we, once again, were on Samoan time and a couple of weeks turned out to be several months.

In the meantime life went on as usual and we prepared for yet another Christmas in Samoa. I continued to do sail repair work and, of course, schoolwork with the boys. Daryl spent most of his time working on the boat but also managed to build cabinets in the kitchen and tile the counter top. The boys played with their friends and we baked and delivered Christmas cookies. In mid December a huge planeload of fir trees arrived on the island so we were able buy a real Christmas tree this year. The boys and I made decorations for the tree and it really did look quite festive. We had hoped that Jerad would be home for Christmas but his father had sent him a plane ticket to California which Jerad felt obligated to use. This would make two years in a row that Jerad was away for Christmas. I was sad but at least Jerad would be with family. I think Liai missed Jerad almost as much as we did. She was spending more and more time at our house and had become like one of the family. We were still upset that she would not be able to go with us when we would eventually leave the island for good. It would be like losing another child.

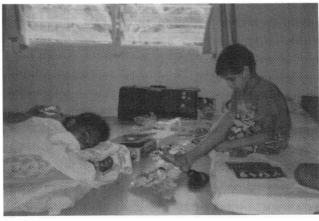

CHAPTER SEVENTY-FOUR

HOSPITAL, WAR, AND SO MUCH MORE

The weeks following Christmas were both busy and confusing. Our plans for the future changed almost weekly. Jerad would fly back to Samoa in late May and help us work on the boat. We agreed to pay him for the work he did as he was trying to earn money to go on a church mission. He also had some fun surfing trips planned for later in the summer and then would go to work for his dad in the Bay Area for a while. He was trying to talk us into sailing the boat back to the states by way of Hawaii. We weren't too excited by that idea as sailing in that direction was a lot of hard work and Jerad wasn't willing to make the trip with us.

Next was the war. The Gulf War had broke out which made me really nervous. I now had two sons that were of draft age. I prayed that the war wouldn't last long but I refused to leave Samoa until it was over. In the event that my sons were called to war I wanted to be somewhere where I could be notified about what was going on.

Then there was a medical problem that had to be dealt with. Back in

1973 when Jerad was just a baby, I had silicone breast implants done. It was a silly thing to do but frankly I just got tired of the boy's father always making jokes in public about my boobs being the size of eggs ... fried! Anyway, I had had the surgery to stop the jokes and keep what was left of my self-esteem and now some 18 years later one of the implants had ruptured.

I went to the the medical clinic because of the lumps in my left breast. Once again, I should have known, but there was not a doctor on the entire island who had ever seen let alone dealt with breast implants. This was early in 1991 and Samoa was still a long ways from catching up with the rest of the world. I felt like a lab rat as several doctors leaned in to examine my breasts while I laid prone on the exam table. After each of them had taken a turn at poking and prodding it was concluded that they would need to do a biopsy. We scheduled a date for the following week.

I had to go back the day before the biopsy so that they could do blood work, take a chest x-ray, do a Pap smear, and an EKG. I also had to meet with the surgeon who decided to call a plastic surgeon at the military hospital in Honolulu to find out what to look for and how to proceed. I can tell you this did nothing to build my confidence. This whole process took up most of the day.

I returned the following morning, they knocked me out, did the biopsy and that was that. I could have gone home that night but I got sick when I sat up and tried to eat dinner so I had to stay the night. Oh yeah. And my surgeon still hadn't heard back from the plastic surgeon in Hawaii. Great.

It was weeks before the results of my biopsy came back. It was determined that the lumps were actually caused by silicone leaking out of the left breast implant. I decided to have the implants removed. The original surgery back in 1973 had lasted less than 30 minutes. This shouldn't take much longer I reasoned. Wrong.

Once again I was knocked out and taken into surgery. I learned later that every available doctor there was in the operating room looking on at the lab rat. My surgeon had the plastic surgeon from Hawaii on the phone and was being walked through my operation. Good thing I was knocked out. I don't remember how long the surgery took but it was way more than 30 minutes. I ended up spending two more days in the hospital and it was not a fun experience. At least it didn't cost much; just the standard $2.00 as was the price for all services there.

I had to return to the clinic once a week after that which lasted up until the time we left the island. For some reason, and nobody seemed to know why, my left breast kept filling up with fluid. I would go to the clinic where with the use of a huge syringe they would aspirate large amounts of amber colored fluid from my swollen breast. This resulted in my going into the clinic with a very lopsided chest and coming out with breasts of equal size, only to become lopsided again by the following week as my left breast refilled with fluid.

I had bought Jerad a plane ticket for the 28th of May when I figured he would be finished with his first year of college. He surprised us, however, when he knocked on our front door at 6am in the last week of April. You couldn't even walk through our living room on the morning of his arrival as I had seven huge sails which I was repairing spread out over the floor. We didn't care. We were just happy to have Jerad home again.

Our boat still hadn't been taken out of the water but we had heard that the government crane was operational again. Jerad, our hired hand, was here and we needed to get this show on the road.

CHAPTER SEVENTY-FIVE

HAUL OUT ... SAMOAN STYLE

We went to see Captain Patane once again and stressed our urgency in getting *Lunar Glow* taken out of the water for repairs. He assured us that he would have everything arranged soon.

The water in Pago Pago Harbor is very dirty and polluted. On a nice sunny day we sailed the boat out into some clear blue water and anchored her there. We spent an enjoyable day in the water cleaning the bottom of the boat and inspecting the damage to get ready for our haul out. A split in our main keel had grown larger and there was a crack under one of our wing decks that would have to be repaired. We also needed to paint the exterior and especially put a new coat of bottom paint on the hulls. We had already done about as much to the inside as we possibly could. We had sanded, painted, and varnished pretty much the whole interior. I had made new curtains, a bimini top for the cockpit, and seatee cushions. The boat looked better than it ever had.

The day finally arrived for the crane to lift us out of the water. I don't believe this arrangement had ever been made for a private vessel before and I would venture to say it hasn't been done again since. We pulled *Lunar Glow* up alongside the customs dock. The huge yellow crane was sitting off to the side. On the dock were four big 55 gallon drums with planks of wood on top of them. Two drums would be placed under each of our ama hulls to hold the boat up off the ground. This was just high enough so that our main center hull cleared the ground by just inches.

When our boat had been built it had four long, flat pieces of stainless steel with a big ring at the top built right into our cabin top. The steel plates had been built in for this very purpose; to lift the boat. Daryl and Jerad attached heavy chains to each of the four steel rings and pulled the other end of the chains up to a single huge hook hanging down from the crane. Next, before exiting the boat, they attached guide ropes to the stern and bow of the boat in order to guide it onto the barrels once the crane had it in the air. This was a very nerve racking experience. The crane made a couple of jerks and groaned as it lifted *Lunar Glow* up clear of the water and even higher up into the air in order to clear the side of the dock. Our boat looked like a huge gull hovering in the air. If something went wrong here we were doomed. I think we were all holding our breath as the boat dangled in the air, rotated to the side, and then was slowly lowered down. The men on the ground were now using the guide ropes as well as physically grabbing onto the ama bows to set her in place on the 55 gallon drums. There was a collective sigh of relief when the boat settled down into place on the dock.

Someone would always be there working on the boat during the day but we were concerned about it being broken into at night. Jerad would spend his nights on the boat and sometimes Dustin would spend the night there too. Jerad had volunteered to be Dustin's teacher for the remainder of Dustin's 8th grade schoolwork. He had planned to have 8th grade completed before Jerad arrived home but between Jerad's early arrival and Dustin dragging his feet he still had more work to do. Their evenings together gave them a good time not only to work on schoolwork but to just spend time together. Dustin had a very hard time when Jerad left for college as they were so close to each other even with a four and a half years age difference.

The boat was out of the water for nearly a month but we wanted to make sure we took advantage of this time and did every bit of work we could. It looked great. Now to get it back into the water. The government crane was a little faster this time. It only took days to get it to the dock as compared to the months it took before.

Once the work on the boat was completed and we had her back in the water it was time to do some heavy provisioning and finish up our business in Samoa.

CHAPTER SEVENTY-SIX

MOVING ON

Our sailing plans had changed almost weekly over the past months. We had abandoned the plan to sail back to the states via Hawaii. We knew that we would continue sailing west. At one point Jerad was going to sail with us to Tonga and then on to Fiji. From there he would fly back to the Bay Area, go surfing in Mexico with his friends, then go to work for his dad. He changed his mind about this plan when he realized that it would probably be mid August or even early September before we reached Suva, Fiji. No, he would fly back to California from Samoa and then figure out the rest of his plans.

We still hadn't told Mrs. Tiai our plans to leave for good, and, as I had feared, she was upset. She had been quite happy with our private "taxi" service and the other things we were able to do for her. I decided I would use my parents as the excuse for leaving.

"Good morning, Mataua. How are you today?" I asked Mrs. Tiai, calling her by her given name.

"Oh, Talofa, Dear. Good, and how are you?"

"We are all good. Only we really miss Jerad now that he has gone back to the states. We sure did like having him here … and I need to let you know that we will all be leaving soon also."

"Oh, you go on vacation again?" she questioned.

"Well, no. As soon as we can get our car and furniture sold we are going to be leaving Samoa for good."

"Why you go? You family here. You stay."

"We can't do that. It's my parents. They are getting older and need us to be close by. Samoa is just too far away." I thought that this would be something she could relate to and make our leaving a little bit easier. She didn't need to know our real plans to keep traveling.

"Oh, that be okay. They your family, they my family. You tell them that they can live here too." Great! That didn't go as I had planned.

"I don't think that will ever happen. We just need to sell our things here and be on our way. We are so grateful to be part of your family and will miss you all so much. We would still like to take Liai along with us, too."

"No. Liai have much work to do here. She no go. I buy your things myself."

"Okay. I'll check with Daryl and see what price we need for the car and furniture and let you know." I gave her a hug and left.

In the end, Mataua had no money to buy anything so we sold the car, refrigerator, big sewing machine, couch and chair and just left the rest of the household things there. She was happy with that.

It was the afternoon of July 1, 1991 when we finally left Samoa for the last time. Our departure had been delayed for a couple of days due to bad weather. The boat was fully provisioned including a good supply of birdseed for our little Sweetie Pie. Saying good bye to Liai tore my heart out. I prayed that she would be alright and promised to write.

We averaged nearly seven and a half knots all the way to Tonga. We had a steady 18 - 25 knots of wind on our beam and nobody got sick. We used Mike, our autopilot, so nobody had to stand at the wheel and steer. The boys were happy. Life didn't get any better than this.

We met up with our friends on *Mikasa* who we had met in Samoa. The father, Bill, was a doctor and had been working at the medical clinic in Pago Pago while they were there and, in fact, Bill had been the doctor that Daryl was seeing for his high blood pressure. It was rather reassuring to have your doctor anchored right next to you. They had three children on board. Michael, the oldest son, was Dustin's age. They had become the very best of friends. Next was a daughter, Castle, a year younger. Dustin was rather taken with her as well. The youngest was another boy, Sean, who was a little bit younger than Nathan.

We also met some new folks from Australia, Jan and Alan Teal. They had a trimiran, *Tri-Reality,* which they had built in New Zealand and was the same design as ours. They had no children but were loads of fun to be with. They gave us lots of information on where we could safely sit out the cyclone season in Australia. They also had a crew member sailing along with them; a 70 year old gentleman from Dublin, Ireland. He was making his way around the world crewing on whatever boat he could. He was always laughing and having fun. He was continually quizzing the boys on their spelling. John was a retired pilot for Irish Airways and had also flown for the RAF in WWII. Anyway, he said he nearly failed his exam for the RAF because he couldn't spell diarrhea correctly so he considered that a most important word to spell.

After the schoolwork routine in the mornings the boys would swim, dive, fish, sail, hike, play games with their friends, and have fires on the beach after dark. I found plenty to keep me busy as well. We still had our hand cranked sewing machine onboard. I used it to make tote bags, a guitar case, covers for all of our boat bumpers, as well as shorts for Daryl, Dustin, and Nathan. I also made handmade flags for each of the countries we would visit. They were usually a lot of work but we were required to fly those flags along with our own when in a foreign country. We were having a wonderful time and felt bad that Jerad wasn't here to enjoy this with us. We wondered how he was doing but knew we wouldn't be receiving any mail until we arrived in Suva, Fiji.

We remained mostly in the outer islands of Tonga. There was no electricity except for in Neiafu. We were able to get lots of wonderful produce like yams and breadfruit, etc. These usually came by way of the locals who would row out to the boat with their wares. Sometimes they had shells and baskets for sale as well. Not all of the islands were inhabited. We anchored by one such island, a beautiful place, where we went to shore and got all of the drinking nuts, grapefruit, lemons and limes we wanted. These made wonderful drinks. We also ran our water desalinator for a couple of hours each day which supplied us with all the fresh water we needed.

Daryl and I had an interesting dining experience on one of the islands. We had heard of a unique little restaurant in an out of the way place and made arrangements along with two other couples to have dinner there. All of our kids had dinner and a party of their own on *Lunar Glow*. To reach this place was an adventure all on its own. We went the first distance by dinghy. Next we followed a very narrow trail up and down for about 10 minutes time through some very dense trees. The trail was marked periodically with white paint to show you the way. The restaurant turned out to be a tiny hut with a palm leaf roof and sat completely isolated from any other habitation. It was a Spanish restaurant which had opened about a year and a half before when a couple from Spain sailed in and decided to stay. They spoke very little English and there were no menus. In fact, they had to be notified ahead of time in order for you to eat there. One of our cruising couples had already done that for us, thus we were expected. There were three rickety tables but overall the atmosphere was nice with interesting things hanging all about. I love Mexican food and in my mind that was what we would be having. I was wrong. The fare was "Spanish" and nothing like Mexican cuisine. It was okay but I liked Mexican food better.

After dinner we were entertained with live music. The cook, Maria, played the drums and the saxophone. Her husband played the guitar, harmonica, and sang. Besides the six of us there was a honeymoon couple from Sydney, Australia. They were lots of fun and before long the little hut had become lively with music and dancing.

Most of the boats we met now were from Australia, New Zealand, and some from Europe. We loved listening to them talk. Although they spoke English, many of the words they used were different than ours and it was almost like listening to a foreign language. Dustin and Nathan thought it was great fun to speak "Aussie" and after a while it was hard to understand them too!

We were getting excited to get to Fiji. We had been in Tonga only three weeks and had planned to stay longer but the weather was perfect for sailing and we were ready to see what lay ahead to the west. After filling our water and fuel tanks and washing our clothes in a bucket on the dock (no laundry mat in Tonga), we checked out and left Neiafu for the last time. It was July 23, 1991.

CHAPTER SEVENTY-SEVEN

FIJI HERE WE COME

Our sail to Fiji was rather slow and leisurely. We had very light winds for the most part but the days were sunny and warm and there was a full moon at night. Nobody got sick. Nathan was now beginning to take on more jobs on the boat. Although we used "Mike" a lot during the day, Nathan still felt quite important standing at the wheel during his watch. *Tri-Reality* had left Tonga the same time as we did so it was fun to be sailing along with friends. We crossed the International Date Line the day before arriving in Fiji. We had a celebration at that moment and I gave the boys their Golden Dragon certificates that I had carried along with us since leaving San Diego four years earlier. It was a fun day.

We picked up a little bit of tailwind on our second day out.

Daryl thought this might be a good opportunity for us to try to fly our big colorful spinnaker once again. It hadn't even been taken out of its sail bag again since the disastrous day in Puerto Escondido, Mexico when Nathan had let go of the halyard and sent the spinnaker over the bow of the boat and into the water.

Once again, Daryl gave each of us our assignments. Dustin and I would take care of handling the sail from up on the bow. Nathan would be positioned at the mast where he would control the halyard. Daryl would be at the wheel. Hoisting the spinnaker and getting it adjusted went smoothly. The huge sail filled with air and was pushing us along quite nicely. We relaxed and went about our normal boat routine. Later in the day as the sun was beginning to drop the winds began to increase and Daryl announced that we should get the spinnaker down and bagged while we still had some daylight.

We all returned to our previously assigned stations.

"Nathan," Daryl instructed. "Remember, when I give you the word let off on the halyard. Slowly. You might need to take a wrap or two off the winch but whatever you do, Do Not let go of that rope."

Nathan nodded his head.

"Do you understand?"

"Yes, Sir. Do not let go of the rope."

"Good. Okay. Dustin and Kay. As soon as you feel some slack on the sail start gathering it into your arms just as fast as you can. And whatever you do, Do Not let it fall into the water. Got it?"

"Got it", Dustin and I called back.

"Okay. Here we go. Nathan, let off on the halyard."

"It's still too tight. We can't pull it in," Dustin yelled.

"Take a wrap off the winch."

"It's still too tight. We can't get the sail down."

"Nathan, get the wraps off the winch so they can pull the sail in," Daryl instructed.

With that Nathan whipped the remaining wraps off the winch and Dustin and I gathered the huge sail into our arms. "Good job, guys. We did it!"

We unclipped the halyard form the sail and attached it to the forestay. It was then that we noticed that Nathan was no longer standing at his station by the mast. In fact he wasn't even in the cockpit. Then from somewhere overhead we heard a rather shaky voice, "Moooooom". We looked up and saw Nathan up at the first spreader still holding on tight to that halyard! Well he had followed Daryl's instructions. He didn't let go of the halyard and instead rode it up the mast as we had pulled the sail down.

As we sailed closer to the islands we made sure to stay well offshore until we had good daylight. There are many shallow reefs surrounding the islands and we had heard several stories about boats running up onto the reefs and going down. We didn't want that to happen to us. Even though we were a shallow draft boat we wanted to be careful. Once it was daylight, Dustin put on a pair of Polaroid sunglasses and climbed the mast to sit on the first spreaders. From there and with the aid of the glasses he was able to see the reefs in the water and direct our course into Suva.

The following is taken from a letter I wrote home on September 7, 1991:

We are anchored off one of the villages on the island of Waya in Fiji. These villages are remote and extremely simple. There are no stores of any kind and no electricity. The houses are beautiful. Real grass huts but quite well done. Sand floors with mats. No furniture. Most of the cooking is done outdoors. The men fish and grow some small crops up on the mountain. Lots of children. The first thing we have to do when arriving in a village is to take kava root to the chief. It is presented in a certain way. You hold it in both hands and place it on the ground in front of the chief. You then ask for permission to stay in his village. If he picks it up he is accepting you as his guest and assumes responsibility for you. He also gives you free run of the village and surrounding waters. Actually several men participate in the kava ceremony. The chief closes his eyes like he's praying and says something, then the men clap twice, then the chief says something else, more clapping, etc. This goes on for about 3-4 minutes. We don't know what he is saying but we figure it's something like, "Here come more suckers bringing us kava"! It's interesting at any rate. The people are extremely friendly and like visitors.

At this village and the one before this we were anchored with our Australian friends on 'Tri-Reality'. Alan gives the villagers a big treat by showing them videos. He takes his TV, VCR, and generator to shore in the evening. I pop a big garbage bag full of popcorn and we have a big movie night on the beach. Last night we had over 100 people clustered around an 11 inch TV screen watching movies and eating popcorn. They were soooo excited.

We had lots of locals on the boat all morning visiting and looking around but they are gone now. The boys are with 'Micasa' for a few days so we are having a real holiday. We are always busy here. We've done lots of hiking and spend hours in the water snorkeling on the coral reefs. It's truly beautiful; sort of like being in a tropical fish tank. We've done a lot of fishing and have done quite well. We caught a great barracuda the other day. It was 59 inches long. I didn't know what to do with it so we gave it to the village people. They cut it up right there on the beach and everyone got a chunk.

We still haven't received the text books yet. The post office said it could take up to three months. It's just been two months so far. It won't be hard to spend another month here.

We will be going back into Lautoka on the main island maybe tomorrow to get the boys. We'll take a bus trip from there to Suva to check our mail. It's a 5-6 hour bus ride so we'll spend the night there. It should be fun. I tried two weeks ago to get my mail sent from Suva to Lautoka but it didn't get sent so we'll check it ourselves.

Well here it is September 10th and I've covered a lot of ground and water since starting this letter. Very early on Sunday morning it started to rain and blow hard, so as the wind direction had also changed we had to get out of where we were anchored. Daryl and I sailed back to Lautoka. Dustin was surprised we did so well without him. It would have been nice having him to help but we did fine anyway. Then yesterday we put our boat along with 'Tri-Reality' up at the dock in the marina. We left Dustin there (his choice) and Daryl, Nathan, and I along with Jan and Alan from 'Tri-Reality' left on a bus for Suva. It was a four and a half hour trip and boy did that bus go fast. A real white knuckle ride!

We checked our mail and found that the boy's text books still hadn't arrived so we knew we would be making this trip at least one more time. There were no letters from home either so we could only assume that Jerad was back in Hawaii but we had no address for him there. We found a back packers hotel where we were able to stay the night. The cost was $10.00 US which included a room with a bathroom down the hall. Oh well. It fit our budget.

By the third week in September we had received the text books and were provisioning the boat once again to take off. We had planned to go to Vanuatu and then on to Cairns, Australia, however, we heard that there was an outbreak of malaria in Vanuatu this year and even though we had anti malaria pills Daryl didn't want to chance it. We would head to New Caledonia instead. Daryl also announced that once the boat was secured in Cairns we would all be returning to the states for Christmas. Wow! The whole family. Now this was something new. It probably had more to do with the fact that he was having ongoing urinary tract infections and had a prostate problem that needed medical attention than anything else, but, what the heck, a trip home was a trip home no matter what the reason.

Tri-Reality was heading for the Solomon Islands before returning home to Cairns. They wanted us to go along with them there but the malaria outbreak had also reached the Solomon's so we chose not to go. But then, for two reasons, our New Caledonia plan would have to be changed as well. First, we couldn't find the chart for New Caledonia that we were almost positive we had. And, second, our Sat Nav that we used to navigate with went on the blink and we just couldn't chance going into a new place which was surrounded by reefs with no chart and no navigational equipment. We would start taking our anti malaria pills and go to Vanuatu as was our original plan. At least we had good charts for Vanuatu.

CHAPTER SEVENTY-EIGHT

VANUATU

Our last minute change of plans to go to the islands of Vanuatu turned out to be one of the better plan changes we had ever made. We left Suva, Fiji at 7 am on Saturday morning and arrived in Port Vila, Vanuatu Tuesday evening at 7 pm; a beautiful and uneventful three and a half day sail. Our friends on *Micasa* were already sitting at anchor in the harbor and the boys were beyond happy to be with their good buddies once again. *Tri-Reality* would also be coming in here as Vanuatu was the logical stopping off place before heading further north to the Solomon's.

Our Sat Nav had been acting up while we were in Fiji and we were getting nervous about its reliability. Our first order of business once we had completed our check in process for Vanuatu was to make a phone call to Downwind Marine in San Diego and order a new navigation system. It was an expensive transaction for us. The phone call alone cost us a dear $75.00. This time we purchased a GPS which at the time was new for small boats but we felt certain that it would keep us from hitting a reef. It would be shipped to us in Port Vila.

It's always fun to see more of an island than just the shoreline. Along with some of our friends we rented a 12 passenger mini-bus which was just right for all of us. Daryl was appointed driver. Alan said there was no way he could drive. In Vanuatu the cars drove on the right side of the road unlike Australia, New Zealand, Fiji and many other countries where cars drive on the left side. Actually, we felt lucky to get out of Fiji alive. Between the cars traveling super fast, even through town, driving on the left side of the road, and cars, not pedestrians, having the right of way we narrowly escaped being reduced to road kill several times while just trying to cross a street.

We took several detours off the main road as we explored the island. Such a beautiful place. We drove out onto an old airstrip that was built by the military during the war. There were bunkers and other old relics left over from the war days. We stopped along the way to eat the picnic lunch we had packed. We swapped stories of our sailing adventures and all in all just had a wonderful time.

There was to be a yacht race in Port Vila sponsored by the yacht club. Jan and Alan wanted to enter *Tri-Reality* into the race. They didn't have a big head sail so we loaned them ours off of *Lunar Glow*. Daryl and I went along as part of their racing crew. This was a new experience for us as we had never done any sort of racing before save for the little dinghy races the boys did from time to time in the harbors. The race was exciting and loads of fun. I don't remember who won the race. What I do remember was that we pushed the boat so hard that our big head sail had about 18 inches of one end blown completely out. There was some other damage to the sail as well. Daryl and I spent the better part of the next two days doing sail repair work. In the end the sail was as good as new even if it did look patched.

Up until now we had never taken on an outside crew member. We had had an overnight guest from time to time but never crew. It was here that Jan and Alan introduced us to Don, a young college graduate from Chicago who was spending a year traveling the world before settling down. He had actually crewed for Jan and Alan on their boat before 70 year old John moved aboard. Don didn't crew for money; he just worked for his room and board and transportation to his next destination, which in this case was Australia. Don was nice, clean-cut, well mannered, and came to us highly recommended. He wasn't yet finished exploring Port Vila so he would meet up with us at Santo, one of the other islands in this group.

Our GPS arrived in just 10 days. Daryl got it installed and we played around with it for a couple of days to get ourselves familiar with all its bells and whistles. We continued our normal routine of schoolwork, boat cleaning, and having a general good time with our other boat friends. We thought of Jerad celebrating his 19th birthday in Hawaii and hoped he was having as good a time there as we were having in Vanuatu. We knew he would have loved these islands.

After two weeks in Port Vila we pulled our anchor and headed out again. We took four days to reach Santo Island stopping a couple of times along the way to anchor and explore some of the little bays. We sailed past a shipwrecked boat that had gone up onto a reef and felt grateful that we now had a GPS to keep us away from such disasters.

Santo was one of the northern islands of Vanuatu which we liked even better than the other islands. Santo was still quite primitive. There were no tourists and it was known as a custom village. Many of the local men walked through town wearing nothing but a lap lap; a small flap of cloth about 10 inches long by 8 inches wide worn front and back which was tied around their waist with a thin length of leather or vine. Many of the women wore only a few leaves hung from the waist in the same fashion and no tops. The children wore nothing at all. (Boy, that would really cut down on the laundry!) It was hard to know where to look as we walked down the dirt roads of town so we mainly just looked down at our feet as we walked thinking it might be impolite to look at the scantily dressed locals.

We didn't have to check into Santo as we had taken care of that in Port Vila for the entire island group of Vanuatu. We met a local man with a 4 WD pick up; one of the few vehicles on the island. He offered to take us on an all day tour of Santo. He took us to out of the way places that we never would have been able to find on our own. Jan and Alan from *Tri Reality* as well as our friends on *Micasa* went with us and we were all happy to sit in the bed of the pick up as we navigated through the dense, lush, vegetation of the island. There were lots of WWII relics and old bunkers all over the place. The USS Coolidge had actually been sunk just around the bend from where we had *Lunar Glow* anchored. It sunk when it hit one of our own mines. We also went by Million Dollar Point. That was where at the end of the war the U. S. wanted to sell all its vehicles and equipment to the local people. The natives weren't interested so the U.S. military drove everything into the water where it was now just a huge pile of rusty metal.

Our driver took us to an incredibly beautiful, turquoise blue colored swimming hole where we all went for a swim. The water was deep here; maybe 30 feet or more surrounded by large trees which had long vines hanging from them. I wouldn't have been surprised if Tarzan himself had swung by. The kids made good use of the vines, however, hanging on to them, climbing up a tree, and swinging way out over the water before letting go to plunge into the pristine water below.

We picked up Don, our new crew hand, a couple of days before leaving Santo. He had actually been out to the most primitive of all the islands in Vanuatu

where the men still wore penis wraps and many of the natives had never seen any kind of civilization at all. I felt bad that we had missed this experience ourselves but we were glad to hear Don's telling about it anyway.

CHAPTER SEVENTY-NINE

HEADING ... DOWN UNDER

It was Saturday, October 19, 1991 when we left Santo Island, Vanuatu and headed west towards Cairns, Australia. We had plenty of wind and towards evening the rain started. The wind and rain continued on throughout the first two days and nights. The seas were steep so we had to hand steer the boat. Daryl, Dustin, Don, and I each took two hour watches which worked out well. We were able to get a few hours sleep in between our time at the wheel. By Tuesday the skies were clear and the rain had stopped. We still had good wind so were able to make good time.

On Wednesday we picked up another passenger; a sea bird that landed on *Lunar Glow* and rode along with us for a couple of days. He was shy at first but then became overly friendly, even trying a couple of time to go down below into the galley. We fed him some of the flying fish that were always landing on the boat. He stayed with us for two days and nights, sometimes leaving for about 30 minutes and then returning.

We found different ways to entertain ourselves as we sailed along. I had a bag of prunes onboard. Now most people wouldn't think that prunes could be entertaining, but they were. All of us would line up along the lifelines at the side of the boat. We would each put a prune in our mouth and eat the meat off the pit. Then when the signal was given we would each lean over the side of the boat and spit the prune pit as far out over the water as we could. The one who's pit went the furthest was the winner.

Don wanted to make a Christmas card for his family back home in Chicago. We found a large piece of cardboard and some markers which he used to write a Christmas greeting on then he sat with it in the cockpit where we took his picture while holding the greeting. We got it developed in Cairns and it turned out well.

I'm not sure how he did it but on Friday Nathan had gone down into the forward cabin where a few minutes later we heard a bunch of racket and Nathan yelling. We rushed down the stairs to see what was wrong and it looked as if a snow storm had hit us. Nathan had somehow set off the fire extinguisher and it had sprayed white "snow" all over the cabin. I'm not sure if that qualifies as entertainment or not. It's funny now but not so much so at the time.

The wind continued strong and steady for about a week, then tapered off and suddenly about 250 miles from Cairns it was gone altogether. A sailboat without wind isn't much fun. You just sort of slosh around and sometimes drift in directions you don't want to go. After doing this for almost a full day we gave in and did something we almost never did while out at sea; we started our motor. A 25 H.P. motor wouldn't get us very far, especially with the limited amount of fuel we carried, but it did lift our spirits a bit. By nightfall we had enough light wind to sail again so we turned off the motor and sailed on through the night. By the time the sun came up the wind was gone too. We started the motor once again and used it for a few more hours during the day. About 50 miles off the coast of Australia a customs plane flew over the top of us. They called us on the radio and asked us all sorts of questions. They are just like the U.S. about patrolling their shores.

At this point we had two problems. First of all it would be dark before we could reach Cairns and second, we were about out of fuel. We didn't want to pull into an unfamiliar port at night, especially under sail, and we didn't have enough fuel to motor into Cairns. Our next best option would be to pull into Fitzroy Island which was about 11 miles off the coast from Cairns. Our sailing books indicated that it was a resort island and there would be fuel available there. It also had good range lights leading into it. We arrived at Fitzroy Island just after dark and just as we were running out of gas. We anchored in a small anchorage amongst some other boats, stowed our sails and gear, and went to bed for the night. The next morning Don and the boys took the empty fuel jugs to shore and filled up with enough gas to get us into Cairns.

We arrived in Cairns about 3:45pm and were greeted by our friend, Marilyn, off of *Spindrift*. She brought us a welcome gift of a carton of cold milk, apples, a loaf of bread and a newspaper. We were really happy to see her. The "officials" came out to the boat a short time later to clear us in. They went through every inch of our food stores and began loading all "restricted" items into huge black plastic bags. They took all of our eggs, fresh produce, tinned meats with pork, honey, noodles, beans, milk powder, dairy products, soup mixes with noodles, all of the bird's seeds, etc., etc. They said we could keep our fresh potatoes as long as we peeled them first. How ridiculous was that! There was no doubt in my mind but what the families of these "officials" would eat well for the next couple of weeks.

Because we were friendly, honest, and quite up front with the "officials", we encountered some problems. When we told them of a welcome visit from our friend Marilyn they freaked out. What did we mean we had "contact" with someone before being cleared into Australia. Very bad! And then we told them about running out of gas and stopping for the night at Fitzroy Island and getting gas there. Now they really freaked out. Very, very bad! Now they took all of our passports and told us to report to the Customs office the following day to see the top man there.

We all headed down to the Customs office the next day. Don was still with us and would need to retrieve his passport before he could continue on his way. As captain, Daryl was taken into a separate room where he had to dictate a statement and was given about a 20 minute lecture on breaking this very serious law for which the total fine could be as much as $55,000. It was waived, thank goodness. Then came our next problem; our little bird, Sweetie Pie. We had to fill out all sorts of paperwork for her and post a $500 bond to ensure we don't break any of the "bird rules". She must stay on the boat, in her cage, be covered with a net if outside the cabin, and be checked by an inspector at least once a week to make sure the bird is still here. She must be locked down below in the cabin if we leave the boat and we must notify officials if we move the boat. If we leave the boat to travel inland she must be bonded to another foreign vessel. What a pain. This seemed like a bit of an overkill as we looked overhead to see flocks of wild cockatiels flying by.

Other than that, Australia was great!

CHAPTER EIGHTY

LIFE IN AUSTRALIA

Once we were finished with all of the official stuff we really liked Australia. It was an interesting country with so much to explore. *Spindrift* had been in Australia for several months and had a car so Marilyn was kind enough to take us sightseeing in the surrounding areas. We became familiar with the general lay of the land and did some hiking around one of the local lakes. We even stopped for a hamburger lunch at the golden arches.

One big plus about being in Cairns was their yacht club complete with hot showers and laundry facilities. Hot showers were a real luxury and our first trip to shore after our business with the Customs and Immigration officials was to the yacht club. I packed all of our dirty laundry into some canvas bags and took my towel and toiletries in another bag. My first stop would be the showers. This was the first hot water shower I had had in I don't know how long. It felt so good to feel that hot water spraying down on me. I shampooed and towel dried my hair and left to do the laundry.

I washed two loads of clothes in the coin operated machines. I decided to pack the clean laundry back into the canvas bags and take it back to the boat to hang and dry. We returned to the dinghy dock and I got into our dinghy first along with the clean laundry. Dustin got in next but had not sat down yet when Daryl decided to climb in. Daryl somehow managed to get the dinghy off balance and it was obvious that the whole thing was going over. Nathan was still standing on the dock holding the painter and Dustin managed to jump back onto the dock just in the nick of time. The dinghy flipped completely over with Daryl and myself in it. So much for my nice shower and clean hair. All the clean laundry was now full of salt water. And if that wasn't bad enough my cloth purse with our passports, boat papers, checkbook, money, and so forth was also soaked in salt water. The boys thought it was hilarious but knew better than to laugh as Daryl and I came up sputtering. Somehow the motor managed to start after being dunked but didn't last long and Daryl once again had to do motor repairs.

I had picked up some rip-stop nylon fabric and carbon fiber rods at some point and now started sewing wonderful two string kites. The boys spent many hours flying those kites on the beaches and in the parks. I even made some kites for other boats.

Daryl had announced weeks earlier that we would all be flying back to the states for Christmas, but now there was a problem. There were no inexpensive tickets left to be found. It would cost us over $4500 for all four of us to make the trip. Besides that I don't think that Daryl was looking forward to a prolonged visit with my family. They had never warmed up to each other. In the end Dustin, Nathan, and I made the trip while Daryl stayed behind to watch the boat and Sweetie Pie. I think we were all happy with that arrangement.

We had also decided before reaching Australia that we would try to purchase a vehicle of some sort in order to see more of the country during the months that we would be there. Our friends, Jan and Alan, from *Tri-Reality* had convinced us that Cairns was a very safe hurricane hole and a great place to leave the boat while we traveled around for a while. We spent a couple of weeks looking for cars and finally found a 1982 Mitsubishi camper van that we liked. It was in excellent condition and would save us money on food and lodging as we traveled around. Daryl was happy as he would have transportation while the rest of us were in the states. After getting the van insured and registered we took a couple short excursions to nearby lakes and parks.

CHAPTER EIGHTY-ONE

STATESIDE FOR CHRISTMAS

The boys and I had a wonderful flight from Cairns to San Francisco and were met at the airport by my parents. Michael came to see us later that night and the next day, November 23, 1991, we celebrated Nathan's 11th birthday. Jerad wouldn't arrive from Hawaii for another three weeks.

We had a great time visiting aunts, uncles, cousins, and a host of old friends, all of whom thought us to be just a little bit strange if not interesting. Nathan and Dustin were able to spend some time working with their dad, Joe. He owned his own business installing aluminum windows in older houses and let the boys go along to earn a bit of Christmas money. They still had to have their school work done before anything else but the thought of earning money was a good incentive to get their assignments out of the way early each day.

It was fun for me to just do the things that I used to take for granted. Things like decorating the house for Christmas, going to the mall Christmas shopping, driving around looking at the lights, baking cookies with my mom, renewing my driver's license. Nothing spectacular. Just little things that made me happy to be with my family once again.

Jerad arrived from Hawaii on December 14th. It seemed like forever since we had seen him although in reality it had only been just over eight months. It was hard to believe all that had happened during that time. I was also surprised to find that he had brought all of his possessions with him and was not planning to return to BYU Hawaii after the Christmas break. What he hadn't told me before this is that he had submitted all of his paperwork to go on a two year mission for the LDS Church and was hoping to get his mission call in the mail while we were all staying at my parent's house over the holidays. The call did come in about a week later. After all the traveling Jerad had done we expected him to be called to serve in some exotic part of the world and were all a little surprised when we read that he would serve a Spanish speaking mission in Arcadia, California. Well, if that's where the Lord needed him then that's where he would go.

Now in addition to Christmas shopping I also had to get Jerad outfitted with two years worth of suits, shirts, ties, shoes, dress socks, etc. Suddenly my vacation was changing from leisurely to busy. Not to mention expensive.

Daryl finally called us on Christmas day. It was the first time we had heard from him since arriving in California just over a month before. All was well with the boat and he was doing fine. I told him I would let him know via a letter when we planned to return to Australia. I didn't feel any great need to rush our trip. After all, we were going to be in Cairns for several months anyway and Daryl had taken so many trips without us over the years that I felt justified in staying on here for a while.

All four of my boys took a few days trip up north to Mt. Shasta with their dad to do some snow skiing. They had a great time but came back sick. They spent the next few days laying around the house and battling high fevers. All in all they had a great time. They went to the movies, roller skating, and flew kites. They also continued to work with their dad on most days. I made a weekend trip to Nevada to check on our Stagecoach property there. Thank goodness, all was well.

Before we knew it our time stateside was drawing to an end. I had written to Daryl to let him know that we would be flying into Cairns on January 25th. We had had a farewell party for Jerad even though he wouldn't be leaving for another couple of weeks. At least his shopping was complete and he was ready to go.

It was hard saying goodbye to everyone and thinking that it could be years before we saw any of them again. At that time our plan was to remain in Australia until late summer gradually working our way north to Darwin where we would provision the boat to cross the Indian Ocean and head towards Africa.

We stepped aboard our Qantas Airline flight at 8:45pm on Saturday evening and arrived in Cairns at 8:40am on Monday morning. We had actually lost a day when we crossed the International Date Line. Any way you look at it it's a long flight but it had been completely worth it to have been able to spend the time with our family that we loved and missed so much.

CHAPTER EIGHTY-TWO

AUSTRALIAN ADVENTURES

O ur lives picked up right where we had left them in Australia. Daryl picked us up in the van at the airport and we all went for a ride with Daryl showing us some of the local areas he had discovered in our absence. After returning to the boat to drop off our luggage, picking up some supplies, feeding and locking Sweetie Pie in the cabin, we headed out in the camper van again for Lake Tinaroo where we camped for the night. The boys worked on school assignments, flew their kites, swam and explored. They were pretty much happy wherever we were.

We returned to Cairns the following day and did some heavy shopping as our stores of food had diminished during our Christmas vacation. While on shore I wanted to go by the yacht club and use the hot showers there. One of the favorite Christmas gifts I had received from my parents was a curling iron with a voltage adapter so that I could use it in Australia. I was anxious to wash my hair and try out the new curling iron. I found the women's shower room to be empty when I got there. The room had maybe eight shower stalls with curtains along one wall and on the opposite wall a low bench ran the length of the room. There were no counter tops to set toiletries on and the only electrical outlets were on the wall quite a ways above the long bench. I tore open the wrapping on the voltage adapter leaving the instruction sheet tucked inside the plastic wrapping. I didn't need instructions to tell me how to plug in a curling iron. I plugged the adapter into the wall outlet and then plugged my curling iron into that. The little light came on. Great. The cord wasn't long enough to reach all the way down to the bench so I just let the whole thing dangle down along the wall. I figured it might as well be heating up while I took my shower. I was in the shower shampooing my hair when I began to smell something hot. Wow, the curling iron must really be heating up. I rinsed my hair and turned off the water. As I pulled back the shower curtain to grab my towel I almost panicked. My whole curling iron had melted and was hanging in gooey plastic strands from the end of the electrical cord. I pulled the plug from the wall but the iron was too hot to hold. I grabbed it with my towel and tried to mold it back into shape but every time I held it up the whole top half flopped over at a right angle. It was then that I pulled out the instruction sheet that was still tucked inside the discarded packaging. "Use only with appliances of 50V or more". Opps. My curling iron was only 20V. Well, so much for a nice hair style.

We also stopped at the Customs office to obtain a permit to visit Green Island. Green Island is actually a nation park. It's a beautiful coral cay situated about 17 miles off the coast of Cairns and one of the northern most islands of the Great Barrier Reef. We would leave early in the morning, sail to Green Island, and spend the day snorkeling and enjoying the beautiful island life before sailing back into Cairns harbor in the evening.

The boat was in need of a good cleaning so we spent the next couple of days catching up on the many boat chores that needed to be done. The boys continued to do schoolwork and fly their kites in between cleaning. I was able to do laundry at the yacht club. The decks and cabins were looking good once again but the waterline was a mess and we knew the hulls that weren't visible in the dirty harbor water would be a mess too. None of us were willing to get into the dirty water there in the harbor to clean them. Daryl and I had already taken one involuntary dip into that water when the dinghy had overturned and we for sure didn't want to get in again.

Well, we would just have to sail on over to Fitzroy Island where we knew the water was crystal clear and clean our hulls out there.

Fitzroy Island, being a resort island, is rather ritzy. We dropped our anchor in the harbor amid beautiful large sailboats and expensive motor yachts. *Lunar Glow,* complete with clean laundry hanging from the life lines and a rag tag crew running around the deck no doubt dropped the real estate value in that part of the anchorage down a notch or two. Then to make it worse, we all jumped into the water with our little green scrubber pads and started to work cleaning the hulls and waterline. As our "neighbors" looked on from their comfy deck chairs, sipping exotic drinks with little paper umbrellas, we could almost read their minds; "What on earth are these low class Americans doing?" Given the size and obvious expense of their fancy yachts, I was sure that a job such as hull cleaning would be done by some hired hand. Well, we may not have had a lot of money or a big fancy yacht but we were still able to enjoy the same beautiful scenery and pristine water as everybody else. We were happy!

We spent a total of five nights anchored there in the harbor at Fitzroy Island. By the second day our chores were complete so we took the dinghy to shore to begin exploration there. As we knew very little about this island, other than it being a resort generally visited by well-to-do Australians, we just started walking. As we walked along a path we rounded a bend and came upon a lovely beach. We were combing the beach looking for shells when we noticed the sign that read "Nudy Beach". I also noticed that Dustin was no longer interested in looking for shells but in looking at sunbathers. There were several people on the beach working on their "all over" suntans. Nathan, on the other hand, was embarrassed and just wanted to get out of there. As we were all so overdressed for this party we made a quick retreat back to the path we had been on. We opted to take a swim later at the resort pool which we had learned opened its doors to the yachting community. Even to us!

We swam in the resort pool each day and explored more of the island. We walked through beautiful gardens and hiked to the lighthouse perched on top of the island. It was this lighthouse that had guided us in as we were arriving in Australia. It was so relaxing and peaceful out at Fitzroy. We actually spent most of our time over the following two months anchored out there at that island, making trips back into Cairns only as needed to buy groceries or check our mail. Anchoring at Fitzroy was free whereas staying in Cairns harbor cost us money every night we stayed there. We did, however, have to notify the customs people every time we left Cairns and what day we would return.

The boys were doing well. Nathan had finally started his 6th grade schoolwork but probably spent more time complaining about having to do schoolwork then actually doing it. Dustin was plodding along with his algebra and since returning to Australia had been rather quiet but pleasant to be around. He kept saying he was bored yet was always busy doing something. We spent a lot of time swimming at the resort pool and sometimes had the whole thing to ourselves. At other times there were resort guests laying on the lounge chairs. I thought it was comical to watch Dustin sneak peeks at the topless ladies while trying not to look obvious doing so. It was a large kidney shaped pool with an island in the center. The island had several palm trees growing on it and many more palms growing around the perimeter of the pool as well providing some welcomed shade. The boys also loved to go over to the pier and feed the reef fish there. They would lay down on the pier and hold pieces of bread in their hands and as they put them into the water the reef fish would swim up and eat from their hands. They could even pet some of them. Sometimes the boys would fish or snorkel with the large sea turtles there.

An excerpt from a letter I wrote to my folks reads: *We are on our way back into Cairns Harbor now after having spent another six nights out at Fitzroy Island. Prior to that we had gone on a three night camping trip in the van ... The weather is beautiful but a bit on the hot side some days. The boys are being especially good. Nathan is doing very well on his 6th grade and is actually ahead of schedule. I never thought I'd see that! Dustin, too, is doing good but for some reason he's a little slow. I had to force him to sit and do a few days work right with me to get him past some rough spots but once he got through that he was fine again.*

Our camping trip was a nice change. We went as far south as Townsville, about 250 miles. We stopped at several national parks and each had wonderful waterfalls and swimming holes. So refreshing when it's hot. We saw our first kangaroos in the wild on that trip. Actually we saw a couple others but we decided we couldn't count the ones squished on the highway!"

It was during our final visit to Fitzroy Island in March that Daryl tripped over a bucket in the cockpit while doing some maintenance on the boat and hurt his right leg just above the ankle. It got a big purple goose egg on it. We packed it in ice and thought for sure it would heal up okay. Three days later on Dustin's 15th birthday we returned to Cairns. Daryl's leg was still hurting. Two days later the leg was even worse. By now the whole right foot, ankle, and part way up his leg was red and very swollen so Daryl drove in to the local hospital to get it checked. He checked in but after six and a half hours of waiting he finally left without ever being seen.

We wanted to see more of Australia and felt that this would be a good time to travel around a bit. We arranged for some friends on another boat to feed and water Sweetie Pie while we were gone then loaded up the camper van and headed south. We had purchased a used Zodiac dinghy a couple of weeks before from some local folks for $1200. This was a lot of money for us but we really needed to replace the Avon dinghy that we had lost in the storm between Tonga and Samoa the year before. This one was only four years old and looked like new but after a week it began to leak and we found the main seam beginning to pull apart. We had the original bill of sale for the Zodiac which had cost $2350. We were told of a Zodiac dealership down in Brisbane to take the dinghy to so we headed off in that direction; a drive of about 1150 miles.

After an eight hour drive we pulled into a roadside rest area for the night. By the following morning Daryl's leg was hurting worse and he said it was getting hard for him to drive. He decided that I should drive for a while. I'm always a little bit nervous driving a different vehicle for the first time and this was no exception. Being a camper van I couldn't see out the rearview or side windows so had to rely on my side mirrors. As if that weren't bad enough these crazy Aussies drove on the left hand side of the road and I was 100% programmed to drive on the right side. I drove for a couple of hours but I was such a nervous wreck we finally switched back. We found a roadside rest area where we stayed the night but we really weren't too sure how safe these areas were.

We arrived at the Zodiac dealership the following morning and after some negotiating with the salesman left with a new Zodiac. The new model Zodiacs were selling for $2545 but because we had the original bill of sale they gave us full credit for the used one and so we only had to pay $195 for a brand new one. This seemed to cheer the boys up. It was something like getting a new sports car. We drove down to the harbor there in Brisbane to look at the boats and spotted some friends that we had first met in Mexico. The owners, husband and wife, had both worked at the hospital in Pago Pago and were now here on their boat *Princess del Mar*. We stopped for a visit but when they saw Daryl's leg which now looked as if he had elephantiasis they pointed us in the direction of the local hospital.

Daryl was admitted into the hospital in Brisbane where he remained for the next five nights. Not being able to find a parking space when we arrived at the hospital we parked around the backside of the building next to some dumpsters. The boys and I were too nervous to move the van so we just slept there next to the hospital dumpsters that first night.

The following day we knew we couldn't remain parked where we were so went in search of a caravan park. We finally located one in the town of West Holland which was about 10km from the hospital. The boys kept yelling at me about my driving saying that I was going to get us all killed. That made me even more nervous but they were probably right. I just couldn't get the hang of driving on the left side of the road. Changing lanes was especially hard. As I couldn't see out the side or back windows the boys would stick their heads out the side windows and when it was clear they would yell "Now"! Our road trip suddenly changed from enjoyable to a hair raising amusement park ride, only it was anything but amusing. I kept turning into the wrong lane and cars were constantly honking their horns at us as I frantically swerved out of their way. We made it through another day still in one piece. My left handed shifting had improved some and fewer cars were honking at me but my driving was still anything but safe.

The next day I came up with a new plan. I would let Dustin drive. He had just turned 15 the week before and had never driven a car but at least he wasn't programmed to drive on the right side of the road. He did remarkable well. We went to visit Daryl each day then went out exploring, returning to the caravan park at night. Dustin really wanted to visit Surfers Paradise so we drove down to the Gold Coast where the beaches were indeed beautiful.

The hospital wanted Daryl to stay for ten days but finally discharged him after five days with antibiotics and instructions to return in a week for a recheck. We headed back down to the Gold Coast and found a nice caravan park with a pool and showers and made that our base for the next week. We visited Dreamworld Amusement Park which is sort of like a Five Flags Amusement park in the states, and drove down to Byron Bay for a couple of days where Dustin was able to surf and Nathan could use his boogie board. Except for the schoolwork and chores, our everyday lives were like a once in a lifetime dream vacation for most people.

The recheck of Daryl's leg was encouraging. He was getting better but would need yet another ten days of antibiotics and a follow up check in Cairns after that. At least we could leave the area now. We started our return trip to Cairns but this time taking an inland route through the gem fields. We drove to Emerald and toured a mine and panned for gems in the town of Sapphire. There were hundreds of colorful parrots that were not at all afraid of people. If you had anything to eat they were especially aggressive landing on your head and shoulders. Nathan ended up covered with tiny scratches from all the birds landing on his bare arms.

We visited a park that was full of kangaroos. You get up right next to them and one even allowed us to pet her baby joey still in its pouch. What a fun experience for the boys.

We hadn't been able to see nearly as much off this fascinating country as we had hoped to but it was already into April and we knew we had work to do on *Lunar Glow* before heading north through the Great Barrier Reef.

Daryl went to see a doctor in Cairns upon our return. He had completed his course of antibiotics and his leg was much better. He was given clearance to carry on with our travel plans. Most days were rainy but we were able to still get out and have fun when the sun came out. Dustin, Nathan, and I attended church on Sunday as we did whenever we were in port. The boys had an interview with the Branch President at church to get permission to go on an Easter Youth outing the coming week. They were excited to get to go and spent a couple of days packing for their campout.

On Good Friday we loaded the kids camping gear into the van and drove them to the church camp site. It was a bit muddy from all of the recent rains but we felt sure they would have a good time anyway. We spent a rather quiet few days visiting with our Aussie friends and puttering around on the boat while the boys were at camp. We picked them up, tired and muddy, on Monday afternoon.

We made arrangements at the boatyard in Cairns the following day to have *Lunar Glow* hauled out of the water. This would be our last major haul out before crossing the Indian Ocean later in the year. What had been a nightmare of an operation in Samoa was a piece of cake here. Once again we would be lifted out of the water with a huge crane. It would be ready and waiting for us on Friday of that week. That would give us just one night to head back out to Fitzroy Island and clean the hulls again before the haul out.

Nathan wasn't feeling well so Dustin and I got busy scrubbing the hulls. When Jerad had returned to Samoa after his first semester of college he brought all of his newly acquired scuba gear with him. We were still carrying it around with us on the boat. Dustin used it now to clean the bottom of the hulls. The job went a lot faster when he didn't have to come up for air every few seconds like I did.

We left Fitzroy late the following morning. Dustin asked if he could sail the boat back into Cairns singlehanded. Well, if that's what he wanted to do he could go for it. The rest of us just sat back and let Dustin take over. He sailed the boat clear into the harbor and got it tied up alongside the dock by the boatyard. He never even lowered the motor. Over the past five years Dustin had truly become a fine sailor.

Once we had made arrangements to have the boat hauled out we also put an ad in the local paper to sell our campervan. We thought it might take a while and didn't want to get stuck in Cairns waiting to sell it. We didn't have a phone number to contact us so just put down the address of the boatyard where we could be found. As it turned out, *Lunar Glow* was out of the water for exactly four weeks and the camper van actually sold after four days. This was both good and bad. Good because it was one more thing checked off our list of things to get ready to go but bad because the boatyard was a really long walk to town.

Dustin decided that this would be an excellent time to assemble his bicycle. We had bought him a really nice BMX bike while we were in Samoa. Nathan had a bicycle as well. They had been broken down and stored in one of our ama hulls since leaving Pago Pago. They could put them to good use now. We did a lot of walking to and from the boatyard but after a few days and with provisioning to do Jan and Alan loaned us their car. We continued to attend church on Sundays and the boys participated in several church activities during the week. We sent our passports and visa applications to the Madagascar consulate in Sydney as that was to be a major stopping place for us prior to sailing into South Africa. To our surprise our visas came back to us in just a week's time.

The time went quickly and before we knew it the boat work was completed and the huge crane sat us back in the water again. We spent the next five days finishing up the provisioning and saying good-bye to our special Aussie friends.

I mailed one last letter to my folks giving them a new forwarding address for us in the Northern Territory although we knew it would be several weeks before we reached there ourselves. We got our cruising permit from customs and were ready to go. It was May 27, 1992, Daryl's 61st birthday, when we sailed out of Cairns for the last time.

CHAPTER EIGHTY-THREE

THE GREAT BARRIER REEF

There were still several weeks before we figured we would need to leave Australia and continue on our journey west so we would take our time and enjoy our sailing up through the Great Barrier Reef. Whenever possible we hoped to keep our sailing to no more than 50 miles at a time. There would be plenty of long distance stuff once we started across the Indian Ocean and beyond. Our plans changed often but at that time we were going to sail up the east coast of Australia exploring the islands of the Great Barrier Reef and from there we had a couple of options. We could sail on to Darwin or if we could get hold of the charts we would need we could sail on up to Bali which was the only island in Indonesia where boats could stop without first getting an expensive permit. Plus, if we went that way it would mean two shorter legs to Cocos Keeling Island rather than one long one which was alright with me.

We made a slow sail out of Cairns and up to Port Douglas. It was quiet and peaceful there but we only stayed one night as the no-see-ums, those vicious invisible bugs, were trying their best to feast on us. We headed out the following day for Low Islets. It was cloudy and really windy but at least there were no bugs here. After a couple of windy nights at anchor we pressed on to Cooktown.

There were sand dunes in Cooktown that seemed to call out to the boys like mud to a pig. As much as I disliked sand on the boat I didn't have the heart to keep them from playing on those dunes. They filled a good part of two days sliding and rolling down the sand. They also met a local man who took them along with him to go check his crab pots. They brought back one mud crab and two small fish. I took advantage of the town here to do some laundry and pick up a few groceries. Daryl remembered Cooktown as the place he cut his finger really bad trying to bend a spear into a gaff. We stayed here for three days before moving on to Lizard Island.

It didn't take long for us to discover how Lizard Island got its name. This was really a very nice place. The weather was beautiful and the anchorage was great, however, we were the only boat there. After completing our usual routine we headed to shore for swimming and exploring. The beach here was long with fine white sand; a great place for the boys to fly their kites and look for shells. Further back from the shoreline low scruffy foliage grew. We quickly learned to watch where we were walking as we began spotting lizards there. Not the little cute three to six inch ones like we had back home. No. These were BIG. They would have to be measured in feet, not inches. They were called monitor lizards and we made sure not to aggravate them in any way as we had no idea if they mean or aggressive.

On day two with schoolwork completed we hiked up to the top of the island to a place called Cooks Lookout. Captain Cook had truly left his mark on this part of the world. We saw more huge lizards. Sometimes they were clinging onto the trunk of a tree and blended in so well you really had to look hard to see them.

By day three the wind was picking up again. The boys took their kites back down to the beach a short distance in from the waters edge. They let their kite lines out in front of them and with the wind behind them the kites would fill with air like a big sail and pull them a long ways down the beach while they skied on their bare feet. (I suppose that is why today, as adults, Dustin and Nathan are both excellent kite boarders). Nathan did manage to cut his foot on something in the sand during one of his ski runs. With boys it was always something.

After three fun nights at Lizard Island we headed over to Newton Island. We caught a nice tuna on the way but the anchorage was so horrible we only stayed one night and didn't even leave the boat. We pulled our hook early the following morning and sailed on to Stanley Island. The anchorage was bouncy and offered little protection so we moved the boat around to the other side of the island the following morning and anchored in the channel there. We went to visit friends on *Wings* who gave us directions for a hike to some caves that had aboriginal drawings carved into the walls inside the caves. These were the kinds of outings I loved taking my boys to see.

We spent the next several days hopping from one island to the next. From Stanley we stopped at Hannah Island, Night Island, and Cape Weymouth going to shore only long enough to post some mail.

Our next stop was at Cape Grenville. We liked it here and actually stayed for a week. The fishing was the best there we had ever seen and we did a lot of it. And the oysters. Oh my. There were heaps of them. Nathan and I went out and gathered a big bunch of them. These oysters were so big that if they had been served on the half shell you would have had to bite them in half in order to swallow them. The thought of that almost made me sick so instead I made a big pot of fresh oyster soup. Yum.

The one thing we couldn't do in Cape Grenville was to go swimming. The waters there were infested with sharks and huge crocodiles. We had seen plenty of sharks over the years but this was our first experience with crocodiles. There were plenty of other things to do though. The boys took a hike across the cape and did some beach combing, but with a watchful eye out for the crocs. I had been working on a sewing project for the boat since leaving Cairns and took advantage of these days at anchor to get more of it done. I was working on a topper for our cockpit. *Lunar Glow* had an old worn bimini top on an aluminum frame which I had replaced while we were in Samoa. That helped keep some of the sun off of us but did nothing to keep the wind and rain out. During bad weather it could get downright miserable sitting in the cockpit. I was attempting to add panels onto the existing topper in order to enclose the entire cockpit. Some of the panels were of canvas and other areas were made of heavy clear vinyl so that we could see out. It was a lot of work.

Our next stop would be Gove Harbor. This would be about a three and a half days sail. The winds were light as we left Cape Grenville and headed towards Cape York and they continued to be light throughout the second day as we entered the Torres Straights. This all changed, however, as we began day three. The winds had picked up to 20 to 25 knots and the seas were three to four meters high. It was a really rough ride. Nathan was sick. But the worst part were the sea snakes. The water was churning with them. I'm normally (or maybe abnormally!) not afraid of snakes, but sea snakes were a different story. I had been told that the sea snakes were poisonous and I didn't want anything to do with them. Every few minutes the rough water would wash up over our decks bringing with it some of the snakes. They would slide back off the deck again as the water flowed back off the decks and returned to the sea but the idea of them being so close was unnerving to me. I prayed the winds didn't get so high that a sail change would be required. There was no way I was getting out of that cockpit to change a sail on the foredeck.

Our last day out was much better. The seas had calmed way down and a school of dolphins came to play alongside *Lunar Glow*. They always lifted my spirits no matter how hard the sailing had been. It was 9 pm on Sunday when we pulled into Gove Harbor. Father's Day.

The yacht club at Gove Harbor really knew how to make the sailing community smile. Visiting yachts were given a one month's free membership to the Gove Yacht Club which included just about everything we would need; hot showers, laundry facilities, BBQs, and water and so forth. Plus the people here were real friendly. The town itself was about 15km from the boat. About a five minute walk from the yacht club you could catch a free bus that ran down the main road twice a day. It actually ran between town and the aluminium plant, the major place of employment for the people of Gove.

We headed out to the road and waited about 30 minutes before we decided that we had missed the morning bus. Although there would be no bus there were still other vehicles traveling towards town. I stuck my thumb out and before long we had us a ride on the back of a big flatbed truck. It worked. It dropped us about one and a half kilometers from town so we walked the rest of the way. Our first stop was at the post office where we hit the jackpot. We had mail!

A letter from my parents also included a bunch of Dustin's schoolwork. I had to laugh when I pulled out the sheets from Dustin's science teacher on balancing chemical equation. I had spent several days over the past week trying to figure out how to do those things as Dustin was completely lost. I finally did get it all worked out but it would have saved me hours of frustration had I had those sheets to start with. Science had turned out to be one of the most challenging classes we did on the boat; not only the chemical equations but the many experiments as well. My galley was looking more like a science lab than a place to prepare meals.

We also had a very welcome letter from Jerad and the boys received a letter from their dad, Joe. I also had a letter from the consulate of Madagascar giving me the mailing address to use when we were there. I needed to get this sent back home before we left Australia.

Daryl hadn't gone into town with us. He stayed on the boat saying that he had some work to do on the batteries. By the time we arrived back he had managed to break his little toe. It was now quite swollen and very purple. He was doing a lot of moaning and groaning but there wasn't much to be done about it.

The following day the boys decided to put their bikes together again and do a bit of exploring. We gave them instructions that they were not to venture out too far from the harbor and to be back on the boat before dark. The sun was just setting and the sky was becoming darker when we heard a call come over the single sideband radio. Our friends on a boat call *Nina* had lost their motor and with the fluky winds they were nervous about coming into the harbor in the dark. We answered their call and said we would bring *Lunar Glow* out and tow them in. The boys still hadn't returned to the boat. We pulled our anchor and headed out of the harbor. I'm not sure how long after we left that the boys returned. When they looked out and saw that their home had left them behind they were super worried and wondered what they had done for us to be that mad at them. They breathed a sigh of relief when, sometime later, they saw us pulling back into the harbor with *Nina* in tow. Dustin and Nathan spent the next couple of days concentrating on schoolwork rather than exploring.

The next time the boys took their bikes out they had another huge scare. They were riding along and turned off onto a dirt path where they came face to face with a big water buffalo. They stopped, walked their bikes back for a ways, then remounted and peddled out of their as fast as they could. They weren't so keen on exploring the outback after that.

We made more trips into town and I continued the work I was doing on the cockpit topper. We were told of a crocodile farm in the area so took the boys there for a field trip. There were crocodiles of every size from just hatched to several feet long. I liked the little ones best. We even had a crocodile burger … it tasted like chicken!

We left Gove after ten enjoyable days and headed for The Hole in the Wall. This is a gap between two of the Wessel Islands. Aside from some good fishing, rain, and dropping our man overboard pole in the water requiring some strange looking turns and boating maneuvers we found nothing remarkable here. Our two night stay at Hole in the Wall was followed by an overnight sail into Gouburn Island. We arrived about dinner time and the Spanish mackerel we caught coming in made for a fine meal. It was here that Daryl managed to fall off the cabin top so now he had a sore hip to add to his current broken toe.

We sailed back over to the mainland the following day. This was the first time we had anchored off the mainland of Australia since leaving Cairns some weeks before. After doing their schoolwork and cleaning their cabin the boys dropped a fishing line over the side of the boat. They did this sometimes while we were at anchor. They didn't use a rod or reel but would just bait a hook and drop it over the side into the water. They were engaged in this activity when we all decided to go to shore. Instead of pulling their line in they just tied it off to a cleat on the side of the boat and left it there.

After a couple of hours looking around on shore we rode the dinghy back out to the boat.

"Hey, Dust," Nathan called out as we climbed aboard. "Let's check our fishing line and see if we caught a fish."

"Yeah, okay," Dustin replied, walking over to where their line was tied off. "Hey, I think we got a fish. The line is kind of heavy but nothings moving so maybe it's dead."

"Just pull it in so we can see," Nathan replied, leaning over the side of the boat to watch as the line came up. "Whoa, what is that thing? It looks like we caught a jar!"

"Nathan, there's no way we could catch a jar," Dustin chided him. "Wait, you're right. It is a jar, but look, something's moving inside of it. Dustin pulled the line the rest of the way in and sat their catch on the deck.

"Mom, Daryl," Nathan shouted. "Come here, quick. You have to see this!"

As Daryl and I approached we watched as a small octopus emerged, one tentacle at a time from inside a glass jar. Apparently, this little octopus had picked up the hook at the end of the boys fishing line and taken it with him to his cozy home inside and empty, discarded jar sitting on the ocean bottom under the boat.

"Can we keep it for a pet?" Nathan questioned as the octopus began a slow crawl across our deck.

"No, Dummy. It would die," Dustin shot back.

"Dustin, please don't call your brother names. But, he's right. That little guy won't last very long up here on the boat. He needs to live in the ocean."

After a few minutes the boys returned their catch to the water. What were the odds of ever making another catch like that again?

Next we headed over to Port Essington, then on to Popham Bay, finally ending up at Alcara Bay. The boys did some fishing off the boat but were having no luck.

"Can we go to shore and go swimming?" Dustin had hurried through his schoolwork earlier that morning and they had completed their chores for the day.

"I don't see why not. This looks like a pretty nice place for a swim," I answered. We got our things together and took the short dinghy ride to shore.

Daryl and I were sitting on a log on the beach watching the boys splash around in the water. They had just emerged from the water and were walking up towards us when folks off a local boat, *Tahuni*, walked up to us. We had seen their boat out in the anchorage.

"Pardon me, Mate," the man said, "but you might not want to let your kids get into the water here."

"Why not?" Daryl questioned. He hated when people told him what to do.

"Well, this place is known to have lots of crocs about. Those boys of yours would make a mighty nice lunch for one of them," the man said nodding his head over to one side.

Our eyes followed the direction of his nod. We all stared, wide eyed, mouths open, as a huge crocodile emerged from the water and ambled up onto the shore right near where the boys had been playing.

"The splashing about really seems to attract them," the man stated. We thanked him for the warning and made a hasty but watchful retreat back to *Lunar Glow*.

We left early the following morning and sailed on to a place called Escape Cliffs. There were no cliffs in sight and after the crocodile scare the day before we unanimously decided against exploring here. Besides that we were only about a day's sail out of Darwin and Daryl was anxious to get there, provision the boat, and head on across the Indian Ocean.

CHAPTER EIGHTY-FOUR

DARWIN

Because we had never come across the charts we needed to sail up into Bali in Indonesia we would just make a quick stop in Darwin and then be on our way again. We had good wind coming from our back so Daryl decided that we should fly our big colorful spinnaker for awhile. We had actually used it several more times since hoisting Nathan up the mast along with the halyard while sailing between Tonga and Fiji and we had our routine down to a science now.

With the nice weather and good winds we saw lots of local sailboats out for a day sail as we got closer to Darwin. It was almost dusk by the time we got our sails down and were motoring into Darwin Harbor. We had read about the extreme tides here and so we anchored out a long ways from the shore. Boats that anchored too close to shore when the tide was in would find their boats sitting in the mud once the tide went out.

The following morning a dinghy pulled up alongside *Lunar Glow*. It was a local couple who had come out to welcome us to Darwin. Well wasn't that nice. Alan and Bronwyn introduced themselves and we invited them aboard and gave them a quick tour. They were super friendly and told us a little bit about Darwin, especially getting to and from the boat. They told us about the heavy infestation of crocodiles there so to be careful when taking the dinghy to and from the dock. We had no reason to doubt them. They invited us on a tour of Darwin later on that day and then to dinner at their house that evening. They would pick us up at the dock. Wow. These were the most hospitable folks we had ever met! We were happy to oblige.

It was during this outing that they sprang it at us and caught us quite by surprise. They owned a small trimaran themselves and had been one of the local boats we had seen sailing around outside of Darwin Harbor. They had seen us sailing while we had our big, colorful spinnaker flying and had even snapped our picture as we sailed past them. They had been quite impressed with our speed and overall how our boat sailed. They wanted to buy our boat!

"What do you mean, you want to buy our boat," Daryl laughed. "It's not even for sale."

"Yeah. And besides that it's our home," I added. "We can't just up and sell our home in Australia and leave ourselves stranded here." I was sure they were pulling our leg.

"No, we're serious," Bronwyn piped in. "Our kids are getting bigger now and we've been talking about getting a bigger boat. One that would allow us to take some short trips with the family. *Lunar Glow* would be perfect."

This was getting just downright weird. Even though I had just about had my fill of dealing with Daryl I still wasn't ready to hang it up and stop sailing. I intended to keep going at least until the boys had finished high school.

"Even if we did want to sell our boat, which we don't, it would be quite impossible to do here in Australia. As I'm sure you know the boat would first have to be imported into the country and then the government would charge us a huge tax on top of that. Those two fees along would cost us more than the price of the boat. We just can't do it," Daryl reasoned.

"Well, you two be thinking of a price and we'll talk again in a day or two," Alan said as they dropped us off back at the dock.

We climbed down into our inflatable dinghy and picked up the oars. We had been told that it might not be a good idea to leave our nice outboard sitting at the dock for a prolonged period of time. We were silent as we rowed the long distance back to our boat. It was pitch dark out except for the lights coming from some of the boats at anchor and the water appeared black. As we look around us we could see small yellow lights along the surface of the water. It took us a minute or two to realize that they weren't lights at all, but the eerie yellow eyes of the crocodiles just under the surface of the water. It was a long scary ride back to the boat.

"So, what do you think about selling *Lunar Glow*?" Daryl asked me the next morning.

"I think it's a crazy idea. We have our visas and charts and everything we need for Madagascar and South Africa. What do you want us to do? Just hitchhike home?"

"How about this," Daryl suggested. "We'll ask a ridiculous price for the boat. That should scare them off."

"And the import fees and taxes?" I asked.

"We'll tell them they have to pay all of that too."

"Okay. And the money has to be in US dollars. And they will have to buy all of us airfare back to the US," I added.

"And all of our stuff. We'll tell them that they have to pay to have it all shipped back to the US also," Daryl said. Our list of demands was growing by the minute but we felt that this was the only way to discourage these folks.

Sure to their word, Alan and Bronwyn returned again late that afternoon.

CHAPTER EIGHTY-FIVE

FAREWELL TO LUNAR GLOW

It was no surprise when our new friends showed up again as determined as ever to purchase our boat, our home, but we were ready for them. We invited them in and all took a seat at our settee. I handed them the list of everything we would require from them in order for us to sell them our boat. They read through it, smiled at each other, and then Alan said, "This looks perfectly acceptable. We've got a deal!" and with that he extended his hand out to Daryl for a handshake. Daryl and I felt positive that the price of everything on our list was totally high and unreasonable; a real deal breaker. How were we to know that these people had money? I guess we should have asked more.

Now what? I was stunned; shocked beyond words. My whole plan for the future, my lifestyle, everything, had suddenly been pulled out from under me. I think Alan and Bronwyn sensed my despair from the look on my face as they took their leave after just a few minutes. We would meet up again later that evening for dinner.

We broke the news to the boys, who, as usual, took it all in stride. I didn't even know where to start. Daryl seemed to be relieved at not having to do another ocean crossing and as the week wore on I, too, had the strongest impression that we were being told to stop here and not continue on. I'll never know why for sure, but what I do know is that the Lord was speaking to me and that I should listen. Sort of like when you for no apparent reason take a different route home from work and avoid a terrible accident that took place at that time on your regular route.

Alan and Bronwyn were extremely helpful to us during the next two weeks. They brought us boxes so that we could pack up all of our personal belongings for shipping. We would leave lots of things on the boat that would be of no use to us back home in the states. We saw a travel agent to make arrangements to fly home, and had dinner several times on shore with Alan and Bronwyn. I learned that Bronwyn's birthday was the same day as mine which for some reason made me feel a little better about their buying our boat.

Then there was Sweetie Pie, our little parrot. Because of the strict Australian laws regarding 'foreign' birds, we were unable to leave him on shore. He would have to find a home on another boat; one that would be willing to follow the rules governing birds. Our friends on *Princess del Mar* had arrived in Darwin the day after we did. They were provisioning their boat and would be leaving for Madagascar in a couple of days time. We asked them about taking Sweetie Pie and they were happy to do so.

During the days when Alan was at work Bronwyn would take all of us out and about. We visited another crocodile farm and spent the better part of one day at Litchfield National Park. She explained that this was the area where part of Crocodile Dundee had been filmed. The thing I remembered the most, however, were the huge mounds of what looked like dried mud. We were told that they were termite mounds. Some of them had to be at least eight to ten feet tall. Quite impressive.

On the weekend we took Alan, Bronwyn and their kids out for a sail. They had so many questions and took loads of notes. Daryl went over all of the technical stuff with Alan while I went through our stores and the working of the galley with Bronwyn. They were so excited. Me, not so much.

On Monday Alan paid the duty and government taxes on the boat. *Lunar Glow* would no longer fly the flag of the United States of America. She was now, officially, an Australia vessel. We had to go into the immigration office to extend our visas for Australia. Originally we would have been out of the country before they expired but now with this change of events we needed an extension.

Wednesday afternoon Alan and Bronwyn came out to the boat. They had just returned from their attorney's office where they had picked up all sorts of legal documents for us to sign making the transfer of ownership official. They had brought us all of our money as well as our airline tickets. The tickets were for May 2nd so we still had about ten days before we would leave for good. Though I was still a bit sad I was beginning to accept this new plan change. After all, I would be closer to my family and that would be really nice. Also, things with me and Daryl were becoming more and more strained. I had been working hard to get the topper to enclose our cockpit done, and in fact, it was about 90 percent completed by the time we were just a few days out of Darwin. Daryl wouldn't help me do any of the work on it yet he was continually trying to tell me how to do it. This was beginning to sound just like my old real estate days when he didn't want to sell real estate but insisted on telling me how to do my job. Well not this time. I told him if he knew so much about sewing then he could darn well finish the job himself! And I meant it. I refused to do another minutes work on the project. Now it would be up to the new owners to complete it.

Over the next few days we continued to pack our things into boxes and clean the boat. We would ferry the boxes to shore where Alan would pick them up and store them at their house. They wouldn't be shipped until just before we left the country.

We took the boat out for one last sail with her new family the day before we left. It was a beautiful day for sailing and we all had a wonderful time. I was going to miss this boat more than I could imagine but I would forever take with me memories of the many adventures it brought us.

We spent our last night in Australia at Alan and Bronwyn's home as our flight was to be early the following morning. We would fly to Singapore for a day then on to Hong Kong and finally San Francisco where my parents would be waiting for us. I couldn't stop the flow of tears as I stepped aboard our Singapore Air flight. Another chapter of my life had just closed.

EPILOGUE

We had been away for five years. My parents were happy and relieved to have us back on dry land once and for all. Dustin, Nathan, and I remained in the Bay Area with my folks for the next several months. Daryl had flown back to Nevada the day after we landed. We would divorce a short time later. In 1995 I met my soul mate and although he doesn't share my love of sailboats he does accompany me on land and cruise based adventures.

Today, each of my sons are grown with families of their own. Michael became a police officer in Oakland, California and is currently a Sergeant working with his own squad. Jerad completed his church mission and went on to get his master's degree at BYU in Provo, Utah. Today he works with doctors programming pace makers. Dustin, who hated school and had zero computer training throughout all of his school years now has superior computer skills and certifications and is in constant demand by large companies such as Dell. Nathan also served an LDS mission in Canada and then went on to get his bachelor's degree in mechanics management at BYU Idaho. He currently owns his own plane and has worked as a mechanic on both cars and small aircraft as well as being a master craftsman with wood. We lost touch with Liai for a number of years but thanks to social media we were able to reconnect many years ago. She joined the US Army at age 18, married a wonderful man, also in the military and after 25 years retired as a Sargeant Major. They have two beautiful sons. I still call her my daughter and she calls me her ma.

As for me … well that's a whole other adventure!

Printed in the United States
By Bookmasters